Property and Liability Insurance Principles

Property and Liability Insurance Principles

Constance M. Luthardt, CPCU, AAI, AIM, AIS, CPIW
Director, Northeast Region
American Institute for CPCU/Insurance Institute of America

Barry D. Smith, Ph.D., CPCU, CLU, FLMI
Department Head, Finance Department
New Mexico State University

Eric A. Wiening, CPCU, ARM, AU, AAI, API
Assistant Vice President and Ethics Counsel
American Institute for CPCU/Insurance Institute of America

Coordinating Editor
Christine O. Quay, AAI
Assistant Program Director
American Institute for CPCU/Insurance Institute of America

Third Edition

American Institute for Chartered Property Casualty Underwriters/
Insurance Institute of America
720 Providence Road, Malvern, Pennsylvania 19355-0770

© 1999

American Institute for Chartered Property Casualty Underwriters/
Insurance Institute of America

*All rights reserved. This book or any part thereof may not be
reproduced without the written permission of the publisher.*

Third Edition • Fourth Printing • September 2002

Library of Congress Catalog Number: 99-73210

ISBN 0-89462-132-7

Printed in Canada

Foreword

The American Institute for Chartered Property Casualty Underwriters and the Insurance Institute of America are independent, nonprofit organizations serving the educational needs of the risk management, property-casualty, and financial services businesses. The Institutes develop a wide range of curricula, study materials, and examinations in response to the educational needs of various elements of these businesses. The American Institute confers the Chartered Property Casualty Underwriter (CPCU®) professional designation on people who meet its examination, ethics, and experience requirements. The Insurance Institute of America offers associate designations and certificate programs in the following areas:

- Accounting and Finance
- Agent Studies
- Business Writing
- Claims
- Global Risk Management and Insurance
- Information Technology
- Insurance Fundamentals
- Management
- Marine Insurance
- Performance Improvement
- Personal Insurance
- Premium Auditing
- Regulation and Compliance
- Reinsurance
- Risk Management
- Surety Bonds and Crime Insurance
- Surplus Lines
- Underwriting

The American Institute was founded in 1942 through a cooperative effort between property-casualty insurance company executives and insurance professors. Faculty members at The Wharton School of the University of Pennsylvania in Philadelphia led this effort. The CPCU designation arose from the same type of business and academic partnership at Wharton as the Chartered Life Underwriter (CLU) designation did in 1927.

The Insurance Institute of America was founded in 1909 by five educational organizations across the United States. It is the oldest continuously functioning national organization offering educational programs for the property-casualty insurance business. It merged with the American Institute in 1953.

The Insurance Research Council (IRC), founded in 1977, is a division of the Institutes. It is a not-for-profit research organization that examines public policy issues that affect property-casualty insurers and their customers. IRC research reports are distributed widely to insurance-related organizations, public policy authorities, and the media.

The broad knowledge base in property-casualty insurance and financial services created by the Institutes over the years is contained mainly in our textbooks. Although we use electronic technology to enhance our educational materials, communicate with our students, and deliver our examinations, our textbooks are at the heart of our educational activities. They contain the information that you as a student must read, understand, integrate into your existing knowledge, and apply to the tasks you perform as part of your job.

Despite the vast range of subjects and purposes of the more than eighty individual textbook volumes we publish, they all have much in common. First, each book is specifically designed to increase knowledge and develop skills that can improve job performance and help students achieve the educational objectives of the course for which it is assigned. Second, all of the manuscripts for our texts are reviewed widely before publication, by both insurance business practitioners and members of the risk management and insurance academic community. In addition, the revisions of our texts often incorporate improvements that students and course leaders have suggested. We welcome constructive comments that help us to improve the quality of our study materials. Please direct any comments you may have on this text to my personal attention.

We hope what you learn from your study of this text will expand your knowledge, increase your confidence in your skills, and support your career growth. If so, then you and the Institutes will truly be *succeeding together*.

Terrie E. Troxel, Ph.D., CPCU, CLU
President and CEO
American Institute for CPCU
Insurance Institute of America

Preface

Property and Liability Insurance Principles is the textbook for the first course (INS 21) in the three-part Program in General Insurance (INS) of the Insurance Institute of America (IIA). In conjunction with the INS 21 Course Guide, this text will help students prepare for the INS 21 examination given by IIA. The INS 21 course serves as a foundation for studying the other two courses in the INS program. The second course in the INS program is *Personal Insurance* (INS 22), which addresses personal insurance exposures and coverages. The third course, *Commercial Insurance* (INS 23), covers commercial property and liability exposures and coverages. Students who successfully complete the three INS courses by passing the INS 21, INS 22, and INS 23 examinations earn the IIA Certificate in General Insurance, a significant achievement in professional development in the insurance industry.

This text is divided into three segments. Segment A—Fundamentals of Insurance—provides information on what insurance is, who provides it, how it is regulated, and how the financial performance of insurers is measured. Segment B—Insurance Operations—describes the functions of marketing, underwriting, and claims. Finally, Segment C—Insurance Contracts, Loss Exposures, and Risk Management—discusses insurance as a contract, introduces both property and liability loss exposures and policy provisions, and provides a basic discussion of risk management as a means of managing loss exposures.

Educational objectives are shown at the beginning of each chapter as well as before the text pages to which they refer. Students and course leaders should pay careful attention to these educational objectives because they form the basis for understanding the material; the INS 21 examination is based on these objectives. Key words and phrases are shown in boldface throughout this text with their definitions provided in the margin. Definitions for all key words and phrases are also included in a convenient glossary at the end of the text. Students should carefully study the key words and phrases because a basic understanding of insurance terminology is critical for the student's understanding of the insurance industry. (The last educational objective in each chapter requires an understanding of the key words and phrases in the assignment. Therefore, these key words might also be a source of questions on the national examination.) Occasionally, key words are repeated as "reminders" in later chapters. Other words shown in italics are not key words but are included for emphasis or as explanations of important terminology.

We are grateful to many insurance professionals for their contribution to this textbook. A special thank-you goes to the members of the Advisory Committee for the Program in General Insurance, who continuously provide expertise and insight to the INS program and who give unselfishly of their time to promote insurance education and professionalism. In particular, we appreciate the valuable assistance of the following Advisory Committee member, who reviewed the entire manuscript and provided many helpful suggestions and comments:

Patricia M. Arnold, CPCU, ALCM
Staff Associate, Underwriting
State Farm Insurance Companies

The following Advisory Committee members were instrumental in the overall planning for this edition of the INS 21 text and in reviewing portions of the manuscript:

John E. Clark III, CLU
Manager, Workforce Development Services
USAA

Larry R. Hughes, AIM
Vice President of Marketing and Underwriting
Hoosier Insurance/General Casualty

Larry L. Klein, CPCU, AIM, AAI
Director
PricewaterhouseCoopers, LLP

Melissa McBratney, CPCU, AIM, AU
Vice President—Personal Lines Business Development
Farmers Insurance Group of Companies

Dean Ockerbloom, CPCU, ARM, AU
Second Vice President, Product Management
Travelers Property Casualty

George E. Rejda, Ph.D., CLU
V.J. Skutt Distinguished Professor of Insurance
University of Nebraska—Lincoln

Beth Gamble Riggins, CPCU, AIC, AAI
Director of Training
South Carolina Farm Bureau Insurance Companies

Christine A. Sullivan, CPCU, AIM
Director—Property Casualty Claim Service Organization
Allstate Insurance Company

The contribution of numerous people on the staff of the American Institute for CPCU and the Insurance Institute of America has been invaluable. We appreciate the efforts of the following Institute professionals, who spent many hours reviewing various chapters to verify the accuracy of the text and who made many helpful contributions:

James J. Markham, J. D., CPCU, AIC, AIAF (who reviewed the entire manuscript for this edition)
Senior Vice President

Connor M. Harrison, CPCU, AU, AAM, ARP, AIAF, ARe
Director of Underwriting Education

George L. Head, Ph.D., CPCU, ARM, CSP, CLU
Vice President

Daniel P. (Chuck) Hussey, Jr., CPCU, AAI, ARM
Director, Western Region

James R. Jones, CPCU, AIC, ARM
Director of Claims Education

Christine L. Lewis, Ph.D., CPCU, CLU, ARP, ChFC, RHU
Senior Vice President, Chief Academic Officer

Kenneth N. Scoles Jr., Ph.D., AIAF
Director of Curriculum

Gratefully, we also recognize the following Institute personnel, who offered many valuable comments on the text:

Cheryl L. Ferguson, CPCU, AAI, AU, AAM, API, AIM
Senior Director of Curriculum

Arthur L. Flitner, CPCU, ARM, AIC
Assistant Vice President, Senior Director Curriculum Design

Doris L. Hoopes, CPCU, AIC, AAI, AIM, ARe, AAM, ASLI
Senior Director of Curriculum

Helen E. McCormick, AAI, AAM
Marketing Assistant

We are particularly grateful to the members of the Institutes' Publication Department for their hard work in editing the manuscript, typesetting the text, preparing the exhibits, and publishing the final product. We cannot fail to mention the tremendous contribution of Michele Mollo, who edited the entire textbook and, with her keen eye for detail, enhanced it with many valuable suggestions.

We wish to thank all those authors, reviewers, editors, and others who contributed to the first two editions of *Property and Liability Insurance Principles*, particularly to James S. Trieschmann, D.B.A., CPCU, CLU, the Dudley L. Moore, Jr., Professor of Insurance and Associate Dean for Faculty and Research, Terry College of Business, at the University of Georgia, who authored and reviewed portions of both the first and second editions. We also wish to thank the following consulting authors for both previous editions: Anthony F. Gasich, CPCU, CLU, ChFC, AAI, President and Chief Operating Officer of the International Catastrophe Insurance Managers, LLC; and G. William Glendenning, Ph.D., CPCU, Consultant.

The policy provisions that are quoted throughout this text are from insurance policies developed by Insurance Services Office, to whom we are ever grateful for their continuing cooperation.

Finally, we wish to thank all the students and course leaders who have given us their constructive comments regarding the INS text materials. We invite you to help us by sending your comments on the current edition to the Curriculum Department of the Institutes. With your help, we can continue to improve this and other texts to give you the best educational tools for your insurance and risk management studies.

We sincerely hope that the hard work and expertise of the many people who contributed to this text will provide you with a meaningful experience that will enhance your professional development.

Constance M. Luthardt
Barry D. Smith
Eric A. Wiening

Contributing Authors

The American Institute for CPCU, the Insurance Institute of America, and the authors acknowledge, with deep appreciation, the work of the following contributing authors:

Anita W. Johnson, CPCU, CLU, ChFC
Director of Curriculum
AICPCU/IIA

George L. Head, Ph.D., CPCU, ARM, CSP, CLU
Vice President
AICPCU/IIA

Contents

Segment A:

Fundamentals of Insurance

Segment A introduces the concept of insurance as having three aspects: a transfer system, a business, and a contract. You will learn what insurance is, who provides it, and how the insurance business is regulated. The last chapter in this segment discusses the financial performance of insurance companies.

Chapter 1

Insurance: What Is It?

Educational Objectives

After studying this chapter, you should be able to:

1. Explain how insurance works as a system of transferring and sharing the costs of losses. (p. 1-4)

2. Explain the law of large numbers and its significance to the operation of insurance. (p. 1-5)

3. Identify and describe three major types of loss exposures. (pp. 1-5 to 1-7)

4. Identify and describe the characteristics of an ideally insurable loss exposure. (pp. 1-7 to 1-9)

5. Identify the three major types of private insurers. (p. 1-11)

6. Explain the need for government insurance, and give examples of (a) federal insurance programs and (b) state insurance programs. (pp. 1-11 to 1-12)

7. Briefly describe the major operations of insurance companies. (pp. 1-12 to 1-13)

8. Briefly explain why and how state insurance departments regulate insurers. (pp. 1-14 to 1-15)

9. Identify and describe the benefits of insurance. (pp. 1-15 to 1-18)

10. Identify and describe the costs of insurance. (pp. 1-18 to 1-20)

11. Describe and distinguish among the major types of property and liability insurance. (pp. 1-21 to 1-24)

12. Describe and distinguish among the major types of life and health insurance. (pp. 1-24 to 1-25)

13. Define or describe each of the Key Words and Phrases for this assignment. (All Key Words and Phrases appear in bold print in the text and in the margins throughout this chapter.)

Chapter 1

Insurance: What Is It?

Every person, family, and business needs insurance of some type to protect assets against unforeseen events that could cause financial hardship. Sometimes, insurance is needed to satisfy a contractual obligation, such as a homeowner's commitment to purchase insurance on the home to protect the mortgage company's investment in case the home is damaged or destroyed. Almost everyone needs insurance, but few people really understand it. What exactly *is* insurance?

Insurance is actually three things:

- A *transfer system*, in which one party—the **insured**—transfers the chance of financial loss to another party—the insurance company, or the **insurer**

- A *business*, which includes various operations that must be conducted in a way that generates sufficient income to pay claims and provide a reasonable profit for its owners

- A *contract* between the insured and the insurer that states what potential costs of loss the insured is transferring to the insurer and expresses the insurer's promise to pay for those costs of loss in exchange for a stated payment by the insured

An **insured** is a person, a business, or an organization whose property, life, or legal liability is covered by an insurance policy.

An **insurer** is an insurance company.

This chapter provides an introduction to these three aspects of insurance. Insurance as a transfer system is one technique of risk management, which Chapter 10 will cover. The insurance business and its various operations are discussed in Chapters 4 through 6, and insurance as a contract is covered in Chapter 7.

Insurance as a Transfer System

Insurance is a system that enables a person, family, or business to transfer the costs of losses to an insurance company. The insurance company, in turn, pays for **covered losses** and, in effect, distributes the costs of losses among all insureds (that is, all insureds share the cost of a loss). Thus, insurance is a system of both *transferring* and *sharing* the costs of losses.

Covered losses are the events for which insurance pays.

Transferring the Costs of Losses

By transferring the costs of their losses to insurance companies, insureds exchange the possibility of a large loss for the certainty of a much smaller, periodic payment (the premium that the insured pays for insurance coverage). This transfer is accomplished through insurance policies. An insurance policy is a contract that states the rights and duties of both the insured and the insurer regarding the transfer of the costs of losses.

There would be no need to transfer the costs of losses to an insurance company, however, if there were no exposures to loss, that is, no possibility that losses would occur. It is not necessary for a loss to occur for a **loss exposure** to exist; there simply must be the *possibility* of a loss. For example, every home has a fire loss exposure; in other words, the possibility exists that a fire could occur and cause a financial loss to the homeowner.

A **loss exposure**, or simply an **exposure**, is any condition or situation that presents the possibility of a loss.

Sharing the Costs of Losses

As a system of sharing, insurance involves the "pooling" by the insurance company of the premiums paid by insureds. Insureds who incur covered losses are paid from the insurer's funds, and the total cost of losses is thereby spread (or shared) among all insureds. Insurance companies estimate future losses and expenses to determine how much they must collect from insureds in premiums.

The **law of large numbers**, a mathematical principle that is the foundation of insurance, enables insurers to make predictions about losses. According to the law of large numbers, as the number of similar but independent **exposure units** increases, the relative accuracy of predictions about future outcomes based on these exposure units also increases. (Exposure units, such as cars and houses, are independent if they are not subject to the same event. The future outcomes that insurance companies want to predict are losses.) Because insurance companies have large numbers of independent exposure units (the cars and houses of all their insureds, for example), they can predict the number of losses that all similar exposure units combined are likely to experience.

For example, a homeowner is uncertain whether a fire will damage his or her home and transfers this uncertainty to an insurance company. The insurance company insures thousands of homes whose owners face the same uncertainty. Because of this large number of homes, the insurance company can, with a great deal of accuracy, predict the number of homes that will be damaged by fire during a given period. Based on this prediction, the insurance company can determine the amount of premiums that it needs to pay for the fire losses during that period.

The **law of large numbers** is a mathematical principle stating that as the number of similar but independent exposure units increases, the relative accuracy of predictions about future outcomes (losses) based on these exposure units also increases.

An **exposure unit** is a measure of loss potential and is used in pricing insurance. For example, in homeowners insurance, each home insured is an exposure unit.

Educational Objective 3

Identify and describe three major types of loss exposures.

Types of Loss Exposures

On a New Year's Eve some years ago, a fire swept through the ballroom and lower floors of a crowded hotel; more than 200 hotel guests and employees were killed or injured. All of the hotel's rooms were booked at the time of the fire, and it was alleged that the number of people occupying the ballroom exceeded its legal capacity. It was later discovered that disgruntled former employees had started the fire. Regardless of the cause of the fire, however, the hotel owners had not taken proper precautions to deal with a fire emergency. For example, the owners had not installed an automatic sprinkler system, fire walls were insufficient, exits were unlighted, and the hotel had no emergency plan to safely evacuate hotel occupants.

The hotel fire illustrates three major types of loss exposures that are useful in identifying and categorizing potential losses:

- Property loss exposures
- Liability loss exposures
- Human and personnel loss exposures

Property Loss Exposures

A **property loss exposure** is any condition or situation that presents the possibility that a property loss will happen.

Real property consists of land as well as buildings and other structures attached to the land or embedded in it.

Personal property consists of all tangible or intangible property that is not real property.

Every **property loss exposure** involves some type of property that is exposed to potential losses. Property includes real property and personal property. **Real property** is land and any property attached to it. A house, a storage shed, a swimming pool, a factory building, a flagpole, and an underground sewer pipe are all items of real property, as is the land where each is situated. All property that is not real property is **personal property**. Examples of personal property include the inventory of a retail merchant, furniture and fixtures in a restaurant, equipment and machinery in a factory building, contents of a dwelling, computers, money, securities, automobiles, patents, and copyrights.

In the hotel fire example, damage to the building and the personal property of the owners and others totaled several million dollars. For example, the hotel building was badly damaged and had to be repaired. Much of the furniture and carpeting in the hotel was damaged or destroyed and had to be replaced. The hotel guests' clothing and other personal property that were destroyed also had to be replaced.

Net income is income (or revenue) minus expenses during a given period.

Damage to property can also cause indirect losses, such as **net income** losses. All individuals, families, and businesses must generate an excess of income over expenses in order to remain financially sound. A net income loss can be the result of a reduction in revenue, an increase in expenses, or both. The net income losses of a business often greatly exceed the property loss that caused them, as in the hotel fire example.

While the damaged rooms in the hotel were being repaired and cleaned, the hotel's revenue decreased because guest rooms were empty. The hotel had to cancel social and business functions and close its restaurants and shops. Because of negative publicity about the fire, the hotel permanently lost some of its revenue to competition. The hotel also incurred increased expenses for overtime pay for some employees while it was being restored.

Liability Loss Exposures

A **liability loss exposure** is any condition or situation that presents the possibility that a *liability loss* will happen.

A **liability loss** is a claim for monetary damages because of injury to another party or damage to another party's property.

A **liability loss exposure** presents the possibility of a claim alleging legal responsibility of a person or business for injury or damage suffered by another party. Some liability claims result in a lawsuit; even if the lawsuit is groundless, the defendant might incur substantial expenses to defend against the suit. Liability claims might result from bodily injury, property damage, libel, slander, humiliation, defamation, invasion of privacy, and similar occurrences.

A **liability loss** usually results from one party negligently causing injury to another or damaging another's property. In the hotel fire example, the hotel owners were judged to be negligent for various reasons, including failure to take proper precautions to handle a fire emergency. As a result of the fire, the hotel incurred liability losses that included payments for medical expenses, rehabilitation costs, and pain and suffering experienced by the guests, employees, and others injured in the fire. Liability losses also included payments for damage to property belonging to guests and payments to survivors of people killed in the fire.

Human and Personnel Loss Exposures

Human loss exposures (also called **personal loss exposures**) can cause financial loss to individuals because of death, disability, or unemployment. The term human losses refers to the effect of death, disability, or unemployment on individuals or families. For example, a family would face a loss of income if a breadwinner died or became disabled or unemployed.

Personnel loss exposures, on the other hand, affect businesses. The term personnel losses generally refers to losses suffered by a business because of the death, disability, retirement, or resignation of key employees. For example, a business organization could face a financial loss if a key executive, sales representative, or product developer died, became disabled, or resigned and could not be readily replaced.

In the case of the hotel fire, if a key employee (such as the master chef) died in the fire, the hotel owners would experience a personnel loss. The chef's family and the families of others killed or injured by the fire would suffer human, or personal, losses.

A **human loss exposure**, also called a **personal loss exposure**, can be defined as any condition or situation that presents the possibility of a financial loss to an individual or a family by such causes as death, sickness, injury, or unemployment. (In a broader sense, the term *personal loss exposure* can also be used to include all loss exposures faced by individuals and families, including property and liability loss exposures.)

A **personnel loss exposure** is the possibility of a financial loss to a business because of the death, disability, retirement, or resignation of key employees.

Educational Objective 4

Identify and describe the characteristics of an ideally insurable loss exposure.

Ideally Insurable Loss Exposures

Insurance contracts cover events that might or might not happen. If the events do occur, a financial loss usually results. By transferring the potential costs of the uncertain event to the insurance company, the insured reduces or eliminates the possibility of suffering a financial loss. By charging a premium in return, the insurance company gains the opportunity to make a profit if it handles a volume of similar transactions efficiently. Therefore, each party to the contract receives some benefit from the transaction. However, the transaction is not likely to be advantageous to the insurer unless the loss exposure has certain characteristics that make it ideally insurable from the insurer's standpoint. Insurance companies generally prefer to provide insurance for the financial consequences of loss exposures that have the following characteristics:

- Large number of similar exposure units
- Losses that are accidental
- Losses that are definite and measurable
- Losses that are not catastrophic
- Losses that are economically feasible to insure

Large Number of Similar Exposure Units

An ideally insurable loss exposure must be common enough that the insurer can pool a large number of homogeneous, or similar, exposure units. This characteristic is important because it enables the insurer to predict losses accurately and to determine appropriate premiums.

Loss exposures that satisfy this requirement, such as the possibility of damage to homes or automobiles, allow the insurance company to take advantage of the law of large numbers. The insurance company can determine appropriate premiums based on the experience of thousands of similar exposure units and make reasonably accurate predictions about losses.

On the other hand, predicting the number of losses each year to space stations in outer space would be difficult, since there are very few exposure units. Moreover, each loss could drastically affect the profitability of an insurance company and the insurance business as a whole. The inability of insurance companies to predict losses and thus to determine adequate premiums makes most insurers reluctant to insure unusual loss exposures such as those represented by space stations.

Losses That Are Accidental

An ideally insurable loss exposure also involves a potential loss that is accidental from the standpoint of the insured. If the insured has some control over whether a loss will occur, the insurance company is at a disadvantage because the insured might have an incentive to cause a loss. If losses are not accidental, the insurance company cannot calculate an appropriate premium because the chance of a loss could increase as soon as a policy is issued. If the loss exposure involves only accidental losses, the insurer can better estimate future losses and calculate an adequate premium for the exposure.

Losses That Are Definite and Measurable

To be insurable, a loss should have a definite time and place of occurrence, and the amount of the loss must be measurable in dollars. Insurable loss exposures should be definite and measurable for practical reasons. If the time and location of a loss cannot be definitely determined and the amount of the loss cannot be measured, writing an insurance policy that defines what claims to pay and how much to pay for them becomes extremely difficult. Also, losses are impossible to predict if they cannot be measured. For example, the sudden bursting of a water pipe that causes water damage in the insured's bathroom is an occurrence that has a definite time and place and that can thus be insured. However, if a slow leak in the pipe causes decay and rotting of the insured's bathroom floor over several years, the resulting loss does not have a definite time of occurrence and is generally not insurable.

Losses That Are Not Catastrophic

Effective pooling of exposure units assumes that the exposure units are independent. Independence means that a loss suffered by one insured does not affect any other insured or group of insureds. If exposure units are not independent, a single catastrophe could cause losses to a sizable proportion of insureds at the same time. For example, if an insurance company insured all of the homes and businesses in a particular city, the insurance company would probably suffer a financial disaster if a hurricane leveled the city. The insurer would be unlikely to have the financial resources to pay all claims of all the insureds affected by the hurricane.

This tendency of insurers not to insure catastrophic losses does not mean that hurricane damage to property is not insurable. Coverage for windstorm damage, including hurricane and tornado damage, is readily available throughout most of the country. However, an insurance company avoids possible financial disaster by managing its pool of insureds in such a way that it does not have a large proportion of its insureds exposed to loss in any single event. For windstorm coverage, the insurance company must diversify the homes and businesses it insures so that it does not have a heavy concentration of insureds in any one geographic area. Consequently, the insurer maintains as much independence as possible among its insureds. If each of many insurers issued a relatively small number of policies in the city devastated by the hurricane, no one insurer would face financial ruin.

Losses That Are Economically Feasible To Insure

Insurance companies seek to cover only loss exposures that are economically feasible to insure. Because of this constraint, loss exposures involving small losses as well as those involving a high probability of loss are generally considered uninsurable. Writing insurance to cover small losses does not make sense when the expense of providing the insurance probably exceeds the amount of potential losses. Insurance to cover the disappearance of office supplies, for example, could require the insurer to spend more to issue claim checks than it would to pay for the claims. It also does not make sense to write insurance to cover losses that are almost certain to occur. In such a situation, the premium would probably be as high as or higher than the potential amount of the loss. For example, insurers generally do not cover damage due to wear and tear of an automobile, because autos are certain to incur such damage over time.

Insurance as a Business

The insurance business in the United States provides well over 2 million jobs and, in the late 1990s, had combined assets totaling more than $3.1 trillion. Nearly 8,000 insurance companies are based in the United States, of which well over 3,000 sell property and liability insurance and other related types of insurance. Property and liability insurance companies employ over 600,000 people. In addition, over 700,000 people work in insurance agencies, brokerage firms, and insurance service agencies.[1]

Private (non-government) insurance companies vary enormously in size and structure, the products they sell, and the territories they serve; collectively they represent a substantial segment of business in the United States. Despite their size and number, however, private insurance companies do not fill every insurance need in U.S. society. In some instances, federal and state governments provide insurance in order to meet the property and liability insurance needs of the public.

Through their insurance departments, state governments closely regulate the business of insurance. Private insurers must be licensed in the states in which they sell insurance. Since regulation of licensed insurers encompasses all insurer operations, state insurance regulators review insurance rates, policy forms, underwriting practices, claim practices, and financial performance of insurance companies. Regulators can revoke the licenses of insurers that do not fully comply with state regulations.

This section provides a brief overview of the business of insurance in regard to the following:

- Types of insurers
- Insurance operations
- Financial performance of insurers
- State insurance regulation
- Benefits and costs of insurance

Types of Insurers

Many different types of private insurers offer various types of insurance. The federal government and state governments also provide insurance. In some cases, government insurance plans supply the same types of insurance as private insurers; in other cases, government insurance provides coverage that is not available from private insurers.

Educational Objective 5

Identify the three major types of private insurers.

Private Insurers

The three major types of private insurers are as follows:

- Stock insurance companies, which are corporations owned by stockholders
- Mutual insurance companies, which are corporations owned by their policyholders
- Reciprocal insurance exchanges (also known as an interinsurance exchanges), which are unincorporated associations that provide insurance services to their members, often called subscribers

Other private providers of insurance include Lloyd's of London, captive insurance companies, and reinsurance companies. Chapter 2 will discuss these types of insurance providers.

Educational Objective 6

Explain the need for government insurance, and give examples of (a) federal insurance programs and (b) state insurance programs.

Federal Government Insurance Programs

Some federal government insurance programs exist because of the huge amount of financial resources needed to provide certain types of coverage and because the government has the authority to require mandatory coverage. Social Security is the best example of such a program. Private insurers provide some benefits similar to those provided by the Social Security program, but the number of Social Security beneficiaries and the range of coverages are beyond the scope of private insurers.

In addition to the Social Security program, the federal government provides coverage that only certain segments of the population need. The National Flood Insurance Program provides insurance for owners of property located in flood-prone areas and for others concerned about the exposure of flooding. The Federal Crop Insurance Program insures farmers against damage to their crops by drought, insects, hail, and other causes. The federal government also insures depositors against loss resulting from the failure or insolvency of banks (through the Federal Deposit Insurance Corporation) and credit unions (through the National Credit Union Administration).

State Government Insurance Programs

State governments also offer insurance programs to assure the availability of certain types of coverage considered necessary to protect the public. All states require that employers be able to meet the financial obligations based on workers compensation laws. Some states sell workers compensation insurance to employers. Depending on the state, the state workers compensation insurance program might be the employers' only option, or it might be one of several options available to employers to meet their obligations.

In addition, state governments operate unemployment insurance plans, which ensure at least a minimum level of protection for eligible workers who are unemployed. Fair Access to Insurance Requirements (FAIR) plans have been implemented in many states to provide basic property insurance to property owners who cannot otherwise obtain needed coverage. Through automobile insurance plans and other programs, states make auto insurance available to drivers who have difficulty obtaining such insurance from private insurers.

Educational Objective 7

Briefly describe the major operations of insurance companies.

Insurance Operations

An insurance company must take great care in arranging the insurance it agrees to provide, not only to make certain it can meet its commitments to insureds to pay for covered losses, but also to collect enough premiums to earn a reasonable profit after paying those losses. The insurer must market effectively in order to cover enough customers to enable it to operate economically. It must also decide which potential customers to insure, what coverage to offer, and what premium to charge so that customers are adequately insured and the insurer can operate profitably. The insurer must then determine which losses sustained by its customers are covered and the amount to be paid for covered losses.

To accomplish these objectives, insurance companies engage in the following operations, all of which upcoming chapters will discuss:

- Marketing
- Underwriting
- Claim handling
- Ratemaking

Marketing is the process of identifying customers and selling and delivering a product or service. Insurance marketing enables insurers to reach potential customers and retain current ones. Insurance producers are an integral part of insurance marketing because they represent insurance companies in providing insurance products to the public. Other important aspects of marketing are advertising and marketing management. Marketing management comprises producer supervision and motivation, as well as product management.

Underwriting is the process by which insurance companies decide which potential customers to insure and what coverage to offer them. Underwriters are the insurance company employees responsible for selecting insureds, pricing coverage, and determining policy terms and conditions. Effective underwriting enables insurers to provide the coverage needed by insureds and to be reasonably certain that the loss fund will be sufficient to pay for their losses.

Claim handling enables insurance companies to determine whether a covered loss has occurred and, if so, the amount to be paid for the loss. The role of a claim representative is to satisfy the insurer's obligations under an insurance policy by promptly responding to claims and gathering the information necessary to evaluate a claim properly and reach a fair settlement.

Ratemaking, another important insurance operation, is the process by which insurers determine the rates to charge the thousands (or millions) of similar but independent insureds. Insurers need appropriate rates to have enough money to pay for losses, cover operating expenses, and earn a reasonable profit.

To support their operations, insurance companies process vast amounts of data. They rely on computers to process most of that data and to generate information. Insurers use computers to process applications, to issue and renew policies, to generate invoices, to keep records of claims and loss payments, and to maintain accounting records and statistical reports. In addition to insurance-related information, insurance companies use computers in the same way that other businesses do. That is, they use computers to generate management information reports and to store and retrieve data relating to employees, investments, customers, suppliers, and other matters.

All of these operations are aspects of the insurance business. An insurance company's income must, in the long run, exceed the amount it pays for claims and administrative expenses if the company is to remain financially viable. Therefore, an insurance company's financial performance is very important, but not just to the insurance company. State insurance regulators, insurance producers, stockholders, and insureds also need to be assured of the financial health of an insurance company.

Financial Performance of Insurers

The primary sources of income for insurance companies are premiums and investments. Insurance companies have investments because they receive premiums before they pay for losses and expenses. Insurers invest the money in the meantime and receive investment income as a result. One of the goals of insurers is to generate enough revenues from premiums and investments to pay for losses, meet other expenses, and earn a reasonable profit. In addition to loss payments, insurance companies incur several other types of expenses. Insurers have loss settlement expenses, which include the costs of investigating and settling claims. They also incur expenses to acquire new business, such as advertising costs and producers' commissions, and general expenses, such as salaries, employee benefits, utilities, telephones, and computer equipment. Insurance companies pay premium taxes, income taxes, and various licensing and other fees. Insurers have expenses associated with investment activities, such as the salaries of investment department staff members. The ability to pay these expenses and still make a reasonable profit is a measure of an insurance company's solvency, that is, its long-term financial strength.

Educational Objective 8

Briefly explain why and how state insurance departments regulate insurers.

State Insurance Regulation

A major concern of insurance regulators is that insurers be able to meet their obligations to insureds. A financially weak insurer may not have the resources necessary to meet its obligations. Therefore, insurance regulators closely monitor the financial condition of insurance companies and take actions necessary to prevent insurer insolvency.

Every state has an insurance department that regulates the insurers doing business in the state. Almost all aspects of the insurance business are regulated to some degree, but most insurance regulation deals with rates, insurer solvency, and consumer protection.

State insurance departments regulate insurance rates to protect consumers from inadequate, excessive, or unfairly discriminatory rates. Adequate rates are necessary for insurers to earn enough premium income to pay for losses and other expenses while generating a reasonable profit. Alternatively, if rates were excessive, insurers could earn unreasonable profits. Insurance rates should reflect the exposures to loss presented by insureds, and insureds with similar loss exposures are grouped together in a single rating class and charged the same rate. Although other insureds may be grouped in a different rating class and charged a different rate, that rate must reflect the group's exposures to loss. It would be unfair, however, if the different rate reflected characteristics of the group that had no bearing on their exposures to loss. Therefore, rates based on such characteristics would not be permitted because they would be unfairly discriminatory. What constitutes "unfair discrimination" varies by state, and some states no longer allow discrimination based on such characteristics as age and sex for certain types of insurance.

Through solvency surveillance, insurance regulators monitor the financial condition of insurance companies. Such surveillance enables regulators to work with insurers that have financial difficulties to keep the insurers in business and maintain their ability to meet obligations to insureds.

Insurance regulation protects consumers in several ways. Insurance companies must be licensed to write insurance policies in a given state, and licensing requires an insurer to meet tests of financial strength. In addition to licensing insurance companies, states require that certain representatives of insurance companies also be licensed. Such licensing requirements apply to insurance producers and may also apply to claim representatives and others.

Most states require that insurance companies file their policy forms with the insurance department so that the department can approve policy language. States also monitor specific insurance company practices concerning marketing, underwriting, and claims. In addition, state insurance departments investigate complaints against insurance companies and their representatives and enforce standards regarding their conduct.

Educational Objective 9

Identify and describe the benefits of insurance.

Benefits of Insurance

The business of insurance provides many benefits to individuals, families, businesses, and society as a whole. These benefits include the following:

- Payment for the costs of covered losses
- Reduction of the insured's financial uncertainty
- Loss control activities of insurance companies
- Efficient use of resources
- Support for credit
- Satisfaction of legal requirements
- Satisfaction of business requirements
- Source of investment funds
- Reduction of social burdens

Payment for Losses

The primary role of insurance is to **indemnify** individuals, families, and businesses that incur losses. When an insurance company pays an insured for a loss, the company has indemnified the insured.

To **indemnify** means to restore a party who has had a covered loss to the same financial position that party held before the loss occurred.

To recognize the value of payment for losses, consider the aftermath of a loss for those who have no insurance. If fire destroys the home of a family with no insurance, the family members might be left without the financial resources to repair their home or to replace their belongings; they might also face the immediate lack of a place to live. A business can incur bankruptcy as the result of a liability judgment it cannot pay, and the employees and owners of the business will suddenly be unemployed. By indemnifying insureds, insurance provides some degree of financial security and stability for individuals, families, and businesses.

Reduction of Uncertainty

Because insurance provides financial compensation when covered losses occur, it greatly reduces the uncertainty created by many loss exposures. A family's major financial concerns, for example, would probably center around the possibility of a breadwinner's death or the destruction of a home. If the family transfers the uncertainty about the financial consequences of such losses to an insurance company, the family practically eliminates these concerns. Insurance companies have greater certainty than individuals about losses, because the law of large numbers enables them to predict the number of losses that are likely to occur and the financial effects of those losses.

Loss Control Activities

Insurance companies often recommend loss control practices that people and businesses can implement. *Loss control* means taking measures to prevent some losses from occurring or to reduce the financial consequences of losses that do occur. Individuals, families, and businesses can use measures such as burglar alarms, smoke alarms, and deadbolt locks to prevent or reduce losses. Loss control generally reduces the amount of money insurers must pay in claims. As a result, loss control helps to improve the financial results of insurers and to reduce insurance costs to consumers. Thus, society benefits from activities that prevent and reduce losses.

Efficient Use of Resources

People and businesses that face an uncertain future often set aside funds to pay for future losses. Insurance makes it unnecessary to set aside a large amount of money to pay for the financial consequences of loss exposures that can be insured. Money that would otherwise be set aside to pay for possible losses can be used to improve a family's quality of life or to contribute to the growth of a business. In exchange for a relatively small premium, families and businesses can free up additional funds that they would otherwise need to reserve to pay for unforeseen future losses.

Support for Credit

Before making a loan, a lender wants assurance that the money will be repaid. When a lender loans money to a borrower to purchase property, the lender usually acquires a legal interest in that property. The lender can repossess a car or foreclose a home mortgage if the loan is not repaid. However, the lender would be less likely to make loans if it did not have some assurance of getting back its money if the car or house were destroyed or if the borrower died or became disabled before the loan was paid in full. Insurance makes loans to individuals and businesses possible by guaranteeing that the lender will be paid if the collateral for the loan (such as a house or a commercial building) is destroyed or damaged by an insured event, thereby reducing the lender's uncertainty.

Satisfaction of Legal Requirements

Insurance is often used or required to satisfy legal requirements. In many states, for example, automobile owners must prove they have auto liability insurance before they can register their autos. All states have laws that require employers to pay for the job-related injuries or illnesses of their employees, and employers generally purchase workers compensation insurance to meet this financial obligation.

Satisfaction of Business Requirements

Certain business relationships require proof of insurance. For example, building contractors are usually required to provide evidence of liability insurance before a construction contract is granted. In fact, almost anyone who provides a service to the public, from an architect to a tree trimmer, might need to prove that he or she has liability insurance before being awarded a contract for services.

Source of Investment Funds

One of the greatest benefits of insurance is that it provides funds for investment. When insurers collect premiums, they do not usually need funds immediately to pay losses and expenses. Insurance companies use some of these funds to make loans to businesses. Such loans provide investment money for projects such as new construction, research, and technology. Investment funds promote economic growth and job creation. Insurance companies also invest in social projects, such as cultural events, education, and economic development projects. Investment brings additional funding to insurers in the form of interest; this additional income helps to keep insurance premiums at a reasonable level.

Reduction of Social Burdens

Uncompensated accident victims can be a serious burden to society. Insurance helps to reduce this burden by providing compensation to such injured persons. For example, workers compensation insurance provides payment to injured workers for medical expenses, lost wages, and rehabilitation, as well as death benefits to survivors. Compulsory auto insurance is another example, because it provides compensation to auto accident victims who might otherwise be unable to afford proper medical care or who might be unable to work because of the accident. Without insurance, victims of job-related or auto accidents might become a burden to society and need some form of state welfare.

Educational Objective 10

Identify and describe the costs of insurance.

Costs of Insurance

The benefits of insurance are not cost-free. However, the benefits of insurance far outweigh the costs, and insurance is generally considered to be a tremendous economic and social benefit. Among the costs of insurance are both direct and indirect costs, including the following:

- Premiums paid by insureds
- Operating costs of insurers
- Opportunity costs
- Increased losses
- Increased lawsuits

Premiums Paid by Insureds

Insurers must charge premiums in order to have the funds necessary to make loss payments. In fact, an insurance company must collect a total amount of premiums that exceeds the amount needed to pay for losses in order to cover its costs of doing business. For example, an insurance company might use seventy-five cents of every premium dollar to pay for losses and twenty-five cents for other expenses. Although insurance premiums by law must not be excessive, some insureds believe that their premiums are too high. All those who are insured must consider premiums as a cost of living and doing business in an industrialized society.

Operating Costs of Insurers

Like any business, an insurance company has operating costs that must be paid to run the day-to-day operations of the company. Those costs include salaries, agent commissions, advertising, building expenses, equipment, taxes, licensing fees, and many others. In addition, most insurers are in business to make a profit, just like any other business. A reasonable amount

of profit must be calculated in the cost of insurance that insureds pay.

Opportunity Costs

If capital and labor were not being used in the business of
insurance, they could be used elsewhere and could be making
other productive contributions to society. Therefore, whatever
resources the insurance industry uses in its operations represent
lost opportunities in other areas—in other words, opportunity
costs. These opportunity costs represent one of the costs of
insurance.

Increased Losses

The existence of insurance might encourage losses to some
extent. Although insurers have an economic incentive to
provide and to encourage loss control measures, insurance
sometimes provides an economic incentive for insureds to have
losses. Because of insurance, a person might intentionally cause
a loss or exaggerate a loss that has occurred. For example, it was
estimated that 85,500 structural fires and 47,000 vehicle fires in
a recent year were of incendiary or suspicious origin. Property
damage from these fires amounted to more than $1.4 billion in
structural damage and $202 million in vehicle damage; these
figures do not include indirect costs, such as business interruption, loss of use, and temporary shelter costs; nor do they take
into consideration the human suffering and human loss exposure costs, such as medical expenses and funeral costs, associated
with fire losses.[2] Many cases of arson or suspected arson involve
insurance; some property owners would rather have the insurance money than the property.

Inflated claims of loss are more common than deliberate losses.
For example, an insured might claim that four items were lost
rather than the actual three or that the items were worth more
than their actual value. In liability claims, claimants might
exaggerate the severity of their bodily injury or property damage. In some cases, other parties such as physicians, lawyers,
contractors, and auto body shop operators support the exagger-
ated claims, thus driving up the cost of claims and eventually
the total cost of insurance, because insurers must increase
premiums to pay the cost of inflated claims. Insurance fraud,
involving both deliberate and inflated losses, is a serious problem that results in billions of dollars in fraudulent claims each
year. Fraudulent claims increase costs for both insurers (in terms
of both payment for fraudulent claims and the cost of investigating fraud) and insureds (who pay increased premiums to help
cover the cost of those who defraud insurance companies).

Some losses might not be deliberately caused, but they might
result from carelessness on the part of an insured. Sometimes an
insured is not as careful as he or she would be without insurance

and does not try to prevent losses because insurance is available to pay for losses if they occur. Routinely leaving the keys in an unlocked car and storing oily rags in the basement are examples of such carelessness. If the car is stolen or the rags cause a fire, the insured would suffer only minimal financial harm because the insurance company will pay for the loss. The insured's attitude is "Who cares? I have insurance." The additional losses that result from the carelessness of insureds increase the cost of insurance for everyone because insurance companies often pay for injuries and damage that insureds could have prevented.

Increased Lawsuits

The number of liability lawsuits has increased steadily in recent years. One reason for this increase is that liability insurers often pay large sums of money to persons who have been injured. Liability insurance is intended to protect people who might be responsible for injury to someone else or damage to someone's property. However, many people seem to view liability insurance as a pool of money available to anyone who has suffered injury or damage, with little regard given to fault. The increase in lawsuits in the United States is an unfortunate cost of insurance in our society.

Insurance as a Contract

An insurance policy is a contract between the insurance company and the insured. Through insurance policies, insureds transfer the possible costs of losses to insurance companies. In return for the premiums paid by insureds, insurers promise to pay for the losses covered by the insurance policy. As noted, this promise reduces the uncertainty or insecurity that insureds have about paying for losses that might occur. The coverage provided by insurance policies enables individuals, families, businesses, and organizations to protect their assets and minimize the adverse financial effects of losses.

The four basic types of insurance (property, liability, life, and health) are generally divided into two broad categories:

- Property/liability insurance
- Life/health insurance

Property insurance provides coverage for property and net income loss exposures. It protects an insured's assets by paying to repair or replace property that is damaged, lost, or destroyed or by replacing the net income lost and the extra expenses incurred as a result of a property loss. Liability insurance covers liability loss exposures. It provides for payment on behalf of the insured for injury to others or damage to others' property for which the insured is legally responsible.

Life insurance and health insurance cover the financial consequences of human (personal) loss exposures. Life insurance replaces the income-earning potential lost through death and also helps to pay expenses related to an insured's death. Health insurance provides additional economic security by paying medical expenses. Disability insurance is a form of health insurance that replaces an insured's income if the insured is unable to work because of illness or injury.

These types (or *lines*) of insurance are briefly described below. They are discussed in detail in INS 22 (*Personal Insurance*) and INS 23 (*Commercial Insurance*).

"Fire Insurance" and "Casualty Insurance"

The terms "fire insurance" and "casualty insurance" are historical terms that have their roots in insurance regulation, but they are still used in the insurance business today. Before the 1950s, there were three categories of insurers: (1) life, (2) fire and marine, and (3) casualty and surety (bonds).

When these separate categories existed, fire insurers could insure only property. Thus, fire insurance and property insurance became almost synonymous terms. Property insurance is still often referred to as fire insurance, although it generally covers much more than fire losses.

Likewise, the term casualty insurance is sometimes used in place of liability insurance and encompasses liability insurance and other related types of insurance (such as workers compensation) that cover losses resulting from casualties. In the past, when insurance companies were either fire companies or casualty companies, separate policies from different insurance companies had to be issued on a house or a commercial building and the personal property inside (fire insurance) and on the owner's liability exposures (casualty insurance). This fire/casualty division has given way almost entirely to a property/liability division, although many insurance professionals continue to use the terms fire insurance to describe property coverages and casualty insurance to describe liability and related coverages.

Educational Objective 11

Describe and distinguish among the major types of property and liability insurance.

Property Insurance

Property insurance covers the costs of accidental losses to an insured's property. The insured could be a person insuring his or her house and personal property or a business insuring its

Jargon Alert!

Line of insurance is just another way of saying type of insurance. For example, "personal lines insurance" means any type of insurance purchased by individuals and families to cover nonbusiness loss exposures. "Commercial lines insurance" is any type of insurance that covers loss exposures for businesses and organizations.

building, inventory, and equipment. When the insured experiences a loss, such as fire damage to a house, the insured deals directly with the insurance company to settle the loss and receive payment.

Many types of insurance are classified as property insurance, such as the following:

- Fire and allied lines
- Business income
- Crime
- Ocean and inland marine
- Auto physical damage

A brief discussion of these types of property insurance follows.

Fire and allied lines insurance covers direct damage to or loss of insured property.

Fire and allied lines insurance generally covers direct damage to or loss of property, such as buildings and personal property, at a fixed location or locations described in the policy. The term "allied lines" refers to insurance against causes of loss usually written with (allied to) fire insurance, such as windstorm, hail, smoke, explosion, vandalism, and others. Examples of policies that cover fire and allied lines insurance are a dwelling policy and a commercial property policy.

Business income insurance covers the loss of net income or additional expenses incurred by a business as the result of a covered loss to its property.

Business income insurance, traditionally called business interruption insurance, pays a business for its loss of net income or additional expenses as a result of a covered loss such as fire. For example, when a business has a serious fire, it might have to close until repairs to the building are made and personal property is replaced. The resulting loss of net income occurs over time. Business income insurance pays the insured for the loss of income or additional expenses that the insured incurs because of the loss during the time needed to restore the business to its pre-loss condition.

Crime insurance protects the insured against loss to covered property from various causes of loss such as burglary, robbery, theft, and employee dishonesty.

Crime insurance covers money, securities, merchandise, and other property from various causes of loss such as burglary, robbery, theft, and employee dishonesty. Coverage for crime losses that a business might suffer is usually provided by separate policies that insure specific types of property against specific crime losses. Crime losses that a person or family might suffer are usually insured under a homeowners policy.

Ocean marine insurance includes hull insurance (which covers ships) and cargo insurance (which covers the goods transported by ships).

Inland marine insurance covers miscellaneous types of property, such as movable property, goods in domestic transit, and property used in transportation and communication.

Ocean marine insurance, one of the oldest forms of insurance, covers ships and their cargo against such causes of loss as fire, lightning, and "perils of the seas," which include high winds, rough waters, running aground, and collision with other ships or objects. **Inland marine insurance** was originally developed to provide coverage for losses to cargo transported over land. Inland marine insurance now covers many different types of property in addition to goods in transit.

Auto physical damage insurance is usually part of a policy that also provides auto liability coverage, such as a personal auto policy or a business auto policy. Auto physical damage is generally considered to mean loss or damage to specified vehicles from collision, fire, theft, or other causes.

Auto physical damage insurance covers loss of or damage to specified vehicles owned by the insured and sometimes covers vehicles borrowed or rented by the insured.

Liability Insurance

An insurance policy is a contract between the insured and the insurance company, and these two are usually the only parties involved in a property loss. Liability insurance, however, is sometimes called "third-party insurance" because three parties are involved in a liability loss: the insured, the insurance company, and the party who is injured or whose property is damaged by the insured. (The third party is usually called the claimant.) The insurance company pays the claimant *on behalf of the insured* if the insured is legally liable for the injury or damage. An insured's legal liability for injury or damage is often the result of a negligent act, but there are other sources of liability as well. Examples of liability insurance include the following:

- Auto liability
- Commercial general liability
- Personal liability
- Professional liability

Auto liability insurance provides protection against an insured's legal liability arising out of the ownership or operation of an automobile. The legal costs of defending the insured against lawsuits are also covered when such defense is necessary. The personal auto policy and the business auto policy are the most widely used auto insurance policies. These policies can include coverage for both auto liability and auto physical damage losses.

Auto liability insurance covers an insured's liability for bodily injury to others and damage to the property of others resulting from automobile accidents.

Commercial general liability insurance covers liability loss exposures arising from a business organization's premises and operations, its products, or its completed work. The following examples of liability claims against an appliance store illustrate the various ways that a business can be liable for the injuries or property damage suffered by others:

- *Premises*: A customer whose finger was caught in a revolving door incurred medical expenses for treatment in a hospital emergency room.
- *Business operations*: Employees broke a water pipe while installing a dishwasher in an apartment, causing substantial water damage to property in the apartment below.
- *Products*: A customer's face was cut when an electric mixer sold to the customer malfunctioned and shattered a glass mixing bowl.

Commercial general liability insurance covers businesses for their liability for bodily injury and property damage. It can also include liability coverage for various other offenses that might give rise to claims, such as libel, slander, false arrest, and advertising injury.

- *Completed operations*: A short circuit developed in an electric stove incorrectly installed by employees and caused a fire that damaged the customer's kitchen.

Personal liability insurance pro-vides liability coverage to individuals and families for bodily injury and property damage arising from the insured's personal premises or activities.

Personal liability insurance provides broad liability coverage to individuals and families. As mentioned, in most instances, the liability arises from the insured's negligence. For example, a visitor to the insured's home might slip and fall on the insured's icy driveway, or the insured might hit a golf ball that accidentally strikes a pedestrian in the head. This type of coverage is included in all homeowners policies.

Professional liability insurance protects physicians, accountants, architects, engineers, attorneys, insurance agents and brokers, and other professionals against liability arising out of their professional acts or omissions.

Professional liability insurance provides liability coverage to professionals for errors and omissions arising out of their professional duties. Medical malpractice insurance, which covers doctors and other healthcare providers, is probably the best known type of professional liability insurance, but similar coverage is available to other types of professionals, including insurance producers, attorneys, architects, and engineers.

Educational Objective 12

Describe and distinguish among the major types of life and health insurance.

Life Insurance

One of the most severe causes of financial loss to a family is the premature death of a family member, especially the primary wage earner. Life insurance can greatly reduce the adverse financial consequences of premature death by providing funds to replace lost income and to pay expenses associated with the final illness, when necessary, and the funeral.

Whole life insurance provides life-time protection (to age 100). Whole life insurance policies accrue cash value and have premiums that remain unchanged during the insured's lifetime.

Cash value is a savings fund that accumulates in a whole life insurance policy and that the policy-holder can access in several ways, including borrowing, purchasing paid-up life insurance, and surrendering the policy in exchange for the cash value.

Although there are many variations of life insurance, three basic types are commonly sold today:

- Whole life insurance
- Term insurance
- Universal life insurance

Whole life insurance provides lifetime protection (for the insured's whole life) and is considered permanent insurance. Whole life policies accrue a cash value that the policyholder can borrow after a policy has been in effect for a specified number of years. Whole life insurance is used when a consumer wants lifetime protection with a level premium and a savings element, which is called **cash value**.

Term insurance is a type of life insurance that provides temporary protection (for a certain period) with no cash value.

Term insurance provides coverage for a specified period, such as five or ten years, and is therefore not permanent insurance. A term life insurance policy has no cash value and is used when the consumer wants the maximum amount of life insurance protection available at the lowest cost.

Universal life insurance is frequently sold as an investment vehicle that combines life insurance protection with savings. The policyowner has a cash value account that is credited with the premiums paid less a deduction for the cost of the insurance protection and expenses charged. The balance in the account is then credited with interest at a specified rate. If the policyowner surrenders the policy, the cash value account may be reduced by a surrender charge to determine the surrender value paid to the policyowner.

Universal life insurance combines life insurance protection with savings. A universal life insurance policy is a flexible-premium policy that separates the protection, savings, and expense components.

Some life insurance policies are sold directly to individuals, while other life insurance policies cover a group of insureds. Such group policies are usually term insurance policies arranged through an employer or an association. Life insurance is discussed in more detail in INS 22.

Health Insurance

Health insurance is designed to protect individuals and families from financial losses caused by accidents and sickness and, like life insurance, is issued on either an individual or a group basis. The various types of health insurance policies can be classified as either medical insurance or disability insurance. **Medical insurance** covers medical expenses that result from illness or injury. **Disability income insurance** provides periodic benefits to an insured who is unable to work as a result of an accident or sickness. Disability insurance is primarily income replacement insurance that pays weekly or monthly benefits until the insured can return to work or until a maximum period has elapsed. Health insurance is also discussed in INS 22.

Medical insurance covers the cost of medical care, including doctors' bills, hospital charges (including room and board), laboratory charges, and related expenses.

Disability income insurance is a type of health insurance that provides periodic income payments to an insured who is unable to work because of sickness or injury.

Educational Objective 13

Define or describe each of the Key Words and Phrases for this assignment. (All Key Words and Phrases appear in bold print in the text and in the margins throughout this chapter.)

Summary

Every individual, family, and business organization needs insurance. Insurance is actually three things: a transfer system, a business, and a contract.

The key elements of insurance as a transfer system are transfer and sharing. An insured transfers the financial consequences of loss to an insurance company, thereby exchanging the possibility of a large loss for the certainty of a much smaller periodic payment (the premium). The sharing element of insurance requires the insurance company to pool the premiums paid by insureds into a loss fund from which covered losses are paid. Although the insurance company does not expect all insureds to experience a loss, all insureds share in the cost of losses because their premiums make up the loss fund. Because of the law of large numbers, insurers can accurately predict the number of losses that are likely to occur and thus the amount of premium to be paid by each insured.

The need for insurance exists because everyone faces exposures to loss, that is, the possibility that a loss will occur. Loss exposures can give rise to three major types of loss: property loss (including net income loss), liability loss, and human and personnel loss. The role of insurance is to protect insureds' assets from the financial consequences of loss. However, insurance companies prefer to provide insurance for loss exposures that are considered ideally insurable.

The business of insurance provides more than 2 million jobs in the United States; property and liability insurance companies, agencies, and brokerage firms employ almost 1.3 million people. Private insurers provide most insurance, but federal and state government insurance programs also exist.

The states regulate many of the operations of insurance companies. These operations include marketing, underwriting, claim handling, and ratemaking, as well as information processing. Regulators, insureds, and others need to be assured of the financial stability of insurance companies. To protect consumers, state insurance departments regulate insurance rates and policy forms, monitor insurer solvency, and investigate complaints against insurance companies.

In addition to payment for losses, the business of insurance offers several benefits to insureds and to society as a whole. However, both direct and indirect costs are associated with insurance.

An insurance policy, which is a contract between the insured and the insurer, states the rights and duties of each party with regard to losses. The four basic types of insurance are property insurance, liability insurance, life insurance, and health insurance. Each of these types of insurance is provided through contracts between the insured and the insurer.

Chapter Notes

1. Insurance Information Institute, *The Fact Book 1998: Property/Casualty Insurance Facts* (New York: Insurance Information Institute, 1997), p. 5.
2. *The Fact Book 1998*, p. 65.

Chapter 2

Who Provides Insurance and How Is It Regulated?

Educational Objectives

After studying this chapter, you should be able to:

1. Describe and compare the various types of private insurers that provide property and liability insurance. (pp. 2-3 to 2-10)

2. Describe common federal government insurance programs. (pp. 2-10 to 2-11)

3. Describe common state government insurance programs. (pp. 2-11 to 2-13)

4. Describe the purpose and activities of the National Association of Insurance Commissioners (NAIC). (pp. 2-14 to 2-15)

5. Explain how insurance rates are developed. (pp. 2-15 to 2-16)

6. Explain why and how insurance rates are regulated. (pp. 2-16 to 2-19)

7. Explain: (pp. 2-19 to 2-22)

   a. How insurance regulators monitor insurance company finances

   b. What else insurance regulators do to protect consumers

8. Explain how the excess and surplus lines market meets the needs of various classes of business that are often unable to find insurance in the standard market. (pp. 2-22 to 2-24)

9. Define or describe each of the Key Words and Phrases for this assignment. (All Key Words and Phrases appear in bold print in the text and in the margins throughout this chapter.)

Chapter 2

Who Provides Insurance and How Is It Regulated?

Insurance, as introduced in Chapter 1, is a transfer system, a business, and a contract, and it is provided by several types of insurance companies. This chapter continues the exploration of these different types of insurers and of how state governments regulate them.

Types of Insurers

Private (nongovernment) insurers provide most of the property and liability insurance in the United States. Private insurers also provide some insurance through government-sponsored insurance programs, and the federal government and the various state governments act as insurers for some types of loss exposures.

Educational Objective 1

Describe and compare the various types of private insurers that provide property and liability insurance.

Private Insurers

Numerous kinds of private insurers provide property and liability coverages for individuals, families, and businesses. Private insurers differ from one another in several ways. Some of the differences among insurers developed through historical circumstances. Other differences, however, result from legislative action or the interests of the parties that formed the insurer.

All insurers provide a means to indemnify insureds if a covered loss occurs and to spread the costs of losses among insureds. Although all insurers perform these basic functions, the underlying motives of the parties forming different types of insurers are not the same. Some types of insurers are formed in the expectation that the insurer's operations will make a profit or provide some other direct financial benefit for its owners. Other insurers are formed by or on behalf of groups of insureds with the motive of making insurance more readily available or making insurance available at a cost lower than if it were purchased through the general insurance market.

This section discusses various types of private insurers, primarily in terms of:

- The purpose for which they were formed
- Their legal form of organization
- Their ownership
- Their method of operation

Exhibit 2-1 outlines these differences for the major kinds of private insurers discussed in this chapter. In addition to these differences, insurers differ according to their licensing status, the marketing systems they use, and the types of insurance coverage they provide. Licensing of insurers is covered later in this chapter. Chapter 4 examines the different types of marketing systems used by private insurers. Various types of insurance coverage provided by insurers are the subject of the last segment of this textbook.

Stock Insurance Companies

Insurers formed for the purpose of making a profit for their owners are typically organized as for-profit (stock) corporations. For-profit corporations are owned by their stockholders. By purchasing stock in a for-profit insurer, stockholders supply the capital the insurer needs when it is formed or the additional capital needed by the insurer to expand its operations. These stockholders expect to receive a return on their investment in the form of stock dividends, increased stock value, or both. Therefore, one of the primary objectives of a **stock insurance company** is returning a profit to its stockholders. Many of the largest property and liability insurance companies in the United States are stock insurance companies. Such companies include The Hartford and the SAFECO Insurance Companies. These companies have been able to attract and retain stockholders by providing sufficient investment returns.

A **stock insurance company** is an insurer that is owned by its stockholders and formed as a corporation for the purpose of earning a profit for these stockholders.

Exhibit 2-1
Differences Among Major Types of Private Insurers (and Lloyd's of London)

Type	Purpose for which formed	Legal form	Ownership	Method of operation
Stock insurer	To earn profit for its stockholders	Corporation	Stockholders	The board of directors, elected by stockholders, appoints officers to manage the company.
Mutual insurer	To provide insurance for its owners (policyholders)	Corporation	Policyholders	The board of directors, elected by policyholders, appoints officers to manage the company.
Reciprocal insurance exchange (interinsurance exchange)	To provide reciprocity for subscribers (to cover each other's losses)	Unincorporated association	Subscribers (members)	Subscribers choose an attorney-in-fact to operate the reciprocal.
Lloyd's of London	To earn profit for its individual investors ("Names") and its corporate investors	Unincorporated association	Investors	The Committee of Lloyd's is the governing body and must approve all investors for membership.

Stockholders have the right to elect the board of directors, which has the authority to control the activities of the insurer. The board of directors creates and oversees corporate goals and objectives and appoints a chief executive officer (CEO) to carry out the insurer's operations. The chief executive officer and a team of top-level management personnel are given authority by the board of directors to implement the programs necessary to operate the company.

The stock form of ownership also provides financial flexibility for the insurer. For example, the management of a stock insurance company may decide to expand its operations by purchasing another insurance company, by developing new territories or product lines, or by purchasing a noninsurance company in order to diversify its operations. One way that a stock insurance company can finance such expansion is by selling additional shares of common stock. The ability to raise additional funds by selling common stock is an important aspect of the stock form of organization.

Mutual Insurance Companies

A **mutual insurance company** is a corporation owned by its

A **mutual insurance company** is an insurer that is owned by its policyholders and formed as a corporation for the purpose of providing insurance to its policyholder-owners.

Demutualization is the process by which a mutual insurer, which is owned by its policyholders, becomes a stock company, which is then owned by its stockholders.

A **reciprocal insurance exchange** (or an **interinsurance exchange**) is an unincorporated association formed to provide insurance coverage to its members. One of the distinguishing features of a reciprocal is that the *subscribers* empower an *attorney-in-fact* to manage it.

Subscribers (also known as members) are the policyholders of a reciprocal insurance exchange who agree to insure each other.

The **attorney-in-fact** of a reciprocal insurance exchange is the contractually authorized manager of the reciprocal who administers its affairs and carries out its insurance transactions.

policyholders. The corporation of a traditional mutual insurer issues no common stock, so it has no stockholders. The policyholders of a mutual company have voting rights similar to those of the stockholders of a stock company. They elect a board of directors that performs the same functions as the board of directors of a stock company. Large mutual companies include the State Farm Insurance Companies and Liberty Mutual Insurance Company.

Although initially formed to provide insurance for their owners, mutual insurers today have approximately the same incentive to earn profits in their ongoing operations as stock companies. A mutual insurer needs profits to assure the future financial health of the organization.

Several types of mutual insurance companies exist. One traditional difference among mutual insurers involves the insurer's right to charge its insureds an assessment, or additional premium, after the policy has gone into effect. Known as an assessment mutual insurance company, this type of mutual insurer is less common today than in the past.

From the perspective of the insured, differences between stock and mutual insurance companies are becoming less significant. Such things as potential assessments, which were a disadvantage, and dividends, which could be a competitive advantage, are not prevalent features of mutual insurers today. In fact, the structure of mutual companies is gradually changing, making them more similar to stock companies. Some state laws now allow mutual insurers to sell stock to the public by creating a mutual holding company, and other states are considering the adoption of similar regulations. In recent years, some mutual companies have converted to stock companies through a process called **demutualization**. Some mutuals have made these structural changes because they wanted to raise additional capital through the sale of stock to compete with stock companies, which have benefited from favorable stock market conditions.

Reciprocal Insurance Exchanges

A **reciprocal insurance exchange** (or an **interinsurance exchange**), also simply called a reciprocal, consists of a series of private contracts among the **subscribers**, or members, of the group, with subscribers agreeing to insure each other. The name "reciprocal" comes from the reciprocity of responsibility of all subscribers to each other. Each member of the reciprocal is both an insured and an insurer. Because the subscribers are not experts in running an insurance operation, they contract with an individual or organization to operate the reciprocal; this manager is called an **attorney-in-fact**. The subscribers empower the attorney-in-fact to handle all the duties necessary to manage the reciprocal. Typically, the function of the attorney-in-fact is to administer the affairs of the reciprocal and to carry out its insurance transactions. An agreement (known as a subscription agreement) authorizes the attorney-in-fact to act on behalf of the subscribers to market and underwrite insurance coverage, collect premiums, invest funds, and handle claims. The existence of an attorney-in-fact, empowered by the subscribers, is one of the main features that distinguishes a reciprocal from other types of insurers.

Today, reciprocals make up a small percentage of the total number of insurance companies in the United States; however, they include some major companies such as Farmers Insurance Exchange, which is part of Farmers Group and United States Automobile Association (USAA), which markets insurance to military persons and their families. Small regional reciprocals also operate on a state-by-state basis.

Lloyds Associations

Among the providers of insurance is a unique type known as Lloyds. Two types of Lloyds associations exist: Lloyd's of London and American Lloyds.

Lloyd's of London

Although not technically an insurance company, Lloyd's of London is an association that provides the physical and procedural facilities for its members to write insurance. In other words, it is a marketplace, similar to a stock exchange. Members of Lloyd's of London do not take an active part in the day-to-day operation of Lloyd's. They are investors who hope to earn a profit from the insurance operations that occur at Lloyd's.

Each individual investor (called a "Name") of Lloyd's belongs to one or more groups called *syndicates*. A syndicate's underwriter or group of underwriters conducts its insurance operations and analyzes applications for insurance coverage. Depending on the nature and amount of insurance requested, the underwriters for a particular syndicate might accept only a portion of the total amount of insurance. The application is then taken to other syndicates for their evaluations.

The insurance written by each individual Name is backed by his or her entire personal fortune. However, each individual member is liable only for the insurance he or she agrees to write, not for the obligations assumed by any other member. In 1993, Lloyd's began admitting corporations as members. Unlike its individual members, corporate members of Lloyd's have limited liability.

Lloyd's of London has earned a reputation for accepting applications for very unusual types of insurance, such as insuring the legs of a famous football player against injury. These applications may be the subject of newspaper articles, but the bulk of

Lloyd's business does not involve such unusual coverages. In fact, most of the insurance written through Lloyd's is commercial property and liability insurance.

Lloyd's has operated continuously for more than three hundred years, and Lloyd's underwriters are considered to be some of the world's leaders in their fields. The integrity of Lloyd's stems from the influence of the Committee of Lloyd's, which is the governing body of the association. The Committee of Lloyd's accepts only members who meet rigorous financial standards. Over the years, despite serious natural disasters and occasional mistakes in underwriting judgment, Lloyd's members have had the financial resources to survive catastrophes, pay claims, and move forward to more profitable times. Until recently, many members have received an excellent return on their investments, and Lloyd's has had little trouble attracting new members. Recent large losses over several years have created a strain on some of Lloyd's syndicate members. Nevertheless, Lloyd's remains one of the world's most important sources of insurance.

American Lloyds Associations

American Lloyds associations are much smaller than Lloyd's of London, and most are domiciled in Texas, with a few in other states. Most of the Texas Lloyds associations were formed or have been acquired by insurance companies. Unlike the individual Names of Lloyd's of London, members (called underwriters) of American Lloyds have limited liability. The liability of underwriters at American Lloyds is limited to their investment in the Lloyds association. State laws require a minimum number of underwriters (ten in Texas) for each Lloyds association. American Lloyds are usually small and operate as a single syndicate under the management of an attorney-in-fact.

Other Private Insurers

In addition to stock insurers, mutual insurers, reciprocals, and Lloyds associations, several other types of private insurers or groups provide insurance, including captive insurance companies and reinsurance companies.

Captive Insurance Companies

A **captive insurance company** (or simply a **captive**) is an insurer that is formed as a subsidiary of its parent company, organization, or group, for the purpose of writing all or part of the insurance on the parent company or companies.

When a business organization or a group of affiliated organizations forms a subsidiary company for the purpose of having the subsidiary provide all or part of the insurance on the parent company or companies, the subsidiary is known as a **captive insurance company**, or simply a **captive**. Although captive insurance companies have been in existence since the early part of the twentieth century, the widespread use of captives is more recent, with the major growth occurring since the late 1970s.

Three factors have contributed to the growth of captives in recent years: low insurance cost, insurance availability, and improved cash flow. First, captives might be able to provide insurance coverage at a lower cost than other private insurers because acquisition costs are eliminated. For example, captives might not have to pay agents' commissions or advertising expenses because they provide insurance primarily to the parent company. Second, a captive helps eliminate the problems some corporations might face because necessary or desired insurance coverage is unavailable or costs more than the corporation is willing or able to pay. Forming a captive insurance company eases the problems of availability and affordability for a parent company that has loss exposures that are difficult to insure. The third and most important factor is cash flow. A premium paid to a captive remains within the corporate structure until it is used to pay claims. Instead of paying premiums to an unrelated insurer, the corporation is able to invest its funds until the time they are needed for claims. Thus, the corporation can receive a significant cash flow advantage by creating a captive. This advantage becomes even greater when interest rates are high, as was the case during the late 1970s and early 1980s, when the number of captives increased dramatically.

Captives have become an important alternative in the insurance-buying decisions of corporations. The relative importance of the factors affecting the growth of captives changes over time, but it appears that captives will remain an important source of insurance.

Reinsurance Companies

Some private insurers provide **reinsurance**, which is a contractual arrangement that transfers some or all of the potential costs of insured losses from policies written by one insurer to another insurer. The insurer that transfers the loss exposures is the **primary insurer**, and the insurer that accepts the loss exposures is the **reinsurer**. Some reinsurers are companies or organizations that specialize in the reinsurance business. Other reinsurers are also primary insurers that enter into reinsurance arrangements with other insurers.

A primary insurer might buy reinsurance for a variety of reasons. One of the most important reasons is that reinsurance permits the primary insurer to share its exposures with the reinsurer. For example, an insurer that writes a large amount of property insurance in an area where tornadoes commonly occur can use reinsurance to reduce its exposure to claims from its insureds arising from windstorm damage to their property.

Reinsurance also enables a small insurer to provide insurance for large accounts (such as large national or multinational corporations) whose insurance needs would otherwise exceed the insurer's capacity. For example, suppose a primary insurer writes a commercial liability policy for a large company that manufactures sports helmets. Since the potential for heavy liability losses resulting from injuries caused by defective

Reinsurance is a type of insurance in which one insurer transfers some or all of the loss exposures from policies written for its insureds to another insurer.

In reinsurance, the **primary insurer** is the insurance company that transfers its loss exposures to another insurer in a contractual arrangement.

A **reinsurer** is the insurance company that accepts the loss exposures of the primary insurer.

helmets is great, the primary insurer might arrange with a reinsurer to cover all of its liability losses for this insured over a certain amount, such as $1,000,000. Therefore, the primary insurer and the reinsurer are sharing the liability loss exposures for this insured.

Government Insurance Programs

Reminder

Characteristics of Ideally Insurable Loss Exposures

- Large number of similar exposure units
- Losses that are accidental
- Losses that are definite and measurable
- Losses that are not catastrophic
- Losses that are economically feasible to insure

Despite the size and diversity of private insurers in the United States, private insurers do not provide some types of insurance. As discussed in Chapter 1, some loss exposures do not possess the characteristics that make them ideally insurable, but a significant need for protection against the potential costs of losses resulting from these loss exposures still exists. Both the federal government and state governments have developed certain insurance programs to meet specific insurance needs of the public.

Educational Objective 2

Describe common federal government insurance programs.

Federal Government Insurance Programs

Some federal government insurance programs serve the public in a manner that only the government can. For example, only the government has the ability to tax in order to provide the financial resources needed to insure some loss exposures and the power to make the system viable by requiring mandatory participation. One federal government insurance program that requires mandatory participation is the Social Security program.

The Social Security Program

The Social Security program, formally known as the Old Age, Survivors, Disability, and Health Insurance program (OASDHI), is a comprehensive program that provides benefits to millions of Americans. The Social Security Administration, a federal governmental agency, operates the program and provides four types of benefits to eligible citizens:

- Retirement benefits for the elderly
- Survivorship benefits for dependents of deceased workers
- Disability payments for disabled workers
- Medical benefits for the elderly (under the Medicare program)

Mandatory participation in the Social Security program for those eligible for coverage eliminates the need for individual underwriting and helps to generate premium revenues to operate the system. Private insurers provide similar benefits (retirement benefits, life insurance, disability insurance, and health insurance) to some insureds, but they cannot approach the scope of the Social Security program. Some private insurers provide protection to supplement specific Social Security benefits.

Other Federal Insurance Programs

Other federal government insurance programs provide coverage for loss exposures that private insurers have avoided largely because of the potential for catastrophic losses. Some of the insurance plans operated by the federal government were created to overcome availability problems. Examples of such plans are the National Flood Insurance Program and the Federal Crop Insurance Program. The need for each of these programs is highly concentrated. Only a specific portion of the population needs the coverage: those who have property in areas exposed to flooding need flood protection, and farmers in areas subject to hailstorms need crop insurance. This concentration of exposure units generally makes private insurers reluctant to provide coverage for flood and crop losses. In other words, the exposure units are not independent and thus are subject to catastrophic losses that private insurers cannot insure economically.

Educational Objective 3

Describe common state government insurance programs.

State Government Insurance Programs

State governments are actively involved in insuring certain loss exposures of their citizens. Among the most common types of insurance programs provided or operated by state governments are:

- Workers compensation insurance funds
- Unemployment insurance programs
- Automobile insurance plans
- FAIR plans
- Beachfront and windstorm pools

In addition, all states have some type of insurance guaranty fund designed to pay for covered losses in the event that an insurer is financially unable to meet its obligations to its insureds.

State Workers Compensation Insurance Funds

Many states offer workers compensation insurance. North Dakota, Ohio, Washington, West Virginia, and Wyoming operate **monopolistic state funds**, which means that the state fund is the only source of workers compensation insurance in the state. All employers in the state who need workers compensation insurance must obtain it from the monopolistic state fund. (Until 1999, Nevada also had a monopolistic state fund,

A **monopolistic state fund** is a state workers compensation insurance plan that is the only source of workers compensation insurance allowed in that state.

A **competitive state fund** is a state workers compensation insurance plan that competes with private insurers to provide workers compensation insurance.

A **residual market plan** (or **shared market plan**) is a program that makes insurance available to those who cannot obtain coverage because private insurers will not voluntarily provide such coverage for various reasons.

but Nevada now allows private insurance, making its fund a *competitive state fund*. Puerto Rico and the U.S. Virgin Islands operate territorial funds, similar to monopolistic state funds.)

Some states have a **competitive state fund**, which means that employers may choose between the state fund or some other means of meeting their obligations under workers compensation statutes. Still other states provide workers compensation through residual market plans. A **residual market plan** (also known as a **shared market plan**) is an insurance source of last resort. When an applicant is unable to obtain insurance from a private insurer, the applicant applies to the state fund to obtain coverage. In this way, the state is performing the function of satisfying a demand for coverage that private insurers are unwilling or unable to meet.

Other State Insurance Programs

All state governments operate unemployment insurance programs, and the benefits provided vary by state. Minimum federal standards, however, as well as some federal financing, ensure that eligible workers have some unemployment insurance protection. Private insurance covering the loss of income due to unemployment is not available because of the catastrophic potential of widespread unemployment.

Most states now require that owners of motor vehicles have auto liability insurance before registering an automobile. However, applicants with poor driving records or persons with little or no driving experience might have difficulty obtaining automobile insurance. As a result, all fifty states and the District of Columbia have implemented automobile insurance plans through a residual market system to make auto liability insurance available to nearly every licensed driver. The form and operation of these plans vary by state, but all of the plans spread the cost of operating the plan among all private insurance companies writing business in the state. In most cases, the state has mandated the creation of automobile insurance plans but has left the administration of the plans to private insurers, which then share the costs.

In most states, FAIR (Fair Access to Insurance Requirements) plans make property insurance available where it would otherwise be unavailable. These state-run plans spread the cost of operating the plan among all private insurers selling property insurance in the state. FAIR plans were originally created in response to the urban riots of the 1960s so that property owners in urban areas could have access to property insurance. These plans now make property insurance more readily available to property owners who have exposures to loss over which they have no control. Therefore, eligible property includes property in urban areas as well as property exposed to brush fires, for example.

Beachfront and windstorm insurance pools are residual market plans similar to FAIR plans. These plans exist in states along the Atlantic and Gulf Coasts, and they provide insurance to property owners against wind damage from hurricanes and other windstorms. Since these states have been severely affected by hurricanes in recent years, some property owners along the coasts have had difficulty obtaining windstorm coverage from private insurers.

Insurance Guaranty Funds

Each state (as well as the District of Columbia) has a property and liability insurance **guaranty fund** that covers the unpaid claims of insolvent insurers licensed in the state. The money to pay the claims of insolvent insurers comes from assessments made against private insurers doing business in the state. In most states, the claims that must be paid after an insurer becomes insolvent are estimated, and then other licensed insurers operating in that state are assessed for their proportionate share of the obligation.

A **guaranty fund** is a state fund that provides a system to pay the claims of insolvent insurers. Generally, the money in guaranty funds comes from assessments collected from all insurers licensed in the state.

Insurance Regulation

The possibility that an insurance company might not be able to pay legitimate claims to or for its policyholders is the primary concern of insurance regulators, who monitor the financial condition and operations of insurance companies. This scrutiny helps to protect the public from irresponsible, unwise, or dishonest activities that could leave consumers with worthless insurance policies.

Historically, state governments have regulated the insurance business. State regulation of insurance began when state legislatures granted charters to new insurance companies and specified certain conditions regarding their minimum capital requirements, their investments, and their financial reports. During the latter part of the nineteenth century, states established insurance departments to monitor the operations of insurance companies and to investigate complaints from insureds. State insurance departments generally have broad powers to regulate the insurance business in the public interest.

Insurance regulations vary by state. Although many insurance professionals believe that state regulation of insurance has advantages over federal regulation, inefficiency can result when over fifty different insurance departments separately perform similar tasks and address the same issues and problems.

Educational Objective 4

Describe the purpose and activities of the National Association of Insurance Commissioners (NAIC).

National Association of Insurance Commissioners

The **National Association of Insurance Commissioners (NAIC)** is an association consisting of the commissioners of the insurance departments of each state, the District of Columbia, and U.S. territories and possessions. The NAIC coordinates insurance regulation activities among the various insurance departments.

The **National Association of Insurance Commissioners (NAIC)** was established to encourage coordination and cooperation among state insurance departments. The members of the NAIC are the heads (usually called commissioners) of the insurance departments of each of the fifty states and the District of Columbia. (The commissioners of Puerto Rico, Guam, American Samoa, and the U.S. Virgin Islands also belong to the NAIC.) The NAIC facilitates cooperation, coordination, and uniformity in insurance regulation among the states.

The NAIC meets quarterly, but it functions throughout the year with the assistance of its staff. NAIC standing committees meet periodically during the year and report to the NAIC at its regularly scheduled meetings.

A **model law** is a document drafted by the NAIC, in a style similar to a state statute, that reflects the NAIC's proposed solution to a given problem and provides a common basis to the states for drafting laws that affect the insurance industry.

When a new problem or issue arises, the NAIC studies the matter and issues a statement describing its position. In many cases, the NAIC develops a **model law**, written in a style similar to that of a state statute, that reflects the NAIC's proposed solution to a given problem or issue. Each state legislature then considers the model law for possible enactment. A model law might not be passed in its exact form by every state legislature, but it provides a common basis for drafting state laws. In this way, certain aspects of insurance regulation have a degree of uniformity among states.

The NAIC has also created a uniform financial statement for property and liability insurance companies. Each insurance company completes an annual financial statement in the prescribed manner and submits it to the insurance department in each state in which the company is licensed in order to satisfy the financial reporting requirements of that state. This uniformity not only lessens the reporting burden for insurance companies but also simplifies the insurance department's task of comparing the financial reports of many different insurers.

In a further effort to help states monitor the financial condition of insurers, the NAIC has implemented an accreditation program to increase uniformity and improve state regulation of insurance. The program's purpose is to ensure that states have the appropriate legislation and authority to regulate the solvency of the insurance industry. It also attempts to ensure that states apply the required legislation consistently. Under this program, states that have been accredited by the NAIC cannot accept the results of insurance company examinations performed by states that have not been accredited.

Through its various programs and committees, the NAIC enables state regulators to pool their resources while preserving state regulation of insurance. The NAIC encourages uniformity, but each state can tailor its regulatory approach to meet the state's unique needs. Despite the differences among the states, the primary objectives of insurance regulation are:

- Rate regulation
- Solvency surveillance
- Consumer protection

Rate Regulation

Because insurers develop insurance rates that affect most people, the laws of nearly all states give the state insurance commissioner the power to enforce regulation of insurance rates.

Educational Objective 5

Explain how insurance rates are developed.

Ratemaking

An insurer must collect sufficient premiums to pay for the insured losses that occur, cover the costs of operating the insurance company, and allow a reasonable profit. Determining the proper rate to charge each insured for coverage involves the process of ratemaking.

Ratemaking is the process by which insurers calculate rates that determine the premium to charge for an insurance policy. The **rate** is the cost of a given unit of insurance (for example, $100 worth of coverage). The **premium** is the price of the coverage provided for a specified period. To arrive at the premium, the rate is multiplied by the number of insurance units purchased. For example, if an insurer charges a rate of $1.20 per $100 of coverage on jewelry, the premium for a ring insured for $1,000 would be $12.00, according to the following formula:

Rate × Number of exposure units = Premium

$1.20 × 10 units = $12.00

Developing rates that accurately reflect each insured's share of predicted losses is one of the most important operations performed by insurance companies. Since a given rate is the basis of an insured's premium, it is important to both the insured and the insurer that the rate, and therefore the premium, be a fair measure of the insured's exposure to loss.

Ratemaking is the process insurers use to calculate the *rates* that determine the *premium* for insurance coverage.

A **rate** is the price of insurance for each unit of exposure. The *rate* is multiplied by the number of exposure units to arrive at a *premium*.

A **premium** is a periodic payment by an insured to an insurance company in exchange for insurance coverage.

To determine the premiums to charge, insurance companies predict, as accurately as possible, the expenses they will incur to pay for losses, recognizing that this prediction is uncertain. Insurers add an amount sufficient to cover the expected administrative costs of company operations to the predicted claim expenses. In addition, the premium includes a charge to cover a margin for error and a charge for profits and contingencies, such as possible catastrophic losses. This amount is generally modified to reflect the investment income that can be earned on the funds held for future claim payments.

Insurance companies use rate classification systems that differentiate among insureds based on each insured's loss potential. For example, insureds with frame houses are placed in one classification for fire insurance and insureds with brick houses are placed in another, because the probable severity of a fire loss is greater for a frame house. Similarly, insurers group drivers into separate classifications so that young, inexperienced drivers are charged more than experienced drivers, and insureds who use their cars for business are charged more than insureds who do not. Insureds with similar characteristics are placed in the same class and charged the same rate. Insurers use technology extensively in the rating process; computers can be programmed to develop rates according to rating specifications.

An **actuary** is a person who uses complex mathematical methods and technology to analyze loss data and other statistics and to develop systems for determining insurance rates.

An **actuary** analyzes data on past losses and the expenses associated with losses and, combining this with other information, develops insurance rates. Actuaries usually have an education in mathematics and statistics as well as other specialized training. Advances in information technology in recent years have enabled actuaries to perform their jobs more efficiently by using computers.

The goal of an insurer's actuarial staff is to develop a ratemaking system that generates fair, equitable rates and meets corporate objectives. Attaining this goal requires actuaries to constantly monitor and update loss data to develop rates that state regulatory authorities will approve.

Educational Objective 6

Explain why and how insurance rates are regulated.

Objectives of Rate Regulation

Although the objectives of rate regulation are generally the same for all states, the approaches used differ significantly. Rate regulation serves three general objectives:

- To ensure that rates are adequate
- To ensure that rates are not excessive
- To ensure that rates are not unfairly discriminatory

Ensuring That Rates Are Adequate

When rates are adequate, the price charged for a given type of insurance coverage should be high enough to meet all anticipated losses and expenses associated with that coverage while generating a reasonable profit for the insurer. Rate adequacy helps insurers remain solvent so they can meet obligations to policyholders. Therefore, rate regulation attempts to ensure that rates are adequate.

Adequacy is not always easy to achieve. It is virtually impossible to guarantee that premiums paid by insureds will be adequate to cover insured losses. Even when a large group of similar exposure units is covered, unexpected events—such as a natural disaster—might lead to losses significantly higher than those predicted when rates were originally set. For example, when Hurricane Andrew hit the eastern United States in 1992, the resulting unexpected losses exceeded the predictions that had been used to rate the policies that covered these losses.

The goal of rate adequacy conflicts with pressures to hold down insurance premiums. An insurer might have difficulty competing if its rates are substantially higher than those charged by other insurers providing similar coverage and service. Also, although insurance regulators desire rate adequacy to maintain insurer solvency, other pressures encourage regulators to keep rates low.

Ensuring That Rates Are Not Excessive

To protect consumers, states also require that insurance rates not be excessive. Excessive rates could cause insurers to earn unreasonable profits. Determining whether rates are either excessive or inadequate is difficult, especially since insurers must price insurance policies long before the results of the pricing decision are known. Nevertheless, when regulators determine that insurers have earned substantial profits in a particular type of insurance, they may require insurers to reduce rates retroactively or to return the "excess profit" to policyholders.

Ensuring That Rates Are Not Unfairly Discriminatory

Since insurance is a system of sharing the costs of losses, each insured should pay a fair share of the insurer's losses and expenses. Some disagreement exists as to how this fair share should be determined.

One concept involves **actuarial equity**—basing rates on actuarially calculated costs of losses. Actuaries define rate classifications and calculate rates based on the loss experience of each given class. Insureds with similar characteristics are placed in the same rating class and charged the same rate. Thus, the premium should accurately reflect each insured's expected contribution to the losses of a group of similar insureds.

Actuarial equity is a ratemaking concept through which actuaries base rates on actuarially calculated loss experience and place insureds with similar characteristics in the same rating class.

Social equity is a rating concept that considers rates to be *unfairly discriminatory* if they penalize an insured for characteristics (such as age or gender) that are beyond the insured's control.

Unfair discrimination would involve applying different standards or methods of treatment to insureds who have the same basic characteristics and loss potential. Insurers generally establish rates based on "fair discrimination," which is the grouping of individuals with similar characteristics who have similar loss exposures. Members of that group are then charged the same actuarially developed rate. *Unfair discrimination* in insurance rating would include charging higher-than-normal rates for an auto insurance applicant based solely on the applicant's race, religion, or ethnic background.

Types of Insurance Rating Laws

• **Prior-approval laws**—rates must be approved by the state insurance department before they can be used.

• **Flex rating laws**—prior approval is required only if the new rates are a specified percentage above or below previously filed rates.

• **File-and-use laws**—rates must be filed but do not have to be approved before use.

• **Use-and-file laws**—rates must be filed within a specified period after they are first used in the state.

• **Open competition (no-file laws)**—rates do not have to be filed with the state.

• **State-mandated rates**—state-specified rates must be used by all insurers of a particular type of insurance in the state.

On the other hand, **social equity** holds that rate structures discriminate unfairly if they penalize an insured (through higher rates) for factors, such as age or gender, that are beyond the insured's control. In certain states, age and gender are no longer allowed as factors in rating auto insurance on the grounds that they are unfairly discriminatory. Rate regulation attempts to balance the concepts of actuarial equity and social equity in determining whether a particular rating plan involves **unfair discrimination**.

Insurance Rating Laws

In attempts to balance conflicting objectives, states have developed a variety of laws to regulate insurance rates. Rate regulation varies by state. Moreover, within a state, different laws might apply to different types of insurance. Despite these differences, the various insurance rating laws fall into the following categories:

• **Prior-approval laws**—Under these laws, which are used in most states, insurers must file their proposed rates with the state insurance department. Insurers must also provide data that show that the rates are not excessive, inadequate, or unfairly discriminatory. The commissioner has a certain time period, typically thirty to ninety days, to approve or reject the filing. Some states have a deemer provision (or "delayed effect" clause) that causes the rates to be deemed approved if the commissioner does not respond to a rate filing within the specified time period.

• **Flex rating laws**—Under this type of law, prior approval is required only if the new rates are a specified percentage above or below previously filed rates. Insurers are permitted to increase or reduce their rates within the specified range without prior approval. Percentage ranges vary by state and by type of insurance, but they are generally between 10 and 25 percent.

• **File-and-use laws**—Some states require insurers to file rates with the state insurance department before the rates become effective. However, insurers are not required to wait for approval from the commissioner but rather may begin using the rates as soon as they are filed.

• **Use-and-file laws**—These laws require that rates be filed within a specified period of time, often fifteen or thirty days, after they are first used in the state.

• **Open competition (no-file laws)**—In some states, insurers are not required to file rates or rating plans with the state regulatory authorities. This approach is called open competition, because it permits insurers to compete with one another by quickly changing rates without review by state regulators. Market forces rather than administrative action determine rates under this approach.

- **State-mandated rates**—This system requires all insurers to adhere to rates established by the state insurance department for a particular type of insurance, such as private passenger automobile insurance. Rates for all other types of insurance are subject to another type of rating law.

Modified versions of these laws also exist. For instance, modified prior-approval laws permit an insurer to revise rates without prior approval if the revision is based solely on a change in the insurer's loss experience. Another example is a modified open competition law, which allows open competition as long as certain tests are met, such as evidence of competitive markets or rate increases of less than a certain percentage per year.

The insurance rating laws that do not require prior approval of rates do not relieve insurers of their obligation to use rates that are adequate, not excessive, and not unfairly discriminatory. State insurance departments can and do exercise their legal right to request, at a later date, the statistics that support the fairness of the new rate.

Educational Objective 7

Explain:

a. How insurance regulators monitor insurance company finances

b. What else insurance regulators do to protect consumers

Solvency Surveillance

In an effort to ensure insurer **solvency**, insurance regulators carefully monitor the financial condition of insurance companies. Two major aspects of **solvency surveillance** are insurance company examinations and the Insurance Regulatory Information System (IRIS).

Insurance Company Examinations

Regulatory authorities periodically conduct examinations of insurance companies. An examination consists of a thorough analysis of an insurance company's operations and financial condition. This analysis usually occurs every few years under the direction of the insurance department of the state where the insurer's home office is located.

During an examination, a team of state examiners, working at the insurance company home office, reviews a wide range of activities, including claim, underwriting, marketing, and accounting procedures. Of particular interest to the examiners is the financial condition of the insurer. The financial records of the insurer are carefully analyzed to ensure that the company is meeting all state financial reporting requirements and to determine whether the insurer has the ability to meet its obligations. If the examination uncovers problems, the insur-

Solvency is the ability of an insurance company to meet its financial obligations as they become due, even those resulting from insured losses that might be claimed several years in the future.

Solvency surveillance is the process, conducted by state insurance regulators, of verifying the solvency of insurance companies and determining whether the financial condition of insurers enables them to meet their obligations and to remain in business in the long term.

ance department usually has broad powers to take control of the situation in an attempt to correct whatever problems are identified.

The Insurance Regulatory Information System

The **Insurance Regulatory Information System (IRIS)**, begun in the early 1970s as the Early Warning System, is an analytical system designed by the NAIC to monitor an insurer's overall financial condition.

The NAIC designed the **Insurance Regulatory Information System (IRIS)** to help regulators identify insurance companies with potential financial problems. IRIS takes data from insurers' financial statements and develops eleven financial ratios to determine insurers' overall financial condition. If a particular insurer has ratios that are outside predetermined norms, IRIS identifies the company for regulatory attention.

IRIS provides all state insurance departments with a timely and objective method of identifying companies that might have financial problems. Although the system does not always identify a problem before a financial crisis occurs, it is an important tool for solvency surveillance.

Consumer Protection

In addition to rate regulation and solvency surveillance, the activities that regulators undertake to protect insurance consumers include:

- Licensing insurers
- Licensing insurance company representatives
- Approving policy forms
- Examining market conduct
- Investigating consumer complaints

Licensing Insurers

A **licensed insurer** (or an **admitted insurer**) is authorized by the state insurance department to transact business within that state.

A **domestic insurer** is incorporated in the same state in which it is transacting business.

A **foreign insurer** is licensed to operate in a state but is incorporated in another state.

An **alien insurer** is licensed in a U.S. state but incorporated in another country.

Most insurance companies must be licensed by the state insurance department before they are authorized to write insurance policies in that state. A **licensed insurer** (or an **admitted insurer**) is one that the state insurance department has authorized to sell insurance in that state. An insurance company that is incorporated in the same state in which it is writing insurance is known as a **domestic insurer**. If an insurance company is licensed to operate in a state but is incorporated under the laws of another state, that company is known as a **foreign insurer**. A licensed insurer that is incorporated in another country is known as an **alien insurer**.

For example, an insurer that is incorporated in Massachusetts is considered a *domestic* insurer in that state. However, if the same insurer is also licensed to operate in New Hampshire and Vermont, it is considered a *foreign* insurer in those two states. An insurer that is incorporated in London, England, is considered an *alien* insurer in the United States.

A primary requirement for obtaining an insurance license involves tests of financial strength. Each state has specific requirements concerning the minimum amount of surplus (assets minus liabilities) an insurance company must have to be licensed in the state. The required amount of surplus varies, depending on the state and the type of insurance for which the company wants to be licensed. If an insurer fails to meet financial standards or fails to operate in a manner consistent with state insurance laws, state regulators have the authority to revoke or suspend the company's license in order to protect consumers' interests.

Licensing Insurance Company Representatives

In addition to licensing insurance companies, all states have licensing requirements for certain representatives of insurance companies. All states require insurance agents to be licensed to transact insurance business in the state. A license is usually granted only after the applicant passes an examination on insurance laws and practices. Most states have similar requirements for insurance brokers. Claim representatives (also known as adjusters) are also required to be licensed in some states before they are allowed to handle claims. (Chapter 4 explains the roles of insurance agents and brokers, and Chapter 6 describes the duties of claim representatives.)

In most states, continuing education requirements specify that, before renewing a license, the agent, broker, or claim representative must complete a prescribed amount of continuing education during a specified period. Licensing and continuing education laws vary widely by state, but all attempt to ensure that these insurance company representatives have a prescribed minimum level of insurance knowledge.

Approving Policy Forms

Most states require insurance companies to file their policy forms with the state insurance department in a manner similar to the method used for rate filings. Whenever an insurer wants to change the language of a particular policy, it must submit the new form for approval.

By regulating policy language, the state insurance department prevents insurers from including unfair or unreasonable provisions in insurance policies. Although the possibility always exists that an insured might misinterpret the policy, regulatory approval of policy forms reduces the possibility of misleading wording. Having clear and readable insurance policies is a goal of most regulators. In many cases, states also prescribe specific wording that must be included in insurance policies, such as cancellation requirements and procedures.

Examining Market Conduct

Market conduct regulation consists of state laws that regulate the practices of insurers in regard to four areas of operation: sales and advertising, underwriting, ratemaking, and claim handling.

Regulators also scrutinize specific insurance company practices. **Market conduct regulation** focuses on the treatment by insurance companies of applicants for insurance, insureds, and others who present claims for coverage. Market conduct examinations involve four areas of insurance company operations: sales and advertising, underwriting, ratemaking, and claim handling.

Most states have statutes, usually called unfair trade practices laws, that identify certain practices that are considered unfair to the public. State regulators could suspend or revoke the licenses of insurance agents or brokers who engage in any of these unfair trade practices. Similarly, an insurance company guilty of unfair underwriting practices could be fined or have its operating license suspended or revoked in the state. Most states also have statutes that prohibit unfair claim practices and assess stiff penalties against claim representatives and insurance companies that engage in such practices.

Investigating Consumer Complaints

Regulatory examinations of insurance companies identify some of the abuses mentioned above, but other abuses are exposed only when an insured or a claimant lodges a complaint. Every state insurance department has a consumer complaints division to enforce the consumer protection objectives of the state insurance department and to help insureds deal with problems they have encountered with insurance companies and their representatives. The state insurance department investigates consumer complaints and often holds formal hearings as part of the investigation process.

Educational Objective 8

Explain how the excess and surplus lines market meets the needs of various classes of business that are often unable to find insurance in the standard market.

Excess and Surplus Lines Insurance[1]

The **standard market** refers collectively to insurers who voluntarily offer insurance coverages at rates designed for customers with average or better-than-average loss exposures.

Most property and liability insurance policies are standardized, and many insurers use essentially the same policy forms. Insurers who use these policy forms and others who write traditional types of insurance are known collectively as the **standard market** for property and liability insurance. Such insurers write the majority of commercial property and liability insurance in the United States.

In most cases, the standard market provides the policies necessary to meet the property and liability insurance needs of the public. But what about the unique or unusual exposures that the standard market is unwilling or unable to insure? In many instances, the standard market does not adequately meet the public's needs. Poor loss experience or expected losses associated with certain classes of business might not meet the underwriting requirements of standard insurers. Changes in business practices or technology might create new loss exposures not contemplated in traditional insurance policies. These exposures require a creative, nontraditional insurance market. The term **excess and surplus lines (E&S) insurance** is often used to identify this nontraditional insurance market. The term "excess and surplus lines" (or simply "surplus lines") refers to the types of insurance written in this market.

Excess and surplus lines (E&S) insurance consists of insurance coverages, usually unavailable in the standard market, that are written by unlicensed insurers.

Classes of E&S Business

The following classes of business are often insured in the excess and surplus lines market:

- Unusual or unique exposures
- Nonstandard business
- Insureds needing high limits
- Insureds needing unusually broad coverage
- Exposures that require new forms

Unusual or Unique Exposures

One of the requirements of a commercially insurable loss exposure is that a large number of similar exposure units should exist. If a exposure does not meet this requirement, standard insurers are often unwilling to provide coverage. For example, suppose a singer does not show up for a performance. The sponsors of the program can suffer a financial loss if they have to refund money to ticket holders. A coverage known as "non-appearance insurance," written by E&S insurers, covers the losses of the production or show sponsors if the performer named in the policy fails to appear because of a covered cause, such as injury, illness, or death.

Nonstandard Business

Sometimes loss exposures do not meet the underwriting requirements of the standard insurance market. There might be evidence of poor loss experience that cannot be adequately controlled. Perhaps the premiums that standard insurers normally charge are not adequate to cover these exposures. For example, suppose a particular restaurant has a history of grease fires in its kitchen, and its standard insurance company has nonrenewed its policy because of poor loss experience. An E&S insurer might be willing to write this restaurant with a premium substantially higher than a standard insurer would charge.

Insureds Needing High Limits

Some businesses demand very high limits of coverage, especially for liability insurance. A standard insurance company might not be willing to offer limits as high as an insured needs. The E&S

market often provides the needed limits in excess of the limits written by a standard insurer.

Insureds Needing Unusually Broad Coverage

The traditional insurance market uses standard coverage forms developed through advisory organizations, such as Insurance Services Office (ISO) and the American Association of Insurance Services (AAIS). When broader coverage is necessary, however, producers and insureds often seek such coverage from the E&S market.

Exposures That Require New Forms

Creativity has long been a distinguishing characteristic of the E&S market. As new insurance needs arise, the E&S market is usually quick to respond. Producers and consumers often turn to the E&S market when they have an immediate need for a new type of coverage.

Excess and Surplus Lines Regulation

Nonadmitted (or **unlicensed**) insurers are insurers that are not licensed in many of the states in which they operate and that write E&S insurance coverages.

E&S insurance is usually written by **nonadmitted** (or **unlicensed**) **insurers**, which are insurers that are not licensed in many of the states in which they operate. Nonadmitted insurers are not required to file their rates and policy forms with state insurance departments, which gives them more flexibility than standard insurers.

Although nonadmitted insurers are generally exempt from laws and regulations applicable to licensed insurers, the E&S market is subject to regulation. Some states maintain lists of E&S insurers that are approved to do business in the state; others keep lists of those E&S insurers that are not approved. Most states have surplus lines laws that require that all E&S business be placed through an excess and surplus lines broker, also known as an E&S broker. The E&S broker is licensed by the state to transact business through nonadmitted insurers. When an insurance producer seeks to insure a customer with a nonadmitted insurer, he or she must arrange for an E&S broker to handle the transaction.

E&S insurers and brokers provide a valuable service to the insurance industry and to the public. They provide insurance to many insureds who might otherwise be unable to obtain coverage. They also find solutions to many problems created by unusual or unique loss exposures.

Educational Objective 9

Define or describe each of the Key Words and Phrases for this assignment. (All Key Words and Phrases appear in bold print in the text and in the margins throughout this chapter.)

Summary

In the United States, private insurers provide most property and liability insurance, but both federal and state governments also provide some types of insurance. Most private insurers are either stock or mutual companies. Other types of private companies or groups that provide insurance include reciprocal insurance exchanges, Lloyds associations, captive insurance companies, and reinsurance companies.

Private insurers are generally reluctant to insure loss exposures that do not possess most of the characteristics of an ideally insurable loss exposure. In some instances, state and federal governments have intervened to make certain types of insurance available to the public. Government insurance programs have arisen when needs for insurance coverage existed that were not satisfied by private insurers and when society benefitted from the programs. Examples of federal government insurance programs include the Social Security program, the National Flood Insurance Program, and the Federal Crop Insurance Program. State governments also provide various insurance programs, including state workers compensation funds, unemployment insurance programs, automobile insurance plans, FAIR plans, and beachfront and windstorm pools. In addition, all states have insurance guaranty funds that cover unpaid claims of insolvent insurers.

Because insurance is a business that affects the public, state governments are heavily involved in the regulation of the insurance industry. State insurance departments, with the assistance of the National Association of Insurance Commissioners (NAIC), are responsible for most insurance regulation. Insurance departments regulate insurance rates to ensure they are adequate, not excessive, and not unfairly discriminatory. Insurers and their actuaries develop insurance rates in a process called ratemaking. However, these rates are subject to various state insurance rating laws.

Solvency is another major concern of insurance regulators. Through periodic examinations of insurers' financial condition and the Insurance Regulatory Information System (IRIS), regulators conduct solvency surveillance to monitor the solvency of insurance companies.

Regulators also try to protect consumers by licensing qualified insurance companies and their representatives, approving policy forms, examining market conduct, and investigating consumer complaints. Through the licensing of excess and surplus lines brokers, state insurance regulators also regulate the excess and surplus lines market, which provides insurance coverages that are unavailable in the standard market.

Chapter Note

1. The section on excess and surplus lines insurance is adapted from material originally written for the Insurance Institute of America by William R. Feldhaus, Ph.D., CPCU, CLU, Georgia State University.

Chapter 3

How Is the Financial Performance of Insurers Measured?

Educational Objectives

After studying this chapter, you should be able to:

1. Identify and describe the sources of income for a property and liability insurance company. (pp. 3-4 to 3-6)

2. Identify and describe the types of expenses that a property and liability insurance company incurs. (pp. 3-7 to 3-9)

3. Describe and distinguish between admitted and nonadmitted assets of insurance companies. (p. 3-11)

4. Describe the two major types of liabilities found on the financial statements of insurers. (p. 3-12)

5. Identify the typical items found on the balance sheet of a property and liability insurer. (pp. 3-14 to 3-15)

6. Identify the typical items found on the income statement of a property and liability insurer. (p. 3-15)

7. Calculate and explain the significance of the following profitability ratios: (pp. 3-16 to 3-19)

   a. Loss ratio

   b. Expense ratio

    c. Combined ratio

    d. Investment income ratio

    e. Overall operating ratio

8. Calculate an insurance company's capacity ratio, and explain its importance. (p. 3-20)

9. Define or describe each of the Key Words and Phrases for this assignment. (All Key Words and Phrases appear in bold print in the text and in the margins throughout this chapter.)

Chapter 3

How Is the Financial Performance of Insurers Measured?

Sound management of an insurance company requires careful attention to its financial performance. One concern about any insurance company's financial performance is its profitability: Does the insurer generate enough profit to survive? A related concern is the insurer's solvency: Does the insurer have adequate resources to meet all of its financial obligations? Insurance companies prepare financial statements that address these concerns, and analysis of these statements helps insurers, regulators, and other interested parties to monitor insurers' financial performance over time and to identify any financial difficulties.

Insurer Profitability

To survive in the long term, any business must make more money than it spends. In a given month or year, its expenses might exceed its income, requiring the business to pay some of those expenses with accumulated funds. A pattern of this, however, will eventually deplete accumulated funds, and the business will fail. Like any other business, an insurance company must manage its income and expenses to produce an overall gain from its operations and to ensure the profitability on which its survival depends.

Educational Objective 1

Identify and describe the sources of income for a property and liability insurance company.

Income

Insurance companies receive income from two major sources. The first is the sale of insurance, which generates premium income. The second is the investment of funds for the purpose of generating investment income. While some insurers receive other income from the sale of specialized services or other incidental activities, most of the income an insurance company receives comes from either premium income or investment income.

Premium Income

Premium income is the money an insurer receives from its policyholders in return for the insurance coverage it provides. When measuring its total premium income for the year (or any other period), an insurance company must determine what portion of its *written premiums* is considered *earned premiums* and what portion is considered *unearned premiums*.

Written Premiums

Written premiums are premiums on policies put into effect, or "written," during a given period.

During a particular calendar year, an insurer calculates its **written premiums** by totaling the premiums on all policies written with effective dates of January 1 through December 31 of that year. Although written premiums provide a source of cash for insurers, rules of accounting allow insurers to recognize only earned premiums as income.

Earned and Unearned Premiums

Earned premium for a particular policy is the portion of the written premium that applies to the part of the policy period that has already occurred.

Unearned premium is the portion of the written premium that applies to the part of the policy period that has not yet occurred.

Earned premiums represent the portion of written premiums that is recognized as income only as time passes and as the insurance company provides the protection promised under the insurance policies. The remaining portion of written premiums applies to the part of the policy periods that has not yet occurred. The latter portion is therefore called **unearned premiums**, representing insurance coverage yet to be provided.

The concept of earned and unearned premiums is similar to the way in which a magazine subscription might operate. When a subscriber pays a $24 annual subscription fee for a monthly magazine, the publisher does not "earn" the entire $24 subscription income until the magazine has been provided for twelve months. If the subscriber cancels the subscription after receiving only six monthly issues, the publisher might refund $12, or half of the subscription income (the "unearned" portion).

Likewise, when an insured pays a premium of $600 on July 1 for a one-year policy, the $600 premium is not fully "earned" until the end of the twelve-month coverage period. The entire $600, however, is considered written premium for the current calendar year. As Exhibit 3-1 shows, only half of the $600 annual premium paid on July 1 is earned as of the end of the calendar year because only six months, or half of the protection period, has passed. Therefore, at the end of the calendar year, the insurance company records $300 of earned premium for this policy and $300 of unearned premium. During the next calendar year, between January 1 and July 1, the unearned portion of the premium is earned as coverage is provided by the insurance company. If this policy is not renewed on July 1 of the second year, the insurance company records *no* written premium for this policy in the second year (remember that the entire $600 was considered to be written during the first year) and records only the earned premium of $300 from the previous year's written premium. (See the examples on page 3-6.)

Exhibit 3-1
Earned Premium—One-Year Policy Issued on July 1 for $600

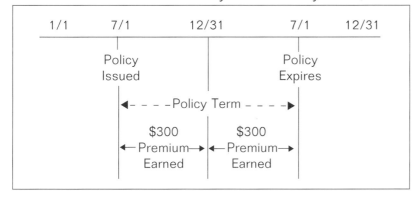

Investment Income

Because an insurance company collects premiums from its policyholders and pays claims for its policyholders, the insurer handles large amounts of money. Insurers invest available funds to generate additional income. Particularly during periods of high interest rates or high returns in the stock market, investment income can be substantial.

An insurance company has funds available for investment for two reasons. First, the insurer is legally required to maintain a certain amount of funds, called *policyholders' surplus*, so it can meet its obligations even after catastrophic losses. As long as an insurance company is operating profitably, its policyholders' surplus is generally available for investment.

The second reason that an insurance company has funds available for investment is that it usually receives premiums before it pays claims on the corresponding policies. Thus,

---

**Examples of Written Premiums,
Earned Premiums, and Unearned Premiums**

Case 1

Annual policy with $600 premium is effective July 1.

At the end of Calendar Year 1:

Written premium = $600

Earned premium = $300 (6 of the 12 months of coverage have elapsed)

Unearned premium = $300 (6 of the 12 months of coverage have not elapsed)

At the end of Calendar Year 2 (assuming the policy is not renewed):

Written premium = $0

Earned premium = $300 (the remaining 6 months of coverage have elapsed)

Unearned premium = $0 (there is no more coverage; all the premium is earned)

Case 2

Annual policy with $600 premium is effective December 1.

At the end of Calendar Year 1:

Written premium = $600

Earned premium = $50 (1 of the 12 months of coverage has elapsed)

Unearned premium = $550 (11 of the 12 months of coverage have not elapsed)

At the end of Calendar Year 2 (assuming the policy is not renewed):

Written premium = $0

Earned premium = $550 (the remaining 11 months of coverage have elapsed)

Unearned premium = $0 (there is no more coverage; all the premium is earned)

In each case, the written premium and the earned premium total $600 by the time the coverage has expired. However, all of the written premium is recorded immediately, while the earned premium is counted as it is earned over time. In both cases, the unearned premium disappears by the expiration date of the policy because all of the written premium has been earned by the time the policy period ends.

---

insurers can invest premium funds and earn additional income until those funds are needed to pay claims. However, when insurance companies settle claims, they must have funds readily available to meet their obligations. Similarly, if a policy is canceled before the end of the policy period, the insurer must be able to refund the unearned premium.

Insurers have investment departments whose objective is to earn the highest possible return from investments while ensuring that funds are always available to meet the insurance company's obligations. Thus, the investment department must have a thorough knowledge of financial markets in order to select high-quality investments that are relatively secure and that can be readily converted to cash.

> **Educational Objective 2**
>
> Identify and describe the types of expenses that a property and liability insurance company incurs.

Expenses

The major expenses incurred by an insurance company are claim payments for insureds who have suffered losses and the costs associated with handling those claims. The insurer also incurs operating expenses in providing and servicing its insurance products. In addition, the insurer has expenses associated with its investment activities. For an insurer to be profitable, its combined premium and investment income must exceed its total loss payments and other expenses.

Losses and Underwriting Expenses

Expenses associated with an insurer's underwriting activity include payment for losses, loss expenses, and other underwriting expenses.

Losses

The major expense category for most insurance companies is payment for losses arising from claims. Claims are demands for payment made by insureds based on the conditions specified in their insurance policies. For property and liability insurers, loss payments often represent 70 to 80 percent of their total expenses.

Claims are not necessarily settled immediately after a loss occurs. Sometimes the loss is not reported immediately. When the loss is reported, the insurer's claim representative usually investigates the loss and verifies whether the loss is covered before the insurer pays the claim. Liability claims might involve lengthy legal proceedings. Some losses occur in one year but are settled in a later year. In any given year, an insurance company knows only the amount of losses it has paid so far, but not a definite amount it will ultimately have to pay. To compare income and expenses, however, an insurer must calculate not only its **paid losses** but also its **incurred losses** for the period.

Because it has been paid, a paid loss is a definite amount. Paid losses, however, do not include those losses in the process of settlement or losses that are *incurred but not yet reported* (IBNR). Therefore, another method to measure losses is to calculate incurred losses for a particular period, as shown below:

Incurred losses = Paid losses + Changes in loss reserves

Loss reserves are based on estimates of future payments for losses that have already occurred. Changes in loss reserves are calculated as follows:

Paid losses are claim payments that an insurer has made.

Incurred losses for a particular period equal the sum of *paid losses* and changes in *loss reserves* (loss reserves at the end of the period minus loss reserves at the beginning of the period).

Loss reserves are amounts designated by insurance companies to pay claims for losses that have already occurred but are not yet settled. A loss reserve for a particular claim is the insurer's best estimate of the total amount that it will pay in the future for a loss that has already occurred.

Changes in loss reserves =
Loss reserves at end of period – Loss reserves at beginning of period

Because setting loss reserves for individual claims is an important part of the claim process, it is discussed in more detail in Chapter 6.

Loss Expenses

Insurers also incur loss expenses, which are expenses necessitated by the process of investigating insurance claims and settling them according to the terms specified in the insurance policy. For property insurance claims, the claim representative must identify the cause of the loss and decide whether this loss is covered by the policy; if the loss is covered, the claim representative must determine the amount covered by the policy.

For liability claims, the claim representative must determine whether the insured is legally responsible for the bodily injury or property damage that is the basis of the claim and, if so, for how much. Determining the legal responsibility of the insured for a loss might require a complex and costly investigation. In addition to paying covered losses, liability insurers often pay the costs to defend the insured in the event of a lawsuit, regardless of whether the insured is ultimately held responsible for the damages. Thus, loss expenses associated with a liability claim can be substantial.

Other Underwriting Expenses

In addition to losses and loss expenses, the costs of providing insurance include other significant underwriting expenses. As much as possible, insurance companies try to classify their underwriting expenses in relevant categories. The major categories of insurer underwriting expenses, other than losses and loss expenses, are:

- Acquisition expenses
- General expenses
- Taxes and fees

Acquisition Expenses The expenses associated with acquiring new business are significant. All property and liability insurance companies have a marketing system to market and distribute their products. This marketing system includes individuals involved directly with sales (usually called agents, brokers, producers, or sales representatives) and the administrative staff that manages and supports the sales effort. Many people who directly generate insurance sales for insurers receive a commission, which is usually a percentage of the premium written by the salesperson. Others receive a salary, or a combination of salary and commission, and sometimes also a bonus based on sales, profit, or some other measure of productivity. While some insurers operate without salespeople (usually through direct response systems such as mail, telephone, and Internet sales), these insurers must still employ and pay staff to manage and administer their marketing operations.

Advertising expenses can be a significant component of acquisition expenses for most insurers regardless of whether the advertising is directed toward the general public or specifically toward insurance producers. Insurers incur still other expenses in the process of underwriting and issuing insurance policies. They need staff to review and analyze applications for insurance, assemble and issue insurance policies, issue billing statements, collect premiums, and record necessary information.

General Expenses   Like other businesses, insurance companies incur certain miscellaneous expenses. While these expenses do not relate directly to activities such as claims, marketing, and underwriting, they are crucial to the insurers' operations. These general expenses include expenses associated with staffing and maintaining departments such as accounting, legal, research, product development, customer service, electronic data processing, and building maintenance. In addition, insurers must provide office space, telephones, and other utility services, as well as office equipment and supplies for these necessary support functions.

Taxes and Fees   Property and liability insurance companies must pay several different types of taxes and fees. All fifty states levy premium taxes, which are usually between 2 and 4 percent of all premiums generated by the insurer in a particular state. Unless they function as excess and surplus lines insurers, insurance companies must hold and pay for licenses in each state in which they operate. In addition, insurers must participate in various state insurance programs, such as guaranty funds and automobile insurance plans.

Investment Expenses

An insurer's investment department includes a staff of professional investment managers who oversee the company's investment program. In addition to devising investment strategy and implementing it through the purchase and sale of stocks, bonds, mortgages, and other investments, the investment department is responsible for a careful and thorough accounting of all invested funds. Investment expenses include the salaries and all other expenses related to the activities of the investment department. On their financial statements, insurance companies deduct these expenses from investment income to show the net income from investments (Investment income – Investment expenses = Net investment income). Gains or losses realized from the sale of invested assets are added to net investment income resulting in net investment gain or loss, which represents the total result from investment activity.

An insurer's **net underwriting gain or loss** is its earned premiums minus its losses and underwriting expenses for a specific period. When an insurer adds its net investment gain or loss results to its net underwriting gain or loss, the resulting figure is its **overall gain or loss from operations**.

Gain or Loss From Operations

Adding net investment gain or loss to **net underwriting gain or loss** shows an insurer's **overall gain or loss from operations**. (Net investment gain or loss + Net underwriting gain or loss = Overall gain or loss from operations.) This overall figure gives a more complete picture of an insurance company's profitability than net underwriting gain or loss, because net investment gains generally help to offset underwriting losses.

Net Income Before Taxes

An insurer's net income before taxes is its total earned premium and investment income minus its total losses and other expenses in the corresponding period. Some adjustments for other income items might be necessary. For example, the insurance company might have to write off some uncollected premiums, or it might have to add premiums that were written off during the previous period but were ultimately collected during the current period. Adjustments might also be necessary for a gain or loss on the sale of equipment or other items.

Income Taxes

Like other businesses, insurance companies pay income taxes on their taxable income. Taxable income might differ from net income before taxes because of the special requirements of the tax code. For example, interest earnings from qualified municipal bonds are not taxed, and deductions for certain expenses are limited. The income tax due is a percentage of the insurance company's taxable income.

Net Operating Income or Loss

After an insurance company has paid losses and reserved money to pay additional losses, expenses, and income taxes, the remainder is net operating income, which belongs to the owners of the company. The owners may receive a portion of this remainder as dividends. The amount that is left after dividends are paid becomes an addition to the insurer's surplus, which enables the insurer to expand its operations in the future. When they evaluate insurers' rates, regulators permit an allowance for profits and contingencies that should provide the owners of an insurance company with an adequate return on their investment. Unless the insurance company generates an adequate return or profit, it will not attract and maintain the investment funds it needs to survive.

Insurer Solvency

For a property and liability insurer to serve its policyholders in the long term, it must remain financially sound. Although comparing an insurer's income to its expenses in a single year reveals whether the company produced a net operating income or loss, this information alone does not indicate the insurer's financial condition. The financial position of an insurance company at any particular time is measured by its assets, liabilities, and policyholders' surplus.

Educational Objective 3

Describe and distinguish between admitted and nonadmitted assets of insurance companies.

Assets

Insurance companies accumulate funds when they receive premium and investment income. As stated previously, insurers do not immediately need all of their premium income to pay claims and operating expenses; before these funds are needed for claim and expense payments, insurers invest them in income-producing assets.

Assets typically accumulated by an insurance company include money, stocks, and bonds; tangible property, such as buildings, office furniture, and equipment; and accounts receivable from agents, brokers, and reinsurers.

Assets are property (both tangible and intangible) owned by an entity, in this case, by an insurance company.

Admitted Assets

For the purposes of filing financial reports with state insurance regulators, an insurance company's assets are classified as either *admitted assets* or *nonadmitted assets*. Regulators allow **admitted assets** to be shown on insurers' financial statements because these assets could easily be liquidated, or converted to cash, at or near the property's market value. In addition to cash, admitted assets include stocks, bonds, mortgages, real estate, certain data processing equipment, and premium balances due in less than ninety days.

Admitted assets are types of property, such as cash and stocks, that regulators allow insurers to show as assets on their financial statements. Such assets are easily convertible to cash at or near the property's market value.

Nonadmitted Assets

Nonadmitted assets could not readily be converted to cash at or near their market value if the insurer were to liquidate its holdings, so regulators do not allow insurers to show them as assets on their financial statements. Nonadmitted assets include office equipment, furniture and supplies, and premiums that are more than ninety days overdue.

The creation of the two categories of assets, admitted and nonadmitted, reflects the financially conservative view that insurance regulators take when evaluating an insurer's financial strength. Regulators do not want insurance companies to overstate their true financial condition. Therefore, certain types of assets are deemed "nonadmitted" and cannot be used to inflate the value of an insurance company's holdings or its financial strength.

Nonadmitted assets are types of property, such as office furniture and equipment, that insurance regulators do not allow insurers to show as assets on financial statements because these assets cannot readily be converted to cash at or near their market value.

> ### Educational Objective 4
>
> Describe the two major types of liabilities found on the financial statements of insurers.

Liabilities

Liabilities are financial obligations, or debts, owed by a company to another entity, usually the policyholder in the case of an insurance company.

An insurance company has a financial obligation to its policyholders; it must satisfy legitimate claims submitted by insureds and other parties. The major **liabilities** of an insurance company arise from this financial obligation to pay claims. Two major types of liabilities are found on an insurer's financial statements: the loss reserve and the unearned premium reserve.

Loss Reserve

The loss reserve is considered a liability because it represents a financial obligation owed by the insurer. It is the insurer's best estimate of the final settlement amount on all claims that have occurred but have not yet been settled. Although establishing loss reserves for claims whose value is not yet definite might seem impossible, insurers use their experience, the law of large numbers, and their statistical expertise to make reliable estimates of future claim settlement values.

Unearned Premium Reserve

The **unearned premium reserve** is the total of an insurer's unearned premiums on all policies at a particular time.

The unearned premium reserve is the other major liability found on the financial statements of property and liability insurance companies. The **unearned premium reserve** is a liability because it represents insurance premiums prepaid by insureds for services that the insurer has not yet rendered. If the insurer were to cease operations and cancel all of its policies, the unearned premium reserve represents the total of premium refunds that the insurer would owe its current policyholders.

Policyholders' Surplus

The **policyholders' surplus** of an insurance company is equal to its total admitted assets minus its total liabilities (Policyholders' surplus = Admitted assets − Liabilities).

Once the total value of an insurance company's admitted assets (cash, stocks, bonds, real estate, and so forth) and liabilities (loss reserve and unearned premium reserve) is known, the insurer can determine its **policyholders' surplus**. Policyholders' surplus equals the insurer's total admitted assets minus its total liabilities. Policyholders' surplus measures the difference between what the company *owns* (its admitted assets) and what it *owes* (its liabilities).

Policyholders' surplus provides a cushion that is available in case the insurer has adverse financial experience. While premium rates may include a margin for error, that margin might not be sufficient to offset unexpected losses, particularly catastrophic losses. If losses exceed expectations, the insurance company has to draw on its surplus to make required claim payments. Policyholders' surplus also provides the necessary resources if the insurance company decides to expand into a new territory or develop new insurance products. Thus, the amount of policyholders' surplus held by an insurer is an important measure of its financial well-being.

Exhibit 3-2 summarizes the admitted assets, liabilities, and policyholders' surplus held by the property and liability insurance industry in 1997.

Exhibit 3-2
Consolidated Balance Sheet for Property-Liability Industry

Consolidated Property-Liability Industry Totals Balance Sheet December 31, 1997 (in millions of dollars)*	
Admitted Assets:	
Cash and short-term investments	$ 39,481
Bonds	512,692
Preferred stock	12,859
Common stock	172,960
Mortgages	2,230
Real estate	9,087
Other assets	120,747
Total Admitted Assets	$870,056
Liabilities:	
Loss and loss expense reserve	$367,181
Unearned premium reserve	112,802
Other liabilities	81,594
Total Liabilities	$561,577
Policyholders' Surplus	308,479
Total Liabilities and Policyholders' Surplus	$870,056

*Based on data from A.M. Best Company, *Best's Aggregates and Averages: Property-Casualty* (Oldwick, NJ: A.M. Best Company, 1998).

Monitoring the Financial Performance of Insurers

Because the objectives of most insurers include being profitable and remaining in business in the long term, insurance companies must carefully monitor their financial performance. Regulators, investors, and others also monitor the financial performance of insurance companies.

Insurers must record and report financial information in a consistent manner, using various financial statements. Interested parties can analyze these financial statements to evaluate the insurers' financial performance. Insurance buyers, agents, and brokers often use the reports and evaluations of financial rating organizations, such as A.M. Best Company and Standard & Poor's Corporation, to select insurance companies that are considered to be in strong and stable financial condition.

Financial Statements

Insurers must prepare accurate financial statements that describe the company's financial position in an objective, standardized format. The two financial statements that provide the most information concerning the financial condition of an insurance company are the balance sheet and the income statement.

Educational Objective 5

Identify the typical items found on the balance sheet of a property and liability insurer.

Balance Sheet

A **balance sheet** is a type of financial statement that shows a company's financial position at a particular point in time and includes the company's admitted assets, liabilities, and policyholders' surplus.

The **balance sheet** shows an insurance company's financial position at a particular time. Exhibit 3-3 shows a condensed balance sheet for INS Insurance Company, a fictitious insurer. It shows the admitted assets, liabilities, and policyholders' surplus on the last day of the year.

Exhibit 3-3

INS Insurance Company Balance Sheet as of December 31

Admitted Assets:	
Cash and short-term investments	$ 50,000
Bonds	1,100,000
Common stock	350,000
Total Admitted Assets	$1,500,000
Liabilities:	
Loss and loss expense reserve	$ 650,000
Unearned premium reserve	350,000
Total Liabilities	$1,000,000
Policyholders' Surplus	500,000
Total Liabilities and Policyholders' Surplus	$1,500,000

Although a balance sheet indicates an insurance company's assets and liabilities only as of a particular date, they change constantly. Insurers establish unearned premium reserves for premiums they receive. The unearned premium reserve for each policy declines with the passage of time. Also, losses occur and insurers establish loss reserves. New policies are written, and old policies expire or are renewed. Meanwhile, the insurance company buys and sells stocks, bonds, and other investments as needed to meet its obligations while earning investment income. Thus, an analysis of an insurance company's assets and liabilities is only as current as the date of the balance sheet, which presents a snapshot of the financial position of the company at that time.

Educational Objective 6

Identify the typical items found on the income statement of a property and liability insurer.

Income Statement

An insurance company's **income statement** shows its revenues, expenses, and net income for a particular period, such as one year. Exhibit 3-4 shows a condensed income statement for INS Insurance Company.

An **income statement** is a type of financial statement that shows a company's revenues, expenses, and net income for a particular period, usually one year.

Exhibit 3-4
INS Insurance Company Income Statement for the Year Ending December 31

Earned Premiums	$1,000,000
Expenses:	
Incurred losses	$ 650,000
Loss expenses	100,000
Other underwriting expenses:	
Acquisition expenses	220,000
General expenses	90,000
Taxes and fees	20,000
Total Expenses	$1,080,000
Net Underwriting Gain (Loss)	$ (80,000)
Net Investment Income	100,000
Net Operating Gain	$ 20,000

During the year, INS Insurance Company's earned premiums totaled $1,000,000. In the same year, the company's expenses totaled $1,080,000. These expenses included incurred losses, loss expenses, acquisition expenses, general expenses, taxes, and fees. Because losses and underwriting expenses exceeded earned premiums, INS Insurance Company experienced a net underwriting loss of $80,000. However, INS also earned net investment income of $100,000 during the year. Therefore, INS Insurance Company realized a net operating gain of $20,000.

Financial Statement Analysis

Analyzing the relationships of different items that appear on insurers' financial statements helps determine how well insurance companies are performing. Comparing two items produces a ratio that highlights a particular aspect of financial performance. Several such ratios are widely used in the insurance industry.

Many people and organizations use these ratios. Managers of insurance companies use such ratios to identify strengths and weaknesses in their companies' operations. Investors analyze these ratios to identify the insurance companies that are most attractive as investments. Regulators examine the ratios to determine whether insurance companies have the financial strength to remain viable in the long term and to meet their financial obligations to policyholders and other parties.

These ratios are important to insurance agents and brokers as well. The financial condition of an insurer should be one of the factors considered when producers select the companies with which they place business. Producers should be reasonably sure that an insurer is financially sound and that it will be able to meet its financial obligations.

Educational Objective 7

Calculate and explain the significance of the following profitability ratios:

a. Loss ratio

b. Expense ratio

c. Combined ratio

d. Investment income ratio

e. Overall operating ratio

Profitability Ratios

Several ratios measure the profitability of an insurance company. These profitability ratios include:

- Loss ratio
- Expense ratio
- Combined ratio
- Investment income ratio
- Overall operating ratio

Profitability ratios are usually converted into percentages for easier analysis of financial performance.

Loss Ratio

The **loss ratio** is calculated by dividing an insurer's incurred losses (including loss expenses) for a given period by its earned premiums for the same period.

The **loss ratio** compares an insurance company's incurred losses to its earned premiums for a specific time period. The figure for incurred losses includes loss expenses. The loss ratio is defined as follows:

$$\text{Loss ratio} = \frac{\text{Incurred losses (including loss expenses)}}{\text{Earned premiums}}$$

When converted into a percentage, the loss ratio provides the percent of earned premiums used to fund losses and their settlement. By looking at this percentage, insurers, regulators, investors, and others can determine how closely actual loss experience compares to expected loss experience. For example, at the beginning of the year, management might have decided that a 75 percent loss ratio is the target for the coming year. As each month progresses, the loss ratio is recalculated based on the company's experience to date to determine whether the insurer is meeting the targeted 75 percent ratio.

Expense Ratio

The **expense ratio** compares the underwriting expenses that an insurer has incurred to its written premiums in a specific time period. The expense ratio is defined as follows:

$$\text{Expense ratio} = \frac{\text{Incurred underwriting expenses}}{\text{Written premiums}}$$

The expense ratio indicates what proportion of an insurer's written premiums is being used to pay acquisition costs, general expenses, and taxes. In other words, this ratio indicates the insurer's general cost of doing business as a proportion of the premiums it has written. (Investment income and investment expenses are not part of either the loss ratio or the expense ratio.) The expense ratio gives a general picture of how efficiently the insurer is operating. Insurers watch the expense ratio carefully over time and attempt to reduce it by managing cash flow and controlling expenses.

Combined Ratio

The **combined ratio** combines the loss ratio and the expense ratio to compare inflows and outflows from insurance operations. The combined ratio is defined as follows:

$$\text{Combined ratio} = \text{Loss ratio} + \text{Expense ratio}$$

In other words, the combined ratio is calculated as follows:

$$\text{Combined ratio} = \frac{\text{Incurred losses (including loss expenses)}}{\text{Earned premiums}} + \frac{\text{Incurred underwriting expenses}}{\text{Written premiums}}$$

Notice that both the numerators (top numbers) and the denominators (bottom numbers) in the loss ratio and the expense ratio are different. The loss ratio attempts to relate the level of losses to the corresponding earned premiums. Both the incurred losses and earned premiums reflect the insurance coverage provided over time. Because these two measurements represent corresponding cash inflows and outflows, they provide the most informative basis for the loss ratio.

Expenses are a different matter. Many of the underwriting expenses incurred by insurance companies involve acquisition

The **expense ratio** is calculated by dividing an insurer's incurred underwriting expenses for a given period by its written premiums for the same period.

The **combined ratio** is the sum of the loss ratio and the expense ratio.

expenses, such as agents' commissions. Because these expenses occur at the beginning of the policy period, the use of written premiums, which recognizes the entire premium as soon as it is written, is appropriate for comparing expenses to revenues. Therefore, written premiums are used in lieu of earned premiums as the denominator in the expense ratio.

While the combined ratio is considered the accepted measure of an insurer's underwriting performance, this ratio does not take into account the insurer's investment income. Therefore, the combined ratio does not measure the insurer's overall financial performance. Overall financial performance includes the results from both the insurer's underwriting activities and its investment activities.

Investment Income Ratio

The **investment income ratio** is calculated by dividing net investment income by earned premiums for a particular period.

The **investment income ratio** compares the amount of net investment income (investment income minus investment expenses) with earned premiums over a specific period. It is defined as follows:

$$\text{Investment income ratio} = \frac{\text{Net investment income}}{\text{Earned premiums}}$$

The investment income ratio indicates the degree of success achieved in the insurance company's investment activities.

Overall Operating Ratio

The **overall operating ratio** is calculated by subtracting the investment income ratio from the combined ratio.

The combined ratio (loss ratio plus expense ratio) minus the investment income ratio (net investment income divided by earned premiums) can be used to provide an overall measure of the financial performance of the insurance company for a specific period. The **overall operating ratio** is defined as follows:

$$\text{Overall operating ratio} = \text{Combined ratio} - \text{Investment income ratio}$$

The investment income ratio must be *subtracted* from the combined ratio because investment income is used to *offset* the insurer's losses and underwriting expenses. Of all the commonly used ratios, the overall operating ratio is the most complete measure of insurance company financial performance. To obtain a true picture of an insurer's profitability, overall operating ratios for a number of years should be analyzed, because any company might have a single bad year that is offset by a pattern of profitability over a longer period. Exhibit 3-5 shows the various profitability ratios for the fictitious INS Insurance Company.

Expressed as percentages, the expense ratio for INS Insurance Company is 30 percent, while its loss ratio is 75 percent. This creates a combined ratio of 105 percent. When the investment income ratio of 10 percent is subtracted, the overall operating ratio equals 95 percent.

Exhibit 3-5

Profitability Ratios for INS Insurance Company

Earned premiums	$1,000,000
Written premiums	1,100,000
Incurred underwriting expenses	330,000
Incurred losses (including loss expenses)	750,000
Net investment income	100,000

$$\text{Loss ratio} = \frac{\text{Incurred losses (including loss expenses)}}{\text{Earned premiums}} = \frac{\$\ 750,000}{1,000,000} = .75 \text{ (or 75\%)}$$

$$\text{Expense ratio} = \frac{\text{Incurred underwriting expenses}}{\text{Written premiums}} = \frac{\$\ 330,000}{1,100,000} = .30 \text{ (or 30\%)}$$

Combined ratio = Expense ratio + Loss ratio = .30 + .75 = 1.05 (or 105%)

$$\frac{\text{Investment}}{\text{income ratio}} = \frac{\text{Net investment income}}{\text{Earned premiums}} = \frac{\$\ 100,000}{1,000,000} = .10 \text{ (or 10\%)}$$

Overall operating ratio = Combined ratio – Investment income ratio = 1.05 – .10 = .95 (or 95%)

An insurer with an overall operating ratio of 100 percent breaks even because revenues from all operations are equal to total expenses plus incurred losses. A ratio less than 100 percent indicates an overall operating gain because revenues are greater than total expenses. Conversely, if the ratio is greater than 100 percent, an operating loss has occurred because total expenses are greater than revenues.

Although these ratios are the clearest indicators of insurance company profitability, they should be used carefully and re-examined frequently. The loss ratio includes incurred losses as a key component. Since the measurement of incurred losses involves an estimate of the amount that will ultimately be paid on claims that were incurred during the current year, the loss ratio is subject to revision as losses develop. Since the loss ratio is part of the combined ratio and the overall operating ratio, these two ratios are also subject to change. The insurance company cannot know exactly how it performed in a specific period until all claims for incurred losses in that period are fully paid, which might not occur for several years. Monitoring financial results from past years helps to determine the accuracy of the insurance company's loss reserve estimates.

> **Educational Objective 8**
>
> Calculate an insurance company's capacity ratio, and explain its importance.

Capacity

An insurer's **capacity ratio**, or **premium-to-surplus ratio**, is calculated by dividing its written premiums by its policyholders' surplus.

In addition to profitability, an important concern for an insurance company is its capacity to write new business and thus to grow. The measure of an insurer's capacity is its **capacity ratio**, also known as its **premium-to-surplus ratio**, as shown below:

$$\text{Capacity ratio} = \frac{\text{Written premiums}}{\text{Policyholders' surplus}}$$

The capacity ratio compares an insurance company's written premiums (which represent its exposure to potential claims) to its policyholders' surplus (which represents its cushion for absorbing adverse results). If losses and expenses exceed written premiums, an insurer must use its surplus to meet its obligations. Therefore, an insurer's new written premiums should not become too large relative to its policyholders' surplus.

Exhibit 3-6 shows the capacity ratio for INS Insurance Company, using data from Exhibits 3-3 and 3-5. The ratio of 2.2-to-1 is not unusual, because insurance companies often have a premium-to-surplus ratio close to 2-to-1. While it is not a magic figure, insurance regulators use the capacity ratio as a benchmark to determine whether an insurer might be headed toward financial difficulty. For example, a premium-to-surplus ratio above 3-to-1 could be a sign of financial weakness. However, regulators cannot determine an insurer's financial condition by this measure alone. In addition to the capacity ratio, regulators use many other measures of financial performance.

Exhibit 3-6
Capacity Ratio for INS Insurance Company

Written premiums	$1,100,000
Policyholders' surplus	500,000

$$\text{Capacity ratio} = \frac{\text{Written premiums}}{\text{Policyholders' surplus}} = \frac{\$1{,}100{,}000}{\$\ \ 500{,}000} = \frac{2.2}{1}$$

> **Educational Objective 9**
>
> Define or describe each of the Key Words and Phrases for this assignment. (All Key Words and Phrases appear in bold print in the text and in the margins throughout this chapter.)

Summary

Sound operation of an insurance company requires that great care be given to its financial condition and performance. To survive in the long term, any business must make more money than it spends. Insurers must operate profitably, remain solvent, and provide financial statements so that their financial performance can be monitored by state insurance departments and others.

The profitability of an insurance company is more difficult to measure than the profitability of many other businesses because of timing differences between the receipt of money (premiums) and the performance of the corresponding service (claim payments). Earned premiums are a better measure of premium income than written premiums during a specific period. Similarly, incurred losses are a better measure of losses during that period than are paid losses.

An insurance company's income includes both premium income and investment income. Its expenses include losses, loss expenses, other underwriting expenses, and investment expenses. The company's overall gain or loss from operations is the sum of its net underwriting gain or loss and its net investment gain or loss for a specific period. Unless there is an overall gain—that is, a profit—the insurance company's financial condition will deteriorate.

Solvency is the primary measure of an insurance company's financial condition. Solvency indicates the insurer's ability to meet its obligations. Its assets, or what it owns, must exceed its liabilities, or what it owes. The difference between admitted assets and liabilities is policyholders' surplus. To be certain that insurance companies do not overstate their policyholders' surplus, regulators require them to follow conservative accounting procedures. These procedures allow insurance companies to show on their financial statements only admitted assets, which include defined categories of assets that can be readily converted to cash. These accounting procedures for insurance companies also require that insurers show as liabilities both their loss reserve and unearned premium reserve.

To monitor the financial performance of insurance companies, regulators and others examine insurers' financial statements. The balance sheet, which measures an insurer's financial position, shows the insurer's assets, liabilities, and policyholders' surplus at a given time, such as the last day of the year. The income statement, which measures profitability, shows the company's revenues, expenses, and net income during a given period, such as a year. Analysis of these financial statements makes it possible to measure an insurer's financial performance over time, to compare one company to another, and to identify financially weak insurance companies. Financial statement analysis often involves using ratios to make these comparisons. Several different ratios measure various aspects of profitability. The most useful ratio for measuring profitability is the overall operating ratio, which is calculated by subtracting the investment income ratio (net investment income divided by earned premiums) from the combined ratio (loss ratio plus expense ratio). The capacity ratio (written premiums divided by policyholders' surplus) is also important because it measures an insurer's capacity to write new business and thus to grow.

Segment B:

Insurance Operations

Segment A presented the fundamentals of insurance and information about the insurers who provide it. This segment discusses the major operations of those insurers: marketing, underwriting, and claims.

Chapter 4

Marketing

Educational Objectives

After studying this chapter, you should be able to:

1. Explain the legal relationship known as agency. (pp. 4-3 to 4-4)

2. Identify and describe the duties of each of the following in any agency relationship: (pp. 4-4 to 4-6)

   a. The agent

   b. The principal

3. Describe each of the following types of insurance agents' authority: (pp. 4-6 to 4-9)

   a. Express authority

   b. Implied authority

   c. Apparent authority

4. Describe and distinguish among the various types of insurance marketing (or distribution) systems. (pp. 4-9 to 4-15)

5. Describe typical compensation arrangements for insurance producers. (pp. 4-15 to 4-17)

6. Describe advertising methods used by various insurers, producers, and producer trade associations. (pp. 4-17 to 4-18)

7. Describe the various aspects of marketing management. (pp. 4-18 to 4-20)

8. Describe ways in which states regulate producers' activities. (pp. 4-20 to 4-24)

9. Identify and describe acts related to insurance that are considered unfair trade practices in most states. (pp. 4-22 to 4-24)

10. Define or describe each of the Key Words and Phrases for this assignment. (All Key Words and Phrases appear in bold print in the text and in the margins throughout this chapter.)

Chapter 4

Marketing

Marketing enables an insurance company to determine which products meet consumers' needs and then to sell and deliver those products to its customers. An insurer might have the best product at the best price available, but if consumers are not aware of this fact, the insurer will sell few, if any, policies. Consumers have many different insurance needs. One insurance company might attempt to fill only a few of those needs; another might attempt to meet a wide range of insurance needs.

Insurance marketing does not stop after the consumer buys the product. People involved in insurance marketing also assist consumers in their dealings with the insurance company after a policy is issued. Insurance companies depend on their marketing personnel to keep them informed about the changing needs and desires of the insurance-buying public.

Many insurance marketing systems exist and most involve a salesperson of some kind. Various terms, such as agent, broker, producer, solicitor, or sales representative, are used to refer to this salesperson. This book uses the term **producer** to refer to any person who sells insurance (produces business) for an insurance company or companies; however, "agent," "broker," "sales representative," and other titles are also used here to denote special categories of producers.

Marketing is the process of identifying customers and their needs and then creating, pricing, promoting, selling, and distributing products or services to meet those needs.

A **producer** is any person who sells insurance products for an insurance company or companies.

Educational Objective 1

Explain the legal relationship known as agency.

The Legal Role of the Insurance Agent

Agency is a legal relationship that is formed when one party, the *principal*, authorizes another party, the *agent*, to act as a legal representative of the principal.

In the agency relationship, the **principal** is the party that authorizes the agent to act on its behalf.

In the agency relationship, the **agent** is the party that is authorized by the principal to act on the principal's behalf.

The legal relationship known as "agency" is not limited to insurance but exists in many situations. An **agency** exists whenever one party, the **agent**, represents or acts on behalf of another party, the **principal**. The principal gives authority to the agent to act as its representative within certain guidelines. The principal may authorize the agent to do anything the principal can do. For example, an insurance company (the principal) can authorize its agent to collect premiums from insureds for new insurance policies and then require the agent to remit those premiums (sometimes after deducting a commission) to the insurance company within a certain amount of time.

The agency relationship requires a high degree of mutual trust between the principal and the agent, since it imposes far-reaching legal obligations on both parties. While the agent has authority to act for the principal, the principal has control over the agent's actions on the principal's behalf. This authority and control are the two essential elements of an agency relationship.

Insurance agents are legal representatives of the insurance company or companies for which they have contractual agreements to sell insurance.

In insurance, an **agency contract**, or **agency agreement**, is a written agreement between an insurance company and an agent that specifies, among other things, the scope of the agent's authority to conduct business for the insurer.

Creation of the Agency Relationship

An agency relationship is usually created by a written contract between the principal and the agent. In insurance, the insurance company is the principal that appoints **insurance agents** to serve as its representatives; a written agency contract specifying the scope of authority given to an agent formalizes this relationship. An **agency contract**, also known as an **agency agreement**, gives the agent the right to represent the insurer and to sell insurance on the insurer's behalf. The contract states the compensation arrangement between the insurer and the agent. The agency contract also specifies how the agency relationship can be terminated. Insurance agency contracts usually have no fixed expiration date and remain in force until one party cancels the contract after giving proper notice to the other as required by the contract.

Educational Objective 2

Identify and describe the duties of each of the following in any agency relationship:

a. The agent

b. The principal

Responsibilities of the Agent and the Principal

The agency relationship, which is based on mutual trust and confidence, empowers the agent to act on behalf of the principal and imposes significant responsibilities on both parties.

Responsibilities of the Agent to the Principal

In an agency relationship, the agent's fundamental responsibility is to act for the benefit of the principal. The laws of agency impose five specific duties on all agents, including insurance agents:

- Loyalty
- Obedience
- Reasonable care
- Accounting
- Relaying information

Two of the agent's most important duties are to be loyal to the principal and to obey the principal's lawful instructions. In addition, an agent must exercise a reasonable degree of care in its actions on behalf of the principal; in other words, the agent must act as a reasonably prudent person would under the same or similar circumstances. Under the duty of accounting, the agent is responsible to the principal for all the principal's money and property that comes into the agent's possession; the agent must account promptly for any of the principal's money that the agent holds. The duty of relaying information requires the agent to keep the principal informed of all facts relating to the agency relationship.

In insurance, an agency contract specifically addresses certain rights and duties of the agent. For example, the contract explicitly describes the insurance agent's right to make insurance coverage effective and any limitations on that right. The contract also specifies how the agent is to handle funds, including stipulations on how and when the agent must remit premiums to the insurer. Insurance agency contracts usually give the agent the right to employ subagents who may act on behalf of the insurance company according to the terms of the agency contract.

Responsibilities of the Principal to the Agent

Just as the agent owes duties to the principal, so the principal legally owes certain duties to the agent. The principal's primary duty is to pay the agent for the services performed. In the case of an insurance agent, this duty entails payment by the insurer of commissions and other specified compensation to the agent for the insurance the agent sells or renews.

The principal also has a duty to indemnify, or reimburse, the agent for any losses or damages suffered without the agent's

Errors and omissions (E&O) are negligent acts (errors) committed by a person in the conduct of the insurance business that give rise to legal liability for damages. E&O claims can also arise from a failure to act (omission) that creates legal liability.

fault, but arising out of the agent's acts on behalf of the principal. If a third party sues the agent in connection with activities performed on behalf of the principal, the principal must reimburse the agent for any liability incurred, *if* the agent was not at fault. However, no reimbursement is due the agent if the agent acts illegally or without the principal's authorization, even though the principal might be liable to others for those acts. An important factor involved in this duty is the exposure of insurance agents to **errors and omissions (E&O)** claims, which might arise from the agent's negligent actions. For example, when an insurance agent gives a customer misleading or incorrect advice regarding the customer's insurance, the customer could bring an E&O claim against the agent if the customer suffers damage because of the agent's poor advice. For further information on errors and omissions issues, the Insurance Institute of America's Accredited Adviser in Insurance (AAI) program, designed for insurance producers, provides tips on avoiding E&O claims.

Responsibilities of the Agent and the Principal to Third Parties

An agency relationship also creates responsibilities to third parties (parties other than the agent and the principal). The agent's authorized acts on behalf of the principal legally obligate the principal to third parties in the same way as if the principal acted alone. Thus, from an insured's point of view, little distinction exists between the insurance agent and the insurance company.

Since the agent represents the insurance company, the law presumes that knowledge acquired by the agent is knowledge acquired by the insurance company. If, for example, the agent visits the insured's premises and recognizes an exposure (such as vacancy of the building) that could suspend or void the insured's policy, the insurance company cannot deny a claim to the insured merely because the agent failed to communicate that information to the insurer. According to agency law, the fact that the agent knew about the exposure means that the insurer is presumed to know about it.

Educational Objective 3

Describe each of the following types of insurance agents' authority:

a. Express authority

b. Implied authority

c. Apparent authority

Authority of Agents

The principal is legally bound by any acts of the agent that are within the agent's authority. Insurance agents generally have three types of authority to transact business on behalf of insurers that they represent:

- Express authority
- Implied authority
- Apparent authority

Express Authority

The terms of the agency contract define the **express authority** of the agent. For example, the contract will state that the agent has authority to sell the insurance company's products or that the agent has authority to bind coverage up to a specified limit.

Binding authority is generally granted to the agent in the agency contract and, thus, is a form of express authority. Binding authority is the power to make insurance coverage effective on behalf of the insurer; binding coverage is usually accomplished by issuing binders. A **binder**, which can be either written or oral, is a temporary contract between the insurance company and the insured that makes insurance coverage effective.

For example, suppose Christopher owns an old car for which he has an automobile policy with no collision coverage. Christopher purchases a new car and telephones his insurance agent, Lisa, to make sure the car is covered before he drives it away from the dealer's lot. Reminding Christopher that he has no collision coverage, Lisa gives him a quote for collision coverage on the new car. Lisa and Christopher agree that Lisa will immediately add the new car to Christopher's policy, including collision coverage with a $250 deductible. Christopher agrees to pay the premium when he receives an invoice, and Lisa assures Christopher that "coverage is bound." Lisa then begins to process the paperwork necessary to have a policy change (called an endorsement) issued that includes collision and other coverages on Christopher's new car.

If Christopher should have an accident before receiving the policy endorsement, he would have collision coverage on his new car because Lisa issued an oral binder. The binder is temporary because it will be replaced by a policy endorsement.

As illustrated by the example, oral binders are often used until the paperwork necessary to have an endorsement or a new policy issued is completed. Such paperwork often includes a written binder completed on a standard form. A written binder provides a brief summary of who is insured, what is insured, and the coverages and limits that apply.

Express authority is authority that the principal specifically grants to the agent.

Binding authority, which is usually granted in the agency contract, is the authority of an insurance agent to effect coverage on behalf of a particular insurer.

A **binder** is a temporary contract of insurance and can be either written or oral.

Binding authority gives an agent the power to put specified types and limits of coverage in force at once rather than waiting for approval from the insurer. When an insurance agent binds coverage for a new client, the agent commits the insurer to covering an exposure for, and possibly paying a claim to, a customer who is unknown to the insurer. Binding authority involves important responsibilities for the agent, and agents are expected to use their binding authority carefully.

Implied Authority

Implied authority is authority that arises from actions of the agent that are in accord with accepted custom and that are considered to be within the scope of authority granted by the principal, even though such authority is not expressly granted orally or in an agency contract.

The scope of an agent's authority, however, can go beyond the terms of the agency contract. In addition to express authority, the agent may have **implied authority** to perform other tasks necessary to accomplish the purpose of the agency relationship. For example, assume that IIA Insurance Company's agency contract with Dutie Insurance Agency does not give Dutie's agents express authority to collect premiums from IIA's insureds. Dutie's agents would have implied authority to do so because collecting premiums is an act that is reasonably necessary for Dutie to accomplish the sale of IIA's policies, and the sale of IIA's policies is expressly authorized in the contract.

Apparent Authority

Apparent authority is authority based on a third party's reasonable belief that an agent has authority to act on behalf of the principal.

An agent can also have **apparent authority** to act on behalf of the principal in ways that the principal does not intend. Usually, an insurance agent has broadly defined powers to represent an insurance company and to transact the company's business. Without actual notice or reason to believe otherwise, a third party cannot be expected to know of any unusual limitations on the agent's authority. The insurance company is bound by all acts within the agent's apparent authority, unless the insurer takes steps to prevent that outcome.

For example, IIA Insurance Company furnishes its agents with application forms showing the IIA name and logo. IIA grants its agents binding authority for routine applications for homeowners insurance. If IIA terminates its agency agreement with Greene Insurance Agency but fails to retrieve the blank application forms, a Greene producer might inadvertently take Maria's application for homeowners insurance on an IIA application form, accept Maria's check for the premium, and tell her that her coverage is bound effective that day. If a fire occurs in Maria's house the next day, IIA Insurance Company would probably be required to pay the claim because it appeared to Maria that the Greene Insurance Agency had the authority to bind her coverage with IIA. From Maria's standpoint, the Greene Insurance Agency *apparently* had the authority to bind coverage for IIA. Maria would not be penalized because she did not know that IIA had terminated its agency contract with the

Greene Insurance Agency. IIA, however, might attempt to recover the cost of the claim from Greene.

Educational Objective 4

Describe and distinguish among the various types of insurance marketing (or distribution) systems.

Insurance Marketing Systems

Insurance companies have many types of marketing systems, also known as distribution systems, designed to meet their particular marketing objectives. Most insurers use one or more of the following traditional marketing systems:

- Independent agency system
- Exclusive agency system
- Direct writing system
- Direct response system

Exhibit 4-1 shows some of the differences among these traditional insurance marketing systems. These marketing systems are not mutually exclusive. Some insurance companies use a mixed marketing system, combining two or more of these traditional distribution systems. In fact, combinations of distribution systems are becoming increasingly common among insurers.

Independent Agency System

The independent agency system is used by insurance companies of all sizes. When an insurance company uses the independent agency system, insurance sales are made through independent insurance agents. An **independent agency** is a business, operated for the benefit of its owner or owners, that sells insurance, usually as a representative of several unrelated insurers. The agency can be organized as a sole proprietorship (owned by an individual), a partnership (owned by two or more individuals), or a corporation (owned by stockholders). Closely related to and often working with independent agencies are brokers and managing general agencies.

An **independent agency** is an independent firm that sells insurance, usually as a representative of several unrelated insurance companies.

Independent Agents

An **independent agent** is a producer who works for an independent agency and can be either the owner or an employee of the agency. In a small independent agency operated by a sole proprietor who is the only producer, the independent agent and

An **independent agent** is a producer who works for an independent agency.

Exhibit 4-1

Differences Among Traditional Insurance Marketing Systems

Type of marketing (or distribution) system	What company or companies do the producers represent?	Are the producers employed by the insurer?	How are producers usually compensated?	Does the agency or agent own the expiration list(s)?	What methods of sales are usually used?
Independent agency system	Usually more than one insurer	No, the producers are employed by the agency	Sales commissions and contingent commissions	Usually, yes	Personal contact, phone, or Internet
Exclusive agency system	Only one insurer or group of related insurers	Usually, no; however, some producers begin as employees	Sales commissions (commissions on renewals might be lower than on new business) and bonus	Usually, no; but the agency contract might provide for the agent's right to sell the list to the insurer	Personal contact, phone, or Internet
Direct writing system	Only the producers' employer	Yes	Salary, bonus, commissions, or combination	No	Personal contact, phone, or Internet
Direct response system	Only the producers' employer	Yes	Salary	No	Mail, phone, or Internet

An **agency expiration list** is the record of an insurance agency's present policyholders and the dates their policies expire. "Owning the expirations" means that the agency expiration list of an independent agency belongs to the agency (not the insurer) and gives the agency the right to solicit those policyholders for insurance.

the independent agency are the same. Larger independent agencies are usually corporations that employ many producers. Independent agencies enter into agency contracts with one or more insurance companies.

One of the main distinguishing features between independent agency systems and other marketing systems is the ownership of the **agency expiration list**, which is the record of present policyholders and the dates their policies expire. The typical independent agency contract specifies that the independent agency—not the insurance company—owns the list of policyholders, the dates their existing policies expire, and, most importantly, *the right to solicit these policyholders for insurance*. If the insurance company ceases to do business with a particular agency, the insurance company cannot legally sell insurance to the agency's customers or give the expiration list, showing policyholders with that agency, to another agency. Under such circumstances, the independent agency has the right to continue doing business with its existing customers by selling them insurance with another insurance company. The customers, however, are not obligated to keep their business with the agency, but might choose another agency or company.

Because of the independent agency's traditional exclusive right to solicit policyholders on an agency expiration list, the ownership of expiration lists is generally considered the agency's most valuable asset when an independent agency is bought or sold. The agency has the right to sell its expiration lists to another independent agent. For example, if the agency were to be sold, the new buyer would want to keep the agency's customers and would thus want the agency's expiration lists.

Sometimes, an independent agent determines that a different insurance company represented by the agency can better meet an existing customer's needs. Occasionally, an insurance company might be unwilling to renew an insurance policy or might have rates that are not competitive. Therefore, the agent must select another insurer for the customer. In either case, the independent agency has the right to switch the coverage to another insurer, subject to the customer's approval.

Exceptions to the General Rule: Independent Agencies That Represent Only One Insurer

Independent insurance agencies generally represent more than one, and sometimes a dozen or more, insurance companies. However, it would not be accurate to state that all independent agencies represent more than one insurance company. Some independent agencies represent only one insurer or a group of related insurers. An agency might not find it practical to represent more than one insurer because the agency is small or just starting in business, the agency might specialize in one type of coverage, or the agency might have a special arrangement with an insurer.

Some independent agents agree to place all or most of their business with just one insurance company. Agents find some advantages in doing a large volume of business with one insurance company rather than a smaller volume with each of several companies. Some insurance companies offer independent agents incentives for special agency agreements. Those incentives might include computer systems, higher commission rates, a more open market for the agent's customers, or other advantages.

Brokers

An insurance **broker** is an independent business owner or firm that represents customers rather than insurers. Brokers shop among insurance companies to find the best coverage or value for their clients—the insurance buyers. Some insurance companies require that brokers purchase insurance through one of the company's agents who, in turn, pays a portion of the agent's commission to the broker. Other insurance companies have contracts with and regularly accept business directly from

An insurance **broker** is an independent business owner or firm that sells insurance by representing customers rather than insurers.

insurance brokers and pay them a fee or commission for the business. Since they are not legal representatives of the insurer, brokers are not likely to have authority to commit the insurer by binding coverage, unlike agents, who generally have binding authority. As discussed in Chapter 2, an excess and surplus lines (E&S) broker is a special type of broker who is licensed by a state or states to transact insurance through nonadmitted insurers.

In practice, despite the technical distinctions between brokers and independent agents, the differences are quite limited. Both brokers and independent agents are intermediaries between insurance companies and insurance buyers, and both collect premiums from insureds and remit them to insurers. Both are in the business of finding people with insurance needs and selling insurance appropriate to those needs. In fact, the same person can act as an agent on one transaction and as a broker on another. A person acts as an agent when placing insurance with an insurer for which he or she is licensed as an agent but might act as a broker when placing insurance with other agents or insurers.

Large brokerage firms have many brokers who generally handle commercial insurance accounts that often require sophisticated knowledge and service. Many brokerage firms operate nationally, with offices in many states, and some operate internationally as well. In addition to insurance sales, large brokerage firms, as well as large agencies, might provide extensive loss control, appraisal, actuarial, risk management, and other insurance-related services that large businesses need. A few large brokerage firms account for a substantial share of the commercial property and liability insurance sold in the United States.

Managing General Agencies (MGAs)

A **managing general agency (MGA)** is an independent business organization that appoints and supervises independent agents for insurance companies that use the independent agency system. The MGA functions almost as a branch office for one or more insurance companies.

A **managing general agency (MGA)** is an independent business organization that functions almost as a branch office for one or more insurance companies. The MGA appoints and supervises independent agents for insurance companies that use the independent agency system. MGAs serve as intermediaries between insurers and agents who sell insurance directly to the consumer, in much the same position as wholesalers in the distribution system for tangible goods. The exact duties and responsibilities of an MGA depend on its contracts with the insurers it represents. The MGA receives a managerial commission—often referred to as an "override"—which is a percentage of the premium or the profits on policies sold by producers placing business with the insurance company through the MGA.

Excess and surplus lines brokers resemble MGAs in that they usually transact business primarily with other brokers and agents and not directly with consumers. In fact, some firms operate as both MGAs and E&S brokers.

Exclusive Agency System

An **exclusive agent** resembles an independent agent in some ways. Like the independent agent, the exclusive agent's business operation is his or her own insurance sales agency. An agency agreement describes the exclusive agent's binding authority and compensation arrangements.

Unlike the agency agreement in the independent agency system, the exclusive agency system limits the agent to selling insurance *exclusively for one insurance company* or group of related companies. If a desired type of insurance is not written by the insurance company represented, some contracts allow the agent to place ("broker") the business with an independent agent or another exclusive agent.

Generally, an exclusive agent is not an employee of the insurance company but a self-employed representative of the company. With some exclusive agency insurance companies, agent trainees begin as employees and later make the transition to owning their own business.

Some exclusive agency contracts provide that the agent owns the agency expiration list and has the right to sell it to another party, but this is often not the case. Usually, the contract contains an agreement that, upon termination of the agency contract, the insurance company will buy the expiration list from the exclusive agent, using a predetermined formula to establish its value. An exclusive agent's expiration list—and the right to consider people on the list as customers *of that agent*—can become a valuable asset as an exclusive agent's business grows.

> An **exclusive agent** is an agent that has a contract to sell insurance exclusively for one insurance company (or a group of related companies).

Direct Writing System

As with the exclusive agency system, producers in the **direct writing system** sell insurance for only one insurance company or group. Unlike most producers in the exclusive agency system, however, producers in the direct writing system are not self-employed. They are employees of the insurance company, and their job is to sell insurance for the company. Employees who work as insurance producers for a **direct writer** are generally called sales representatives. Terminology can be confusing here. A direct writer's sales representatives are sometimes called agents, and they must possess agents' licenses. Legally, they function as agents of the insurance company, and most insurance buyers would not distinguish between an agent and a sales representative.

Like employees in general, a direct writer's sales representatives work from offices or other business locations provided by the employer. The insurance company in this system, unlike insurers using the independent and exclusive agency systems, pays

> The **direct writing system** of insurance marketing uses sales representatives who are employees of an insurance company.
>
> A **direct writer** is an insurer that uses the direct writing system to market insurance.

the office expenses as well. Employees can be transferred from job to job and from office to office to meet the overall needs of the insurer.

Because the direct writer's sales representative is an employee of the insurance company, the expiration list belongs not to the sales representative but to the insurance company, which can use the customer information as a source of prospects for follow-up sales by its other sales representatives.

Brokering Business

Sometimes an agent has a customer who needs a type of policy not available from an insurance company the agent represents. When this happens, the agent might contact an agent who represents another insurance company and apply for insurance through that agent. The agent who represents the insurer usually shares the commission with the agent who has the customer.

In this situation, the original agent acts as a broker—the agent shops for insurance on behalf of the customer. The act of placing the insurance for this customer through another agent is called *brokering*. The insurance sold in this manner is referred to as *brokered business*.

Exclusive agents and direct writers' sales representatives, as well as independent agents, might occasionally broker business for an account whose other coverages are handled by the producer's insurance company. Authority for such transactions would be specified in the agency or employment contract.

Direct Response System

The **direct response system** includes any insurance marketing system that does not depend primarily on individual producers to locate customers and sell insurance. Direct response insurance companies advertise directly by mail, radio, television, Internet, or with the communications of an association, a credit card company, or a bank. These advertisements encourage potential customers to contact the insurance company to purchase insurance.

> The **direct response system** includes any insurance marketing system that does not depend primarily on individual producers to locate customers and sell insurance but relies primarily on mail, phone, and/or Internet sales.

With this system, a person shopping for insurance coverage contacts the insurance company by telephone, through the mail, or on the Internet. An employee of the insurance company, often called a customer service representative (or CSR), handles the telephone call or correspondence. The CSR could be in an office hundreds of miles away from the customer.

Mixed Marketing System

Traditionally, each insurance company used just one of the marketing systems described above. Recently, many insurance companies have departed from this practice. The term **mixed marketing system** refers to an insurance company's use of more than one distribution system. This practice, which has become increasingly popular among insurers, is also referred to as using alternative distribution systems.

For example, some insurers that traditionally sold insurance only through independent agents have also done some direct response marketing, developing business without producers and without paying commissions to producers. These insurance companies generally argue that advertisements and direct mail enable them to reach customers they would not reach through an independent agent. Nevertheless, the company's independent agents sometimes feel they are being bypassed by such practices.

Conversely, some direct writers, seeking to expand their business, have entered into agency agreements with independent agents in some areas. These direct writers have turned to independent agents as a distribution system partly because they have found it relatively expensive to establish offices and develop trained employees—especially in small communities.

A **mixed marketing system** refers to the use by an insurer of more than one marketing system.

Educational Objective 5

Describe typical compensation arrangements for insurance producers.

Compensation of Producers

While some producers receive a salary, commissions provide the primary form of compensation for producers. Two types of commissions that producers typically earn are sales commissions and contingent commissions.

Sales Commissions

An independent agency or an exclusive agency receives commissions from the insurer for all insurance premiums the agency generates. A **sales commission** (or simply, a **commission**) is a percentage of the premium that goes to the agency or to the producer. As mentioned, an insurance broker might receive a sales commission or fee directly from the insurer or might receive a portion of the commission from the agent who placed the insurance.

For insurance agents, the method of premium collection determines how sales commissions are received. If the insurance company handles billings and collections (direct billing), the insurance company periodically mails a commission check to

A **sales commission** (or simply, a **commission**) is a percentage of the premium that the insurer pays to the agency or producer for new policies sold or existing policies renewed.

the agency. If the agency collects the premiums (agency billing or producer billing), it subtracts its commission on each policy and remits the balance of collected premiums to the insurance company, usually on a monthly basis.

In a small agency with only one agent, the entire commission goes to that agent. In a larger agency, a portion of the commission typically goes to the producer who made the sale, and the remainder goes to the agency to cover other expenses.

Usually, commissions are not fully earned at the time of a sale. If policies are canceled or premium is returned to an insured for some other reason (such as deleting or reducing coverage), the producer must also return the unearned portion of the commission to the insurance company.

The commission compensates the agency not only for making the sale but also for providing service before and after the sale. Service provided before the sale includes locating and screening insurance prospects, conducting a successful sales solicitation, getting the necessary information to complete an application, preparing a submission to the insurance company, and presenting a proposal or quote to the prospect. To make a sale, the agent must also evaluate a prospect's insurance needs and recommend appropriate coverages for the client to select. After the sale, the agency often handles the paperwork that accompanies policy changes, billing, and claim handling, among other things. When it is time for the policy to be renewed, the agency must again analyze coverage needs and consider any changes in insurance coverage that have become available.

The producer who is an employee of a direct writer generally receives a salary and perhaps also a bonus that relates to the premiums of the policies the producer sells. The compensation arrangements of direct writers tend to emphasize sales to new customers, since these companies generally assign service after the sale to employees who specialize in the applicable areas, such as claims. With some insurers, drive-in claim service offices and other customer service centers handle most of the services required after the sale, including policy changes and billing problems.

Contingent Commissions

A **contingent commission** is a commission that an insurer pays, usually annually, to an independent agency and that is based on the premium volume and profitability level of the agency's business with that insurer.

In addition to commissions based on a percentage of premiums, many agencies receive a **contingent commission**, sometimes referred to as "profit sharing." The insurance company compares the premiums received for policies sold by the agency with the losses incurred under those policies to determine whether the agency's business has earned a profit. If the business sold by the agency attains a certain volume of premium and level of profitability, the company shares a portion of the profit with the agency. Since this extra commission is *contingent* on earning a profit, it is called a contingent commission. Contingent commissions encourage agencies to sell policies that will be profitable to the insurance company and to avoid selling policies that are likely to be unprofitable. Agencies that practice careful selection can earn sizable contingent commissions as a result. An independent agency is typically eligible to receive a contingent commission annually from each insurer for which the agency's business has been profitable.

Insurance companies that use the exclusive agency system or the direct writing system might offer higher sales commissions, rather than contingent commissions, for agents whose sales generate a given level of profit. Alternatively, these companies sometimes offer bonuses or other forms of compensation to agents whose business is profitable.

Educational Objective 6

Describe advertising methods used by various insurers, producers, and producer trade associations.

Advertising

An independent agency attempts to attract customers *for the agency*, and local advertising often stresses the agency rather than the various insurers it represents. On the other hand, many insurance companies marketing through the independent agency system use national advertising programs intended to enhance the company image. With many products, "name brands"—those that are known and recognized—tend to be most readily accepted by customers. Insurance is no exception. Advertising symbols like the Travelers umbrella, the Hartford stag, and the Fireman's Fund fire helmet are designed to increase public recognition of these companies.

Local independent agents sometimes identify with national symbols or repeat nationally advertised slogans in their advertisements. At other times, their ads focus on the agency itself—its quality of service, reputation, personnel and their qualifications, range of services, or similar themes that might attract an insurance buyer.

In the exclusive agency system, advertising programs emphasize the names of both the insurance company and the agent. Sometimes an insurance company's advertisement lists all its agents in the area and includes a photo of each agent. Advertising for direct writers tends to emphasize the company itself rather than individual producers or office locations.

Since they do not have producers, insurers using direct response marketing must use other ways of attracting new customers.

Some insurers using the direct response system advertise heavily—an activity that can be quite costly. Others, working from an established customer base, have traditionally relied successfully on free word-of-mouth advertising.

In addition to the traditional types of advertising—television, radio, magazines, newspapers, mail, and so forth—insurers and agents of all types are increasingly using the Internet for advertising, and most insurers and many agents now have websites giving information about the company or agency and the products and services it provides.

Producers' Trade Associations

Trade associations serve their members through activities such as education, political lobbying, research, and advertising. The advertising programs are intended to create a favorable image of members of the associations as a group and to make the public familiar with the logo and other symbols of each association.

Independent Agents' Trade Associations

Most independent agents are members of the Independent Insurance Agents of America (IIAA) or the National Association of Professional Insurance Agents (PIA) or both. The IIAA is often called the "Big I" because of the prominent letter "I" in its advertising logo. (In some states, IIAA and PIA have consolidated to form one state insurance agents' association.)

Agents' and Brokers' Trade Association

The members of the Council of Insurance Agents and Brokers (CIAB) are independent agents and brokers associated with large agencies or brokerage firms that primarily handle commercial insurance.

Managing General Agents' Association

Many managing general agents are members of the American Association of Managing General Agents (AAMGA), which, like agents' and brokers' associations, also provides various services to its members.

Educational Objective 7

Describe the various aspects of marketing management.

Marketing Management

All insurance companies need some means of managing the activities of producers—systems to supervise producers, to motivate them, and to provide them with insurance products they can sell. An important function of marketing management is monitoring agency sales and underwriting results to ensure that both the company's and the agency's sales and profit objectives are met.

Producer Supervision

Although selling insurance is essentially a one-on-one activity that often occurs away from the producer's office and the insurer's home office, insurance companies do supervise their producers. An insurance company using independent agents typically has **marketing representatives** who visit the independent agents representing the company. The marketing representative's role is to develop and maintain a sound working relationship with the insurer's agents and to motivate the agents to produce a satisfactory volume of profitable business for the insurer. Marketing representatives also have the responsibility of finding and "appointing" (entering into agency contracts with) new independent agents who can potentially produce profitable business for the company. Some marketing representatives operate from their homes and spend most of their time traveling among agencies in their marketing territories, maintaining a close personal contact.

Marketing representatives are insurance company employees whose role is to visit agents representing the insurer, to develop and maintain sound working relationships with those agents, and to motivate the agents to produce a satisfactory volume of profitable business for the insurer.

Other insurance companies have **production underwriters**, who spend most of their time inside the insurance company office but also travel to maintain rapport with agents and to meet with clients in special situations. Insurers using the direct writing system might have an agency manager or district manager as the supervisor of a group of producers, directing their activities rather closely.

Production underwriters are insurance company employees who work in an insurer's office in an underwriting position but who also travel to visit and maintain rapport with agents and sometimes clients.

Depending on how an insurer is structured, producer supervision and support can be provided from either the insurer's home office or a branch office or regional office. Small insurers, or those doing business in a limited geographic area, might have only one office. When this is the case, producers deal directly with personnel in the home office.

Insurers doing business nationally or over a widespread geographic area usually find it desirable to establish field offices close to producers' offices, and producers usually work closely with a local field office rather than the home office. A small field office, perhaps with only one marketing manager or marketing representative, might be called a service office. A larger office, containing management personnel, underwriters, claim representatives, and others, might be called a branch office or a regional office.

Producer Motivation

Insurance companies need to motivate their producers to sell the types of insurance the companies want sold. This, too, is the task of insurance company marketing management. Some producer motivation results from personal relationships and encouragement by marketing representatives, regional managers, and other people working in field offices. Other motivation comes from programs developed in the home office.

The financial incentives that producers receive for selling can affect their sales performance. The insurance company's marketing department considers this motivational effect when recommending the amount of salaries, bonuses, or commissions to be paid to producers. Insurers often pay contingent commissions to reward producers for producing business that earns a profit for the insurer.

Some insurance companies develop sales contests to encourage some specific production activities, such as selling a particular type of policy or reaching a particular level of sales activity. Sales contests can lead to special recognition or to an all-expenses-paid trip to a resort for a combination of business and pleasure.

Product Management and Development

Insurance production is most successful when producers have a desirable product to sell at a competitive price. The insurance company's marketing department—usually at the home office level—strives to give producers the products and pricing they need. The home office marketing department bases many of its decisions on information provided by producers and by other insurance company personnel in the field. An insurer's product management involves maintaining an ongoing relationship with producers.

People involved with sales are often the first to identify a need that could be addressed by either a new policy or modification of an existing policy. Those involved in marketing are acutely aware of what the competition is doing in regard to product management and development. The response to new product development elsewhere is often critical to satisfying changing market demands.

The home office marketing department cooperates with other departments to determine what coverages the insurer's insurance policies should provide, what price to charge, and what other services the insurer should provide. Decisions in those matters are based partly on claim costs for the particular insurer or for the industry as a whole and on information about the coverages, prices, and services of competing insurers.

Educational Objective 8

Describe ways in which states regulate producers' activities.

Regulation of Insurance Producers

In addition to regulating insurer activities as discussed in Chapter 2, state insurance departments regulate activities of insurance producers. Such regulation occurs primarily through agent and broker licensing laws and other state laws dealing with insurance, such as unfair trade practices laws.

Licensing Laws

To function legally as an insurance agent, a producer must be licensed by the state or states in which he or she wishes to sell insurance. Producers' licensing laws vary by state and change periodically. Some states have several different licenses, including licenses for agents, brokers, and solicitors. The exact titles and the authority that goes with them vary somewhat by state. Generally, insurance agents are defined legally as representatives of the insurance company or companies for which they sell insurance. Brokers, as stated previously, are the representatives of the insurance purchasers rather than of the insurance companies with which they transact business. Some states, such as California, have separate licenses for "solicitors," who work for and are representatives of agents or brokers, often as office employees, and who have more limited authority than agents. Generally, solicitors can solicit prospects but cannot bind insurance coverage. In other states, such office employees who "solicit" insurance must secure an agent's license; they are often called customer service representatives (CSRs) or customer service agents (CSAs).

To obtain a state agent's license, a person must meet several requirements. Usually, a producer must pass an examination and meet other qualifications of the state insurance department to receive a state insurance license. These examinations typically deal with insurance principles, insurance coverages, and insurance laws and regulations. Some states mandate a certain number of hours of classroom study before a candidate can take a license examination. In some states, completing a recognized professional designation program, such as the Chartered Property Casualty Underwriter (CPCU) program, allows the producer to waive the classroom and examination requirements for licensing. Once a state agent's license has been issued, an agent generally must seek to be appointed by one or more insurance companies before he or she can sell insurance.

Producers' licenses generally have a specified term, such as one or two years, and can be renewed by paying a fee specified by the state. Most states also impose a continuing education requirement, requiring that producers periodically complete a specified number of hours of educational study related to the insurance business. Producers in those states must provide evidence that they have completed approved continuing education courses before the state will renew their licenses.

Licensed producers are required to adhere to all laws regulating insurance sales in the state or states in which they conduct business. The state can suspend or revoke licenses under certain circumstances, such as engaging in unfair trade practices.

Educational Objective 9

Identify and describe acts related to insurance that are considered unfair trade practices in most states.

Unfair Trade Practices Laws

Unfair trade practices laws are state laws that specify certain prohibited business practices.

Many states have adopted **unfair trade practices laws** that specify certain prohibited practices. These laws are not specifically limited to the activities of insurance producers. Underwriters, claim representatives, and others could also be guilty of misconduct in these areas. Although they vary by state, these laws typically prohibit various unfair trade practices, such as:

• Misrepresentation and false advertising

• Tie-in sales

• Rebating

• Other deceptive practices

Misrepresentation and False Advertising

It is an unfair trade practice for insurance agents or other insurance personnel to make, issue, or circulate information that does any of the following:

• Misrepresents the benefits, advantages, conditions, or terms of any insurance policy

• Misrepresents the dividends to be received on any insurance policy

• Makes false or misleading statements about dividends previously paid on any insurance policy

• Uses a name or title of insurance policies that misrepresents the true nature of the policies

It is also considered an unfair trade practice to make untrue, deceptive, or misleading advertisements, announcements, or statements about insurance or about any person in the insurance business.

Tie-In Sales

It is an unfair trade practice for a producer to require that the purchase of insurance be tied to some other sale or financial arrangement—a practice referred to as a "tiein sale." It is also an unfair trade practice for a lender to require that a borrower purchase insurance from the lender or from any insurer, agent, or broker recommended by the lender. Each transaction must stand on its own, and insurance on property that is the subject of a loan can be purchased from any insurer the borrower chooses.

For example, assume that Richard, a salesman with New Car Dealership also holds an insurance agent's license with White Insurance Company and sells insurance in addition to selling cars. If Julia purchases a car from Richard, Richard cannot require that Julia purchase insurance on the car from White Insurance Company. Julia is free to purchase insurance from any company or agency she chooses. If Richard were to coerce Julia to purchase insurance from White by telling Julia that the loan on her new car will be denied unless Julia purchases a policy from White, Richard would be guilty of an unfair trade practice because Richard would be requiring a tie-in sale—tying the sale of insurance to the financing of the car.

Rebating

The prohibition of **rebating** means that producers are not allowed to pay a portion of the premium or give any commission to a policyholder. This ban on rebating also means that producers are not permitted to offer to do other business with the policyholder in exchange for the purchase of a policy. Most states have enacted anti-rebating laws.

Rebating is offering anything of value, other than the insurance itself, to an applicant as an inducement to buy or maintain insurance.

However, rebating is permitted in at least one state, California, under many circumstances. Proposition 103, which was passed by California voters in 1988, repealed the law that prohibited insurance agents from rebating part of their commission to clients. As a result, rebates may now be made to California insureds, unless rebates are specifically prohibited by sections of the state's Insurance Code that were not repealed by Proposition 103. A further restriction on rebating exists in California's civil rights laws, which prohibit insurance agents and brokers from offering rebates or varying the size of rebates if the practice arbitrarily discriminates among individuals.

Opponents of anti-rebating laws in other states continue to argue that such laws inhibit competition in the insurance marketplace. Further challenges to these laws might therefore appear in the future.

Other Deceptive Practices

In addition to the specific practices discussed above, unfair trade practices laws prohibit other practices of insurers that are deceptive or unfair to applicants and insureds. For example, these laws prohibit an insurer and its agents from making a false statement about the financial condition of another insurer. Thus, an agent for IIA Insurance Company, could not legally mislead his client by saying that XYZ Insurance Company has a poor financial rating in the hope of discouraging the client from purchasing insurance from XYZ.

It is also an unfair trade practice to put false information on an insurance application to earn a commission from the insurance sale. Occasionally, some information might lead the insurance company to reject the application, resulting in the producer not earning a commission. Producers are required to be honest in the information they enter on application forms. Both insurance companies and policyholders count on insurance transactions being conducted in utmost good faith.

Educational Objective 10

Define or describe each of the Key Words and Phrases for this assignment. (All Key Words and Phrases appear in bold print in the text and in the margins throughout this chapter.)

Summary

Insurance marketing is the process of identifying potential customers and then creating and supplying the insurance products and services they need. Although there are many facets to this process, the initial contact between an insurance company and its policyholders is typically through an agent or another type of producer. Thus, a major marketing concern is the insurance company's relationship with its producers.

The legal relationship of agency empowers the insurance producer, the agent, to act on behalf of the insurance company, the principal. Normally, insurance companies make very specific agency contracts with their producers. An agent owes specific duties, such as loyalty and obedience, to the principal in acting for the principal's benefit; and the principal owes certain duties to the agent, such as compensation for services. The principal is legally bound by any acts of the agent that are within the agent's authority. The agent's authority includes the express authority stated in the agency contract, implied authority that is not expressly granted, and the apparent authority a third party might reasonably expect the agent to have.

The specific relationship an insurance company has with its producers reflects the type of marketing or distribution system the company uses to distribute its products. While there are many insurance marketing systems, the traditional types are the independent agency system, the exclusive agency system, the direct writing system, and the direct response system. Independent agents are in business for themselves, they usually represent several different insurance companies, and they own their expiration lists. Exclusive agents represent only one insurance company, adhering to its programs and procedures, even though they are also in business for themselves. The sales representatives of direct writers are the insurers' own employees. The direct response system relies on direct mail, Internet, or telephone contact with customers. Insurers increasingly use more than one distribution system in a mixed marketing system.

The compensation of insurance producers includes commissions and salaries. The sales commissions paid to agents and brokers are a percentage of the insurance premiums they produce. Sales commissions are often supplemented by contingent commissions, which reflect the volume and profitability of that business for the insurer. The sales representatives of direct writers receive a salary, which might be supplemented by a bonus reflecting sales performance.

Advertising, another aspect of insurance marketing, reflects the marketing system used. Insurers relying on independent agents usually advertise to promote the company image, while independent agents try to attract local customers to their offices; joint advertising campaigns are often used to serve the needs of both the agent and the insurer. Exclusive agency companies tend to emphasize both the company name and the local service. Direct writing insurance companies advertise primarily to promote the company's name and products with the public. Direct response insurers rely heavily on advertising to bring customers to them.

An insurer's marketing management activities include producer supervision, producer motivation, and product management and development. Insurers motivate producers through personal contact and through incentive programs developed in the home office. Through product management and development activities, insurers attempt to provide producers with the products needed to produce business for the insurance company.

State regulators oversee the marketing activities of insurance companies and their agents. Insurance producers must meet the specified requirements to obtain and maintain a license in the state or states where they transact business. States prohibit unfair trade practices such as misrepresentation and false advertising, tie-in sales, rebating, and other deceptive practices.

Chapter 5

Underwriting

Educational Objectives

After studying this chapter, you should be able to:

1. Identify and describe the major underwriting activities of insurers. (pp. 5-4 to 5-12)

2. Identify and describe the ways in which insurers protect their available capacity. (pp. 5-6 to 5-7)

3. Describe the following types of insurance rates, and explain which type would be more appropriate in a given situation: (pp. 5-9 to 5-10)

   a. Class rates

   b. Individual rates

4. Explain the role of underwriting management. (pp. 5-12 to 5-15)

5. Identify and describe the steps in the underwriting process that an underwriter follows in making an underwriting decision. (pp. 5-15 to 5-22)

6. Identify and describe sources that underwriters use in making underwriting decisions. (pp. 5-16 to 5-18)

7. Identify and describe four categories of hazards that under-writers must evaluate. (pp. 5-18 to 5-19)

8. Identify and explain the underwriting options an under-writer has in evaluating an application for insurance. (pp. 5-20 to 5-21)

9. Describe ways in which states regulate underwriting activi-ties. (pp. 5-22 to 5-24)

10. Define or describe each of the Key Words and Phrases for this assignment. (All Key Words and Phrases appear in bold print in the text and in the margins throughout this chapter.)

Chapter 5

Underwriting

Underwriting is the heart of the insurance business. The function of underwriting is to determine who an insurance company's customers will be, what the company's products will be, and at what price those products will be sold. To a large extent, a company's success in achieving its goals depends on the effectiveness of its underwriting.

Insurance companies themselves, rather than their employees, are sometimes referred to as underwriters. However, the term **underwriter** is usually reserved for insurance company employees whose job is to make underwriting decisions for the insurer.

Underwriting is the process of selecting insureds, pricing coverage, determining insurance policy terms and conditions, and then monitoring the underwriting decisions made.

An **underwriter** is an insurance company employee who evaluates applicants for insurance, selects those that are acceptable to the insurer, prices coverage, and determines policy terms and conditions.

A Brief History of Underwriting

In the seventeenth century, English traders and merchants sent ships on hazardous voyages to the New World and the Far East to trade for goods that were in demand in Europe. While the rewards were great, much uncertainty accompanied these endeavors. When merchants or shipowners undertook such ventures, they often obtained a contract of indemnification from independent business people who agreed, in exchange for a fee, to share in the loss if certain perils of the sea destroyed the ship or its cargo.

Seventeenth-century merchants and shipowners gathered at Edward Lloyd's coffeehouse in London to find individuals who would be willing to provide them with a contract of indemnity (an insurance policy). These early "insurers" risked their personal fortunes on their ability to judge the dangers associated with a particular voyage. To enable these potential insurers to evaluate the hazards of a venture, the shipowner described the details of the venture, including the ship and its cargo, the destination, the route to be traveled, and the

---

experience of the captain. If the venture was deemed acceptable, a contract of indemnity was drafted, *under* which each insurer *wrote* his name along with the percentage of the venture he would assume. These individual insurers became known as "underwriters," and each underwriter then collected a fee, known as a premium, from the shipowner in proportion to the percentage of the venture the underwriter assumed.

With their personal fortunes at stake, these early underwriters were not interested in ventures that were likely to fail. They were selective, and they concerned themselves with the history of the shipowners, the captain, the ship, the planned route, the time (season) of the voyage, and the cargo. Through an informal communication network, they monitored the physical, political, and financial condition of various ports and countries around the world. When a problem became known, the underwriters increased their premiums. In the case of a major problem, insurance could become difficult or impossible to obtain because no underwriter was willing to risk his fortune against a likely disaster.

Underwriters' fortunes rose and fell as reports of completed voyages and occasional sinkings and shipwrecks came back to Lloyd's. Some underwriters became wealthy through good luck and good judgment in deciding which ventures to insure. Others, through a combination of bad luck and bad judgment, lost their fortunes.

While people still risk their fortunes at Lloyd's of London today, the insurance industry has become more complex and institutionalized. In most cases, the corporate insurer has replaced the individual insurer. Modern insurers look to their underwriters to perform most aspects of the underwriting function for them. The modern insurance company is similar to the early entrepreneurs at Lloyd's in that its assets increase and decrease according to the soundness of the decisions its underwriters make. The insurer's assets, rather than the underwriter's own funds, are used as a guarantee that covered losses will be paid. Without the insurer's ability to make good on its promise to pay legitimate claims, an insurance policy would be a worthless piece of paper.

Educational Objective 1

Identify and describe the major underwriting activities of insurers.

Underwriting Activities

Underwriting includes the following activities:

- Selecting insureds
- Pricing coverage

- Determining policy terms and conditions
- Monitoring underwriting decisions

The first three activities are not performed in sequence but occur simultaneously. The last, monitoring underwriting decisions, is an ongoing activity. Underwriters attempt to select insureds to whom the insurer can offer reasonable policy terms and conditions. Of course, the price charged for coverage must be high enough to enable the insurer to pay claims and to provide the insurer a reasonable profit or gain.

Selecting Insureds

Insurers must carefully screen applicants to determine which ones it desires to insure. If insurers do not properly select policyholders and price coverages, some insureds might be able to purchase insurance at prices that do not adequately reflect their loss exposures. The underwriting selection process is not limited to underwriters but also includes producers and underwriting managers. All these participants exert a joint effort in the underwriting process.

Insurance companies receive many applications, but not all applications result in the issuance of policies. An insurance company cannot accept all applicants for two basic reasons:

- The insurer can succeed only if it selects applicants who, as a group, present loss exposures that are proportionate to the premiums that will be collected. In other words, insurers try to avoid *adverse selection*.

- An insurer's ability to provide insurance is limited by its *capacity* to write new policies.

Adverse Selection Considerations

Insurance companies expect to pay claims; without claims, insurance would be unnecessary. However, insurers try to select applicants who are not likely to have covered losses greater than the insurance company anticipated when it calculated its insurance rates. On the other hand, people with the greatest probability of loss are the ones most likely to purchase insurance, a situation referred to as **adverse selection**. Poor underwriting results might occur if too many of the applicants accepted for insurance are those most likely to incur serious losses. Underwriters try to avoid adverse selection by screening applicants to identify, and decline coverage to, those who present loss potentials that would be inadequately reflected in the rates.

An extreme example of adverse selection would involve a burning building. No insurer would knowingly write fire insurance to cover a building that is already burning, but the owner of an uninsured building that is on fire would probably be glad to purchase fire insurance on the building.

Adverse selection is a situation that occurs because people with the greatest probability of loss are the ones most likely to purchase insurance. Adverse selection normally occurs if the premium is low relative to the loss exposure.

Adverse selection is particularly prevalent with some kinds of insurance. For example, owners of property next to a river would be more likely to purchase flood insurance than those who own property on a hilltop with no flood exposure.

Educational Objective 2

Identify and describe the ways in which insurers protect their available capacity.

Capacity Considerations

Capacity refers to the amount of business an insurer is able to write, usually based on a comparison of the insurer's written premiums to the size of its policyholders' surplus. An insurer must have adequate policyholders' surplus to be able to increase the volume of insurance it writes.

Reminder

As discussed in Chapter 3, *policyholders' surplus* is the insurer's total admitted assets minus its total liabilities. A commonly used measure of an insurer's capacity is the *capacity ratio*, or *premium-to-surplus ratio* (written premiums divided by policyholders' surplus).

The term **capacity** refers to the volume of business an insurer is able to handle. Capacity is often measured by comparing the insurer's written premiums to its *policyholders' surplus*. Insurance companies often impose voluntary capacity constraints that are more conservative than those used by regulators. This voluntary constraint on capacity provides a buffer or cushion to allow for variability in the insurer's underwriting and investment results.

An insurer's capacity limits its ability to write new business. Selling new policies creates insurer expenses, such as agents' commissions, that reduce the policyholders' surplus in the short term. Reduced policyholders' surplus leads to reduced capacity. Yet, in the long term, if the new policies generate premiums that exceed losses and expenses, the new policies will increase the policyholders' surplus. Barring serious underwriting or investment losses, an insurer can increase its capacity through steady, orderly growth in sales of policies that contribute to the insurer's profits. Planned growth is generally one of the goals of an insurance company.

Insurers attempt to protect their available capacity in three primary ways:

- Maintaining a spread of risk
- Optimizing use of available resources
- Arranging reinsurance

Maintaining a Spread of Risk

Jargon Alert!

The word *risk* has many meanings. In this text, risk is generally used to mean the chance or possibility of financial loss. Risk can also mean the subject matter insured or being considered for insurance. (In other words, a commercial building on which an application for insurance has been submitted is often called a risk.)

Since every insurer has limited capacity, insurance companies must allocate their available capacity. Like businesses of many kinds, insurance companies prefer not to put all their eggs in one basket. In other words, by spreading their risk among various types of insurance and different geographic areas, insurance companies reduce the chances that overall underwriting results will be adversely affected by a large number of losses in one type of insurance or one territory. In other words, an insurer must diversify the coverage it writes and spread its policies among different types of coverage and different geographic areas. For example, a tornado might require an insurer to pay extensive property claims in one community, but these claims would be balanced against premiums from other communities that do not experience a tornado in the same year, as well as from other types of insurance written by the insurance company.

Insurance companies also allocate capacity by setting limitations on the amount of insurance they write for any one insured. Generally, limitations are more restrictive for some types of business than for others, depending on the exposures presented. For example, an insurance company might place a lower limit on the maximum amount of fire insurance it will provide on a rural home with no fire hydrants nearby and no fire department within ten miles than on a home located within a city with excellent public fire protection.

Optimizing Use of Available Resources

In addition to its financial resources, every insurance company depends on other resources. Among these are physical resources, which include offices and equipment, and human resources, which include underwriters, claim representatives, producers, and service personnel.

Underwriting and servicing some kinds of insurance require special skills or experience, and many insurers offer only certain types of insurance and not others. For example, an insurer might choose not to solicit or accept applications for insurance on farms if that insurer does not have personnel experienced in handling farm business. Without some expertise, recognizing unusual hazards that might exist in a farm operation is difficult. Without experienced farm claim representatives, it can be very difficult and expensive to settle farm claims. On the other hand, another insurance company might have personnel capable of handling farm business, and that insurer might wish to use its available capacity to increase the amount of insurance it writes for farmers.

Arranging Reinsurance

In *reinsurance*, the reinsurer receives a portion of the premiums from the primary insurer's policies and assumes some of the losses on those policies. The primary insurer usually retains a portion of the premiums and pays the insured losses on reinsured policies and is then reimbursed by the reinsurer for losses for which the reinsurer is contractually responsible. If reinsurance is readily available, insurance companies can increase the number of new policies they write by transferring some of the premium and loss exposures to reinsurers. Thus, the availability of reinsurance can affect an insurance company's capacity to write business.

Reminder

Remember from Chapter 2 that *reinsurance* is a contractual arrangement whereby one insurer, the primary insurer, transfers some or all of the loss exposures from policies written for its insureds to another insurer, the reinsurer.

Pricing Coverage

Commensurate means showing an appropriate relationship. A premium is **commensurate with the exposure** when an appropriate relationship exists between the size of the premium and the exposure assumed by the insurer.

The underwriting pricing objective is to charge a premium that is **commensurate with the exposure**. In other words, each insured's premium should be set at a level that is adequate to enable the total premiums paid by a large group of similar insureds to pay the losses and expenses of that group and to allow the insurance company to achieve a reasonable profit or gain. Pricing insurance involves classifying the applicant according to its loss exposures and then determining a premium by applying an appropriate rate to the applicant's exposure units.

Premium Determination

As discussed in earlier chapters, the *rate* is the price of insurance charged per exposure unit, and an *exposure unit* is a measure of loss potential used in rating insurance. The exposure unit used depends on the type of insurance, as illustrated below:

Type of Insurance	Exposure Unit
Workers compensation	Each $100 of payroll
Property insurance	Each $100 of insurance
Auto liability insurance	Each car insured

The premium is determined by multiplying the rate by the number of exposure units. For example, the premium for property insurance with a limit of $250,000 at a rate of $.40 per $100 of insurance is $1,000, calculated as follows:

$$\frac{\$250,000}{\$100} = 2,500 \text{ units} \times \$.40 \text{ per unit} = \$1,000$$

The premium is the total amount of money an insured pays the insurance company for a particular policy or coverage for a stated period. For example, an insurer might charge a premium of $400 to provide a one-year property insurance policy with a $250 deductible for a $100,000 brick home located in Anytown, U.S.A. The same insurer might charge $400 to provide identical coverage on an $80,000 brick home located five miles outside Anytown. While the total premium would be the same in both cases, the rate per $100 of insurance is different, probably reflecting a difference in fire protection in the two locations.

Of course, accurately predicting what losses a particular insured will have during a given policy period is impossible. A very good driver might have several auto accidents in a year because of a streak of bad luck. A careless driver might get through the same year without any accidents. However, according to the law of large numbers, prediction becomes more accurate as the number of similar insureds increases. Although one very good driver might have a worse year than one very bad driver, it is highly unlikely that a group of one hundred cautious drivers will have more insured losses than a group of one hundred careless drivers. Each group of drivers should be charged a premium commensurate with the exposure to loss it presents. Therefore, drivers with good driving records are generally charged less than those with poor driving records.

Educational Objective 3

Describe the following types of insurance rates, and explain which type would be more appropriate in a given situation:

a. Class rates

b. Individual rates

Types of Rates

In determining the appropriate premium to charge for coverage, insurers use either class rates or individual rates.

Class Rates

Class rates are common in property and liability insurance. Most personal lines and many commercial lines of insurance involve large numbers of similar insureds grouped into rating classes. Each insured in a given rating class has approximately the same exposures to loss and would therefore be charged approximately the same rate for insurance coverage. Class rates have traditionally been published in rating manuals—books used by underwriters, raters, and producers in pricing individual policies; therefore, class rates are sometimes called **manual rates**. Increasingly, insurers are replacing rating manuals with computerized rating systems based on class rates formerly published in traditional rating manuals. The rating of most personal lines and a growing number of commercial lines of insurance is now computerized. Class rates are based on the loss statistics of the large number of insureds that constitute a rating class. In many different situations, the use of class rates provides a uniform approach to pricing coverage for similar insureds.

> **Class rates**, also called **manual rates**, are rates that apply to all insureds in the same rating category, or rating class. Insureds with similar loss exposures are grouped into rating classes.

Many insureds within a rating class have loss characteristics that might not be fully reflected in class rates. **Merit rating plans** modify class rates to reflect these characteristics. Merit rating serves two purposes:

- It enables the insurer to fine-tune the class rate to reflect certain identifiable characteristics of a given insured.

- It encourages loss control activity by rewarding safety-conscious insureds with a lower premium or rate than those who do not practice loss control.

> **Merit rating plans** are rating plans that modify class rates to reflect loss characteristics of a particular insured.

The following are illustrations of the use of merit rating plans:

- In personal auto insurance, insurers use *safe driver insurance plans* (rating plans in which premiums are based on the insured's driving record) to lower the premiums for drivers with a history of accident-free driving and no major traffic convictions.

- In homeowners insurance, insurers typically provide *premium discounts* for insureds with fire alarms or burglar alarms.

- In commercial insurance, insurers often use *experience rating.* That is, premiums are increased for insureds whose loss experience has been worse than average, and premiums are decreased for insureds whose loss experience has been better than average.

- In commercial insurance, *schedule rating* allows an underwriter to "schedule" (list) credits or debits based on certain characteristics that are not reflected in the class rate. An example of such a characteristic is the attitude of the insured's management toward loss control. If the insured's management encourages loss control activities, the insurer could apply a schedule credit to the property insurance rate. Schedule debits or credits are expressed as percentage increases or decreases from the class rate.

Individual Rates

Class rates are not suitable for some types of insurance. For example, an underwriter would not be able to use a rating manual to determine the rate for fire insurance on a factory building that has an unusual construction and is occupied for a unique purpose. In such a situation, the underwriter would analyze various characteristics of the building to develop a rate that reflects the building's unique characteristics and occupancy. Such a rate is called an individual (or specific) rate.

Individual rates, also called **specific rates**, are used to assign a specific insurance rate that reflects the unique characteristics of an insured or the insured's property.

Individual rates, or **specific rates**, are used for commercial property insurance on unique structures. The rate is developed only after a detailed inspection of the structure and its contents. Each individual rate reflects characteristics such as the building's construction (brick or frame), its occupancy (warehouse or manufacturing), public and private fire protection (distance to the fire department and existence of a sprinkler system), and external exposures (proximity to other buildings or to brush that could spread a fire to the building).

A **judgment rate**, a type of individual rate, is used to develop a premium for a unique exposure for which there is no established rate. With judgment rating, the underwriter relies heavily on his or her experience.

The pricing of insurance coverage for one-of-a-kind exposures must often be based primarily on an underwriter's experience and judgment. An experienced underwriter might examine rates for comparable exposures to determine appropriate rates before arriving at the premium that will actually be charged for the unique exposure. Therefore, a **judgment rate**, a type of individual rate, is not simply arbitrary but is based on the underwriter's experience in covering various unusual exposures. Judgment rating is often used in rating ocean marine insurance covering many types of cargo being transported to ports worldwide.

Insurance Advisory Organizations

In the past, insurer-supported organizations such as Insurance Services Office (ISO) and the American Association of Insurance Services (AAIS) were known as *rating bureaus*. These rating bureaus collected premium and loss statistics from many insurance companies and developed a set of rates based on those statistics. In addition to calculating rates, rating bureaus also prepared rate filings for their members and submitted the filings to state regulatory authorities for approval.

ISO, AAIS, and similar organizations are now called *insurance advisory organizations*. These organizations no longer calculate and file rates for insurers. Instead, they calculate and file *loss costs*, which are the portion of the rate that covers projected claim payments and claim handling expenses. These loss costs now form the basis of rates developed by individual insurers. Each insurer adds a charge (called an expense loading) to the loss costs to cover other predicted expenses that the insured will incur (such as underwriting expenses, marketing costs, and taxes). Insurers generally develop their rates by adding these expense loadings to the loss costs calculated by the advisory organization.

Determining Policy Terms and Conditions

Selection and pricing are intertwined with a third underwriting activity—determining policy terms and conditions. The insurer must decide exactly what types of coverage it will provide to each applicant and then charge a premium appropriate to that coverage.

In addition to developing loss costs, insurance advisory organizations develop policy forms using standard insurance wording. These policy forms, referred to as **standard forms**, can be used by insurance companies that subscribe to the services of the advisory organization. Since many insurers use standard forms, the policy issued by one insurance company is often identical to the policy that would be issued by a competing insurer.

For each type of insurance it handles, an insurer needs to decide whether to use standard forms developed by the advisory organizations or to develop its own policy language, possibly providing coverages that differ in some ways from coverages provided by other insurers. For some types of insurance, such as professional liability insurance, there is no standard form, and many differences in coverage exist among policies.

When advisory organizations develop insurance policies, they also develop rules specifying what kinds of insureds will be eligible for certain policies. Insurers need to decide whether they will adhere to these rules or whether they will modify them.

Standard forms are insurance forms that contain standardized policy wording. Insurance advisory organizations develop standard forms that many insurers use in their insurance policies. Some insurers develop their own standard forms that they use in policies for their insureds.

Monitoring Underwriting Decisions

Underwriters periodically monitor the hazards, loss experience, and other conditions of specific insureds to determine whether any significant changes have occurred. Since underwriting decisions involve an assessment of loss potential, hazards and other conditions must be reviewed periodically.

If an underwriter made loss control recommendations (such as installing fire extinguishers) to a particular insured, follow-up is necessary to ensure that the insured has carried out the recommendations. An increase in hazards might change an acceptable insured into an unacceptable one for the coverage and premium charged. For example, if an insured converts a garage into a laboratory for producing toxic chemicals, the coverage and premium would have to be changed to reflect the increase in hazard, or continued coverage might be denied. Monitoring helps underwriters discover such changes and alter coverage and premium as necessary.

A **book of business** (or **portfolio**) is a group of policies with a common characteristic, such as territory or type of coverage. A book of business can also refer to all policies written by a particular insurer or agency.

Monitoring also applies to underwriting decisions on an entire book of business. A **book of business** (also called a **portfolio**) can refer to all policies in a particular territory or to all policies providing a particular type of insurance. A book of business can also refer to all policies of an insurance company or agency as a whole.

Educational Objective 4

Explain the role of underwriting management.

Underwriting Management

The role of an insurance company's underwriting management involves various responsibilities:

- Participating in the overall management of the insurance company
- Arranging reinsurance
- Delegating underwriting authority
- Making and enforcing underwriting guidelines
- Monitoring the results of underwriting guidelines

Only by constantly adjusting to a changing environment can an insurance company meet its objectives. Insurance companies change underwriting rules and standards as business conditions change. Underwriting management is the conduit for implementing these changes.

Participating in Insurance Company Management

An insurance company's top management team generally includes officers responsible for marketing, product development, claims, finance, actuarial services, and other functions, as well as underwriting. The head of an insurer's underwriting department participates with other members of the insurer's top management team in making broad business decisions regarding the company's objectives and how it plans to meet those objectives. Decisions at this level might determine what type of marketing system will be used, where offices will be located, what emphasis will be placed on personal and commercial insurance, and so forth. Given a top management consensus on the insurer's broad goals and how its capacity should be allocated, underwriting management must decide how underwriting activities can contribute to these goals. An insurer's underwriting management must develop underwriting objectives that complement or support the company's overall goals and then inform underwriters how to implement these specific objectives.

Arranging Reinsurance

Another aspect of underwriting management is arranging reinsurance. There are two broad categories of reinsurance: treaty reinsurance and facultative reinsurance.

Treaty reinsurance is an arrangement whereby a reinsurer agrees to reinsure automatically a portion of all eligible insurance of the primary insurer. The treaty is a contract that defines the eligible insurance. The primary insurer is required to reinsure, and the reinsurer must accept, all business covered by the treaty. There is no individual selection of policies.

> **Treaty reinsurance** is an arrangement whereby a reinsurer agrees to reinsure automatically a portion of all eligible insurance of the primary insurer.

Primary insurers and reinsurers periodically renegotiate the agreement on which treaty reinsurance is based. Before entering into a treaty and agreeing on pricing arrangements, the reinsurer carefully evaluates the primary insurer's past performance and expected future underwriting results. Because the treaty is based on all eligible insurance written by the primary insurer, the reinsurer is more concerned with the group of insureds as a whole than with individual accounts that compose the group.

Facultative reinsurance is not automatic but involves a separate transaction for each reinsured policy. That is, the reinsurer evaluates each policy it is asked to reinsure. Underwriters for the primary insurer decide which policies to submit for reinsurance, and underwriters for the reinsurance company decide which policies to reinsure. Pricing, terms, and conditions of each policy are individually negotiated.

> **Facultative reinsurance** involves a separate transaction for each reinsured policy. That is, the reinsurer evaluates individually each policy it is asked to reinsure.

Delegating Underwriting Authority

Underwriting management focuses on the entire group of insureds of the insurance company. *Line underwriters*, who usually work in field offices, must deal with individual applications. Underwriting management must determine how much underwriting authority to grant to the line underwriters. **Underwriting authority** limits the types of decisions an underwriter can make without receiving approval from someone at a higher level. The amount of authority given to each underwriter usually reflects the underwriter's experience, job title and responsibilities, and the types of insurance handled. Each underwriter's authority is clearly explained in the underwriting guidelines or in the underwriter's job description.

Underwriting authority is the limit on decisions that an underwriter can make without receiving approval from someone at a higher level.

With some insurers, underwriting authority is highly **decentralized**; that is, underwriting management delegates extensive underwriting authority to personnel in the field offices. Other insurers are highly **centralized** with many or all final underwriting decisions being made in the home office. For centralized insurers, field offices serve as a point of contact where insurance company personnel gather information, accept applications, and provide policyholder services. Many insurers are neither completely centralized nor completely decentralized; these insurers strive to maintain a balance between the underwriting authority given to line underwriters in field offices and the underwriting authority reserved for home office underwriters.

Decentralized means that activities are moved away from a central location; for insurance companies, *decentralization* usually means that processes and decision-making authority are moved geographically closer to the insured, usually to a field office.

Centralized means that activities are in a central location; for insurance companies, *centralization* involves many decisions being made in the home office.

Many insurance companies also grant some underwriting authority to the agents who represent the company. Called "front-line underwriters," these agents make the initial decision regarding applications and then forward to the company underwriter those applications that meet underwriting guidelines. Agents usually have the authority to accept applications and bind coverage for the insurer if the applicant clearly meets guidelines and if the limit of insurance is within a predetermined amount. The extent of the authority granted to agents generally depends on the agent's premium volume and loss experience with the insurance company.

Making and Enforcing Underwriting Guidelines

Underwriting management develops the guidelines that line underwriters use in the underwriting process. Company-wide rules guide underwriters toward consistent decisions that enable the insurance company to meet its overall underwriting objectives.

Underwriting guidelines and bulletins explain how underwriters should approach each application. The guidelines list the factors that should be considered by the underwriter for each type of insurance, the desirable and undesirable characteristics of applicants relative to those factors, and the insurance company's overall attitude toward applicants that exhibit those characteristics. Based on the guidelines, underwriters evaluate the applications they receive, decide how to handle the applications, and act on those decisions.

Underwriting management activity does not end with the development of underwriting guidelines. The guidelines must be clearly communicated to all underwriters, which might require training programs. In addition, underwriting management must prepare and distribute bulletins or guideline revisions whenever changes are made.

Monitoring the Results of Underwriting Guidelines

Underwriting management must also monitor the results of underwriting guidelines to see whether they have had the desired effect. Monitoring includes taking steps to ensure that underwriters are following underwriting guidelines and that underwriting objectives are being met. If the guidelines are not followed, there is no evidence as to whether they will work. Periodically, underwriting management sends underwriting audit teams to visit field offices to examine underwriting files. **Underwriting audits** attempt to determine whether underwriters are following the guidelines. Second, if guidelines are being followed, it is necessary to determine whether they are having the desired results. For example, suppose an insurer has broadened its homeowners insurance policies by adding extra coverages, such as an additional theft limit on jewelry, in an attempt to attract new customers. Monitoring would reveal the extent to which insured losses increase because of the coverage addition, whether sales have increased, and whether the revenues from the increased sales more than offset the costs of claims.

An **underwriting audit** is a process in which members of the home office underwriting department examine files to see whether underwriters are following underwriting guidelines.

Many factors affect the success of an insurance company. Constant monitoring of underwriting results enables underwriting management to adjust underwriting guidelines to accommodate changing conditions, objectives, and results.

Educational Objective 5

Identify and describe the steps in the underwriting process that an underwriter follows in making an underwriting decision.

The Underwriting Process

An underwriting decision must be made on every new insurance application, as well as on renewal policies and many policy changes. The underwriting process comprises the following steps:

1. Gathering the necessary information
2. Making the underwriting decision
3. Implementing that decision
4. Monitoring the decision

Traditionally, underwriting has been largely a nonautomated process that depends on human judgment. Increasingly, however, portions of the underwriting process, particularly in personal lines, are computerized. Computerized underwriting processes use software that emulates the steps an underwriter would take. Computerized underwriting is most common with high-volume types of insurance such as personal auto or homeowners insurance. In a common approach, the computer screens applications and accepts those that clearly meet all criteria and rejects those that clearly do not. Questionable applications are referred to an underwriter for evaluation.

Expert systems (also known as **knowledge-based systems**) are computer software programs that supplement the underwriting decision-making process. The system asks for the information necessary to make an underwriting decision, ensuring that no necessary information is overlooked.

Some insurers now use **expert systems** (also known as **knowledge-based systems**) to assist underwriters in the underwriting process. These computerized systems are programmed to emulate the underwriting decision-making process as it would be performed by "expert" (usually senior) underwriters. The expert system asks for the information necessary to make an underwriting decision, thereby ensuring that no necessary information is overlooked. Although expert underwriting systems are capable of "making" an underwriting decision (usually by assigning a grade on a scale of one to ten or one to one hundred), most are used to supplement an underwriter's decision making, not to replace the underwriter.

New underwriters can "ask" the expert system why a certain question was asked or why a certain grade was assigned. The ability of the expert system to interact with the underwriter makes the system an excellent training tool in addition to an underwriting tool.

Educational Objective 6

Identify and describe sources that underwriters use in making underwriting decisions.

Gathering Underwriting Information

Underwriters base their decisions about individual applications on a combination of information and judgment. To make a decision, underwriters need adequate information in order to analyze the potential losses each applicant represents. Underwriters derive information from several sources:

- *Producers*. In addition to completing and submitting applications, producers might supply additional information not included on applications, such as a personal evaluation of the applicant.

- *Consumer investigation reports*. Several independent reporting services investigate and provide background information on prospective insureds. Insurance applications generally inform the applicant that he or she might be investigated.

- *Government records*. Motor vehicle records (MVRs) are commonly used in underwriting auto insurance. Underwriters can also seek underwriting information in court records and public information relating to property ownership.

- *Financial rating services*. Firms such as Dun & Bradstreet (D&B) and Standard & Poor's provide data on the credit rating and financial stability of specific businesses.

- *Inspection reports*. Many insurance companies employ loss control representatives whose duties include inspecting the premises and operations of insurance applicants and preparing reports for underwriters.

- *Field marketing personnel*. Many insurers have marketing representatives or other employees who spend much of their time in the field working with producers. These field personnel can often provide additional insights regarding an applicant based on personal observations.

- *Claim files*. After a policy has been issued, the insured might have claims. Significant information about the insured might thus appear in the insurance company's claim files, and additional information might be available from the claim representatives who handled the claims.

- *Production records*. In evaluating applications, underwriters generally consider the track record of the producer who submits the application. If the producer has consistently generated profitable business, the underwriter might be willing to accept an applicant that might not meet all of the underwriting standards.

- *Premium audit reports*. Rates for some kinds of commercial insurance are applied to estimated payroll, sales, or some other exposure unit whose final measure is not determined until the end of the policy year. Insurance companies employ premium auditors to obtain the final figures from insureds' accounting records in order to compute the final premium on such policies. In addition to providing this exact information, a premium auditor can provide other information about an insured, especially since the premium auditor has probably visited the insured's premises and seen the operations.

- *Applicant's or insured's records*. Underwriters can sometimes obtain information from the applicant's or insured's records, including copies of appraisals of jewelry (for valuation purposes) and bills of sale. For businesses, the annual report, which describes the firm's operations and future plans and includes its financial statements (balance sheet and income statement), provides much useful underwriting information. Many businesses now have Web sites that could also be a source of valuable information to an underwriter.

Making the Underwriting Decision

Hazards are conditions that increase the chance of a loss occurring.

Once the underwriter has gathered the necessary information, he or she must analyze the information to determine what **hazards** the applicant presents. To make an underwriting decision, the underwriter must then evaluate underwriting options and choose the best option.

Educational Objective 7

Identify and describe four categories of hazards that underwriters must evaluate.

Analyzing Hazards

An applicant with hazards that are greater than normal might not be acceptable as an insured, unless the increased hazards can be eliminated or controlled or unless they can be offset by a substantially increased premium. On the other hand, an applicant presenting normal or less-than-normal hazards is generally desirable from an underwriting standpoint. An underwriter must evaluate four categories of hazards:

- Physical hazards
- Moral hazards
- Morale (attitudinal) hazards
- Legal hazards

Physical Hazards

Physical hazards are tangible characteristics of property, persons, or operations that tend to increase the probable frequency or severity of loss.

In evaluating an application for property insurance on a building, the underwriter considers possible **physical hazards**, such as those inherent in the building's construction, occupancy, protection, and external exposures. An office building located next to a restaurant without adequate fire protection clearly represents a greater fire hazard than an office building located next to a retail store with excellent fire protection.

Moral Hazards

Moral hazards are dishonest tendencies in the character of the insured (or applicant) that increase the probability of a loss occurring.

Moral hazards are dishonest tendencies in the character of the insured (or applicant) that increase the probability of loss. The threat from a moral hazard is the possibility that the insured might intentionally cause a loss or file a false claim. For example, an insured might intentionally cause a fire or an auto accident to collect a claim payment on a hard-to-sell building or car and unjustly enrich himself or herself. A moral hazard might be indicated by a weak financial condition (which could be detected in a financial report) or questionable moral character (which could be indicated by a police record).

As stated in Chapter 1, one of the characteristics of an ideally insurable loss exposure is that losses be accidental. Insurance is intended to deal with losses that are unexpected from the standpoint of the insured; it is not feasible to insure against events within the insured's control. The prudent underwriter rejects applicants presenting a significant moral hazard.

Morale Hazards

Morale hazards (also known as **attitudinal hazards**) are more subtle, and thus more difficult to detect, than moral hazards. A particularly dangerous morale hazard is an insured's attitude that "I don't need to be careful because I have insurance." Evidence of a morale hazard might be found in personality traits (some people are naturally careless and therefore accident-prone regardless of insurance), poor management (tolerance of dangerous conditions and practices), or past loss experience (a history of losses caused by carelessness).

Moral hazards and morale hazards are often confused. Someone who represents a moral hazard might, for example, set a fire to collect an insurance settlement. Someone who represents a morale hazard might be careless in allowing smoking in hazardous areas or permit combustible supplies to be piled in a furnace room.

Legal Hazards

Legal hazards are characteristics of the legal or regulatory environment that affect an insurer's ability to provide insurance with appropriate premiums. Hazards in the legal environment might include court decisions that interpret policy language in a way unfavorable to insurers. For example, commercial liability policies at one time provided coverage for pollution losses that were sudden or accidental, but court decisions applied coverage in cases where insurers thought the pollution was clearly not sudden or accidental but gradual. Because of this legal hazard (courts mandating coverage broader than insurers intended), insurers ceased to provide pollution liability coverage in many cases or started charging an additional premium for pollution liability coverage.

The regulatory environment presents legal hazards when it forces underwriters to charge premiums that are too low for the exposures or to provide coverages that are too broad. Legal hazards are also presented when regulatory authorities unduly restrict insurers' ability to cancel or nonrenew policies.

Morale hazards (also known as **attitudinal hazards**) involve carelessness about, or indifference to, potential loss on the part of an insured or applicant.

Legal hazards are characteristics of the legal or regulatory environment that affect an insurer's ability to collect a premium commensurate with the exposure to loss.

Educational Objective 8

Identify and explain the underwriting options an underwriter has in evaluating an application for insurance.

Evaluating Underwriting Options

In evaluating each application, an underwriter faces three options:

- Accept the application without modification
- Reject the application
- Accept the application with modification

The third option requires the greatest amount of underwriting creativity. Often an applicant that is not acceptable for the insurance originally requested can become acceptable if some aspect of coverage is changed. Generally, the underwriter, producer, and applicant all desire that an insurance policy be issued. If the particular policy applied for cannot be issued, the underwriter might be able to offer an alternative that satisfies all parties.

Frequently, a policy can be issued if the applicant agrees to implement loss control measures. For example, an underwriter might agree to write property insurance for the owner of a particular bookstore, provided the store owner installs and maintains an appropriate fire alarm system.

Another possibility is to modify the rate charged for the coverage. A producer might have quoted auto insurance using the insurer's "preferred risk" rate, a rate offered to substantially better-than-average applicants that is lower than the standard class rate. The underwriter might determine that the applicant does not qualify as a preferred risk but would be acceptable for coverage at standard class rates.

Coverage might also be modified—that is, the underwriter might offer terms and conditions that are somewhat different from those that the applicant has requested. For example, an underwriter might be asked to provide an auto policy, including coverage with a $50 deductible for damage to the insured vehicle for an applicant who has had several claims for windshield damage. The applicant might be a preferred risk except for this one coverage. The underwriter could offer the desired coverage with a $250 or $500 deductible and thus avoid rejecting the applicant. This modification would turn a standard risk into a preferred risk. If the applicant agrees, the underwriter has found a way to make an application acceptable through coverage modification.

Reinsurance presents an underwriting alternative in cases where an otherwise acceptable application exceeds the limit in the underwriting guidelines. Suppose, for example, an insurer is asked to provide $10 million of property insurance on a building, but the insurer's acceptable limit on a single building is $500,000. After checking with underwriting management, an underwriter might determine that adequate reinsurance exists to handle the remaining $9.5 million of coverage. By arranging reinsurance in the amount of $9.5 million, the underwriter can accept the application for the limit of $10 million requested by the applicant.

Choosing the Best Option

After careful analysis of hazards and underwriting options, the best underwriting decision for a particular application usually becomes obvious. All alternatives, such as following loss control recommendations or accepting modified coverage, require the agreement of the applicant and might involve further negotiation. In such situations, the underwriter normally contacts the producer to negotiate the modified terms, price, or conditions with the applicant.

Implementing the Underwriting Decision

When asked to deal with an application for coverage exceeding his or her underwriting authority, an underwriter might need to seek a supervisor's or manager's approval. The supervisor or manager might simply approve or reject the underwriter's recommendation, or the entire application might be referred to a more specialized or experienced senior underwriter.

If the underwriting decision is within the underwriter's authority and consistent with underwriting guidelines, the underwriter can approve the policy and pass the file along to another department for processing and policy issuance. This approach is typical with routine applications for auto insurance, homeowners insurance, and small commercial accounts. In more complex cases, it is necessary to communicate the underwriter's decision to the producer, along with a quote showing the premium to be charged and the terms and conditions to be offered. After the producer discusses this information with the client, and possibly compares it with quotes from other insurance companies, the underwriter might be asked to issue the policy or might learn that the applicant has decided to do business with another insurer.

Monitoring the Underwriting Decision

The underwriter's job does not end when a policy is issued. The underwriter must monitor the results of the initial underwriting decision. Among other things, the underwriter needs to reevaluate his or her underwriting decisions by being aware of claims that develop from accounts that were accepted. The nature and number of losses in a given period might indicate that some other underwriting action is required.

The fact that an insured has a serious loss or several losses is not necessarily an indication that the underwriter made a bad decision. Conversely, a lack of serious losses on an account does not necessarily mean that the underwriter made a good decision in accepting the account; the lack of losses might have been a matter of chance. Despite these variations in the experience of individual accounts, the entire group of accounts handled by an underwriter is expected to earn a profit for the insurer. Each account contributes to the underwriter's record in the long term.

If serious problems develop with an account, the underwriter might need to take corrective action. Such action might include recommending additional loss control measures, modifying the terms of coverage, canceling coverage (if permitted), or marking the policy for nonrenewal at the end of the present policy term.

During the policy term, the underwriter might also receive one or more requests for coverage changes. Each request must be carefully considered and implemented as appropriate. Some changes present no increased hazard, while others might increase the potential for losses beyond those intended in the policy or by the price charged. For example, a change of vehicles on an automobile policy from a five-year-old sedan to a newer model does not necessarily represent an increased hazard, but it might if at the same time a young driver is added as an additional operator.

Finally, as the expiration date of a policy approaches, the underwriter might need to repeat the entire underwriting process before agreeing to renew the policy for another term. Renewal underwriting can generally be accomplished more quickly than new-business underwriting because the insured is already known, to some degree, and the amount of information might be increased as claim reports or loss control reports are added to the file. However, the underwriter must determine whether any changes in the exposures have occurred, and, if so, carefully go through the underwriting process again.

Many insurers do not reunderwrite existing personal lines policies such as auto and homeowners at every renewal. Instead, they continue to renew these policies until something triggers an underwriting review. Claims, requests for coverage changes, or the passage of a certain amount of time might cause reunderwriting.

Educational Objective 9

Describe ways in which states regulate underwriting activities.

Regulation of Underwriting Activity

In the interest of protecting the public, every state regulates insurers' underwriting activities and places some constraints on the terms and conditions that insurers offer. Two important examples of the regulation of underwriting activity are:

- Prohibition of unfair discrimination
- Restrictions on cancellation and nonrenewal

Prohibition of Unfair Discrimination

The ability to discriminate fairly among applicants is one of the most important elements of underwriting. However, as discussed in Chapter 2 in regard to insurance rates, state insurance regulations prohibit *unfair* discrimination in insurance. This prohibition also applies to insurance underwriting activities. The challenge lies in distinguishing between fair discrimination and unfair discrimination.

With the attention given to topics such as racial and sexual discrimination, it is easy to forget that "discrimination" itself can be a neutral word. Dictionary definitions of "discrimination" include the following:

- The quality or power of finely distinguishing
- The act or practice of discriminating categorically rather than individually

Teachers discriminate—that is, they finely distinguish—when they assign different grades to students with different levels of performance. Schools discriminate categorically when they admit kindergarten students based on age rather than rating them individually on the basis of physical or mental maturity.

Similarly, underwriting involves distinguishing among properties, businesses, and people and grouping them into categories. An insurer's ability to discriminate fairly is essential if insureds are to be charged a premium commensurate with their loss exposures.

According to state insurance laws, unfair discrimination is prohibited as an unfair trade practice. Examples of unfair discrimination include the following:

- Refusing to issue, canceling, or nonrenewing coverage for an applicant or an insured solely on the basis of geographic location. (This prohibited practice is sometimes called *redlining*—suggesting a bright red line on a map surrounding a prohibited area.)

Reminder

Unfair discrimination involves applying different standards or methods of treatment to insureds who have the same basic characteristics and loss potential.

- Refusing to issue, canceling, or nonrenewing coverage for an applicant or an insured solely on the basis of that person's gender or marital status.
- Refusing to issue, canceling, or nonrenewing a policy solely because of the applicant's or the insured's race.

These examples of unfair discrimination all include some kind of prejudice: judging, with no further information, that property in a given area, persons of a particular gender or marital status, or members of a certain ethnic group are likely to have an unacceptable level of losses. Further information in each case might indicate that the applicant or insured does not meet the insurer's underwriting standards, without regard to his or her address, gender, marital status, or racial heritage. Therefore, if coverage is denied after objective underwriting criteria have been applied, it is not likely that unfair discrimination has occurred.

Restrictions on Cancellation and Nonrenewal

Most states require that insurers notify the insured a specified period (such as thirty days) before a policy is to be canceled or nonrenewed. This notice is intended to give the insured an opportunity to replace the coverage. Generally, restrictions of this kind help insurance to serve its purpose of providing protection for policyholders. However, such restrictions also limit the speed with which an underwriter can stop providing coverage for an insured who has become undesirable.

During the mid-1980s, several widely publicized claims involving allegations of child abuse caused insurance companies to become concerned about the legal hazards associated with the operation of day-care centers. Some policies providing coverage to day-care centers were canceled or nonrenewed. At the same time, insurer capacity was severely restricted for other reasons as well, affecting many kinds of insurance. Insurers canceled or nonrenewed some policies in an attempt to reallocate their available capacity. In response, several states enacted laws that prohibited insurers from canceling insurance policies during the policy term and restricted insurers' rights to nonrenew policies. Even when such noncancellation laws had not been passed, underwriters became much more reluctant to exercise cancellation rights in order to avoid adverse reaction that could lead to further regulatory restrictions on underwriting activities.

Educational Objective 10

Define or describe each of the Key Words and Phrases for this assignment. (All Key Words and Phrases appear in bold print in the text and in the margins throughout this chapter.)

Summary

Underwriting is the process by which insurance companies evaluate applicants for insurance and those currently insured in order to maintain a profitable book of business. The underwriting process consists of the following activities:

- Selecting those applicants who meet the company's underwriting guidelines
- Pricing the coverage to charge a premium commensurate with the exposure
- Determining the proper policy terms and conditions
- Monitoring underwriting decisions

While line underwriters are responsible for day-to-day decisions, they must refer to the insurer's underwriting guidelines. Underwriting management sets the company's guidelines in order to make optimal use of the company's available capacity and avoid adverse selection. The role of underwriting management involves various responsibilities:

- Participating in the overall management of the insurance company in making broad business decisions
- Arranging reinsurance, which can be either treaty reinsurance (on all eligible policies) or facultative reinsurance (involving a separate transaction for each reinsured policy)
- Delegating underwriting authority, which limits the types of decisions a underwriter can make without receiving approval from someone at a higher level
- Making and enforcing underwriting guidelines that reflect the company's overall underwriting objectives
- Monitoring the results of underwriting guidelines to see whether they have the desired effect

In making decisions, underwriters follow several steps in the underwriting process:

- Gathering the necessary information from various sources to evaluate applicants
- Making the underwriting decision, which includes analyzing hazards (which can be physical, moral, morale, or legal), evaluating underwriting options (accepting or rejecting the application or accepting it with modification), and choosing the best option
- Implementing the underwriting decision
- Monitoring the underwriting decision

In the interest of protecting the public, every state regulates insurers' underwriting activities by prohibiting unfair discrimination. In addition, most states require that insurers notify the insured a specified period before a policy can be canceled or nonrenewed.

Chapter 6

Claims

Educational Objectives

After studying this chapter, you should be able to:

1. Analyze the claim representative's responsibilities in the claim handling process. (pp. 6-4 to 6-5)

2. Describe the role performed by each of the following in the claim handling process: (pp. 6-6 to 6-9)

   a. Staff claim representatives (inside and outside)

   b. Independent adjusters

   c. Agents

   d. Public adjusters

3. Identify the steps in the claim handling process. (pp. 6-10 to 6-11)

4. Describe the claim handling process for property insurance claims. (pp. 6-11 to 6-18)

5. Describe the claim handling process for liability insurance claims. (pp. 6-18 to 6-22)

6. Describe the claim representative's role in establishing an insurer's loss reserves. (pp. 6-22 to 6-23)

7. Describe and, in a given situation, analyze the practices prohibited by unfair claim practices laws. (pp. 6-23 to 6-24)

8. Define or describe each of the Key Words and Phrases for this assignment. (All Key Words and Phrases appear in bold print in the text and in the margins throughout this chapter.)

Chapter 6

Claims

On August 24, 1992, Hurricane Andrew devastated parts of southern Florida after causing millions of dollars of damage in the Bahamas the day before. The hurricane then moved across the Gulf of Mexico and, on August 25 and 26, caused further damage in Louisiana and other southeastern states. In southern Florida alone, Hurricane Andrew caused the deaths of thirty-eight people, destroyed more than 85,000 homes, and left at least 250,000 people homeless. Insured losses caused by Hurricane Andrew totaled more than $15 billion, making the hurricane the most costly catastrophe ever experienced by U.S. insurers.

Newspaper reports in the days following the tragedy described the difficulty people would have in rebuilding their lives. The reports also spoke of a more positive side of the catastrophe: the work that several insurance companies had performed to get people back on their feet as soon as possible after the tragedy. Throughout southern Florida, insurers established centers where insureds could walk in and receive emergency checks; some provided trailers for insureds whose homes had been destroyed. In less than a week, despite extensive damage to radio and telephone transmitters, a vast number of insureds were able to contact their insurers and receive emergency funds and other assistance. For most, such assistance was only a beginning. However, in the ensuing weeks and months, many people devastated by Hurricane Andrew were able to begin to reconstruct their homes, their businesses, and their lives.

The human tragedy that follows a catastrophe of this sort cannot be overstated. But the relief delivered through the claim-handling facilities of the insurance companies helped

For insurance purposes, a **claim** is a demand by a person or business seeking to recover from an insurance company for a loss that might be covered by an insurance policy.

A **claim representative**, also called an **adjuster**, is a person responsible for investigating, evaluating, and settling claims.

The term *adjuster* is the traditional name for a person responsible for handling insurance claims; however, the current trend is to use the term *claim representative*. This text uses the term claim representative except to describe specific types of claim representatives where the traditional term adjuster is generally used.

A **claimant** is anyone who submits a claim to an insurance company. In some cases, particularly in liability claims, the claimant is a *third party* that has suffered a loss and seeks to collect for that loss from an insured. In other cases, particularly in property claims, the claimant is the insured (the *first party*).

The *first party* to an insurance contract is the insured. (Although the second party is technically the insurer, the term second party is rarely used in insurance.)

A *third party* to an insurance contract is a person or business that is not a party to the contract but who might assert a claim against the insured.

Insurance professionals generally use the term *claimant* to refer to a third party who submits a claim under an insured's policy. This text uses the term claimant to refer to a third-party claimant.

enormously. The peace of mind created through the purchase of insurance is often taken for granted until a catastrophe causes people to realize the value of an insurance policy. And to those personally affected by the devastation, the existence of a policy that will help in rebuilding their lives is invaluable.

In a recent year, property and liability insurance claim payments and loss settlement expenses exceeded $198 billion. The responsibility for properly investigating, evaluating, and settling the hundreds of thousands of claims submitted annually to property and liability insurance companies rests with the people in various claim departments. This chapter examines how the claim handling process works.

Educational Objective 1

Analyze the claim representative's responsibilities in the claim handling process.

Responsibilities of the Claim Representative

The primary purpose of the claim handling process is to satisfy the insurance company's main obligation under the insurance policy: to pay **claims** for covered losses. To accomplish this objective, the insurer's **claim representative**, also called an **adjuster**, has certain responsibilities:

- To respond promptly to the submitted claim
- To obtain adequate information
- To properly evaluate the claim
- To treat all parties fairly

Respond Promptly to the Submitted Claim

Once a claim is submitted, the claim representative must respond quickly. For the insured or **claimant**, the loss experience might have been painful, frustrating, agonizing, or even embarrassing. These feelings might intensify if the claim representative delays in responding to the claim. The example described at the beginning of this chapter, while an extreme case, underscores the value of a quick response.

Obtain Adequate Information

Once the insurer responds to the first report of the claim, the claim representative must promptly obtain information that is accurate and adequate to properly evaluate the claim. Although obtaining information is usually time-consuming, it is an essential step in the claim handling process.

A claim representative must verify whether the claim is covered under the insured's policy. If a question of coverage exists and the insurer wishes to continue its investigation, the insurer might send a **reservation of rights letter** to the insured. Failure to reserve its rights as facts are gathered might bar the insurer from denying coverage later. Examples of claims that might require a reservation of rights letter include occurrences that might have happened outside the policy period, intentional actions of the insured, and situations involving more than one insurer when there is a question of which insurer pays first.

Properly Evaluate the Claim

Valid and accurate information enables the claim representative to evaluate the claim. This evaluation hinges on two critical elements of the claim handling process:

1. Whether the claim is covered according to policy provisions
2. If the claim is covered, the dollar amount payable under the policy

The determination of whether coverage exists and the valuation of a covered loss are the central tasks involved in the claim handling process.

Treat All Parties Fairly

Throughout the claim handling process, the claim representative must remember that a loss often produces strong emotions. The claim representative is dealing with an insured or a claimant who has been through a trying, if not traumatic, experience, and good interpersonal communication skills are vital. Although constantly dealing with persons in such trying circumstances can be a challenge, the claim representative is often rewarded by his or her ability to help people through a difficult time.

The claim representative must treat all parties fairly by paying valid claims according to the policy provisions and denying uncovered claims. Failure to pay a claim that is covered by an insurance policy hurts the person who is denied a fair settlement. On the other hand, paying a claim that is not covered penalizes the insurer and all of the insurer's policyholders. If an insurer pays claims that are not covered by a particular insurance policy, it is likely that all of the insurer's policyholders will eventually pay higher premiums. It is important to individual policyholders and to policyholders as a group that insurers neither overpay nor underpay claims.

A **reservation of rights letter** is a notice sent by the insurer to an insured advising that the insurer is proceeding with investigation of a claim but that the insurer retains its right to deny coverage later.

A reservation of rights letter serves two purposes:
- To inform the insured that a coverage problem might exist
- To protect the insurer so that it can deny coverage later, if necessary

---

> ### Educational Objective 2
>
> Describe the role performed by each of the following in the claim handling process:
>
> a. Staff claim representatives (inside and outside)
> b. Independent adjusters
> c. Agents
> d. Public adjusters

Types of Claim Representatives

Who performs various claim handling activities? While it might seem obvious to say a claim representative, the answer is a bit more complex. Several different types of people participate in claim handling, depending on the circumstances:

- Staff claim representatives (inside and outside)
- Independent adjusters
- Agents
- Public adjusters

In addition, an organization that has established a self-insurance plan must make provisions to settle its own claims by using either an internal claim department or an outside administrator.

Staff Claim Representatives of Insurance Companies

A **staff claim representative** is an insurance company employee who performs some or all of the insurer's claim handling activities.

Most insurance companies have at least two kinds of **staff claim representatives**: those who work exclusively inside the office and those who travel to the site of the loss and elsewhere to perform claim investigations and evaluations.

Inside Claim Representatives

An **inside claim representative** is an insurance company employee who handles claims that can be settled, usually by telephone or letter, from inside the insurer's office.

The role of an **inside claim representative** is to gather information concerning a claim and to settle relatively simple and straightforward cases. Often, the inside claim representative takes the initial claim information from the insured or the producer. Inside claim representatives generally handle claims that are clearly either covered or not covered and that do not involve questions about the circumstances or validity of the claim.

The inside claim representative usually speaks or writes to the insured to obtain information concerning how and when the loss occurred. If a third party is involved, the inside claim representative might use a tape recorder to take statements about the loss from the insured, the claimant, and any witnesses, after obtaining their permission to tape their statements. In many cases, the claimant's statement is taken first to get a record of his or her version of the occurrence.

For claims involving automobile accidents, the claim representative usually orders a police report and compares this report with the statements of the insured, the claimant, and any witnesses. The inside claim representative also requests repair estimates or assigns appraisers to inspect damaged automobiles. Some insurers have drive-in claim facilities where an appraisal of the damage can be made and the insured can receive payment for the damage. For simple cases, such as a broken window or a minor automobile accident in which no one is injured, the inside claim representative can usually arrange with the insured or claimant to have repairs made or can otherwise settle the claim without involving anyone else. Many cases, however, require an outside claim representative or the services of an independent adjuster.

Outside Claim Representatives

An **outside claim representative** (also called a **field claim representative**) is usually part of the insurer's staff located in a branch office, regional office, or other location, and is assigned to handle claims that occur in the area surrounding that location. An insurer assigns an outside claim representative when it is not practical to settle the claim by telephone or mail. In cases of significant damage, for example, an outside claim representative inspects the property to assess the damage. In addition, if anyone has suffered bodily injuries, an outside claim representative usually gathers information in person, taking statements from the injured parties and interviewing witnesses, physicians, and others.

An **outside claim representative** (also called a **field claim representative**) is an insurance company employee who handles claims that cannot be handled easily by phone or mail. Outside claim representatives spend much of their time visiting the scene of a loss, interviewing witnesses, investigating damage, and meeting with insureds, claimants, attorneys, and other persons involved in the claim.

Independent Adjusters

Insurance companies usually find it efficient to locate staff claim representatives only in those areas where the company has a significant number of policyholders who will presumably submit a large volume of claims. Generally, it is inefficient for an insurer to have a staff of claim representatives in an area where few claims are filed. To handle claims in areas where they do not have large numbers of policyholders, insurers often hire independent adjusters.

Independent adjusters are independent claim representatives who offer claim handling services to insurance companies for a fee. While some independent adjusters are self-employed, many independent adjusters work for one of several large, national independent adjusting firms. These firms have offices located throughout the country and handle all types of claims.

Independent adjusters are independent claim representatives who offer claim handling services to insurance companies for a fee. These independent adjusters can either be self-employed or work for an independent adjusting firm.

Although a particular insurance company might not have sufficient numbers of policyholders to set up its own staff of claim representatives in a specific area, it is feasible for an independent adjusting firm to open an office as long as there are sufficient numbers of people within a reasonable distance from the office. These firms offer their services to any insurance company needing claim handling services in that geographic area.

In some situations, an insurer might hire independent adjusters even if the insurer has staff claim representatives in the area. A staff claim representative might work with an independent adjuster when a claim involves a unique or complex situation and the staff claim representative does not have sufficient expertise to handle the claim. Many insurers, for example, use independent adjusters to handle particular types of claims, such as those involving business income or ocean marine insurance. By providing independent adjusters who have the expertise to handle such claims, independent adjusting firms can meet the special claim handling needs of insurance companies.

Insurers might also need independent adjusters in addition to staff claim representatives after a natural disaster, such as a severe hurricane. Because of the volume of claims generated by natural disasters, insurers not only send staff claim representatives to work with insureds, but also hire independent adjusters to assist in handling claims.

Agents

In an independent or exclusive agency, the agency usually receives the first notification of a claim. Depending on the size of the office, the agency can have one person, several people, or a department responsible for handling claims.

In some cases, the agency does little more than communicate the claim information to the insurer. Other agencies take a more active role in the claim handling process. The agent immediately sets up a claim file and collects information concerning the loss. In some cases, the agent's role is then to monitor the progress of the claim and the insured's satisfaction with the insurer's claim service.

Draft authority is authority expressly given to an agent by an insurer to settle and pay certain types of claims by writing a claim *draft* up to a specified limit.

A *draft* is similar to a check, but it requires approval from the insurance company before the bank will pay it.

If the agent has **draft authority**, he or she might actually settle claims. For example, an insurance company might give an agent draft authority up to a certain limit (such as $1,000 or $2,500) per claim. That authority allows the agent to settle claims and make payments on behalf of the insurer in cases involving settlements up to the specified limit.

Why do insurance companies grant draft authority to agents? Insurance companies have found that allowing agents to handle small or routine claims results in both expense savings and increased goodwill. Without the direct involvement of the insurer on small claims, the claim can be handled more quickly and with less expense to the insurer. Since the agency personnel obtain the loss information, verify coverage, and issue the draft for the claim, delays and expenses involved in contacting the insurer's claim staff are eliminated. This reduction in claim handling expenses benefits both the agent and the insurer because it contributes to a more competitively priced product.

The insured benefits from the quick payment of claims, and the agent and the insurer also benefit from the goodwill thus created. The agent can give personal service to the insured, and both the insurer and the agent benefit from having a satisfied customer.

Public Adjusters

In certain circumstances, an insured might decide to hire someone to represent his or her interest in the claim handling process. This claim representative who represents the insured is called a **public adjuster**. Usually an insured hires a public adjuster either because a claim is complex or because the loss negotiations are not progressing satisfactorily. The public adjuster acts as an advocate for the insured in the negotiations. The insured generally pays the public adjuster a percentage of the settlement as compensation for this assistance.

A **public adjuster** is a person hired by an insured to represent the insured in handling a claim.

Internal Claim Administration

Many organizations have developed self-insurance plans to cover part or all of their loss exposures. Under a **self-insurance plan**, an organization uses its own funds to pay for losses. However, many companies with self-insurance plans purchase insurance to pay losses that exceed a predetermined amount. Organizations with self-insurance plans must make provisions for handling claims. Two options for this purpose are an internal claim department and a third-party administrator.

A **self-insurance plan** is an arrangement in which an organization pays for its losses with its own resources rather than purchasing insurance. However, the organization might choose to purchase insurance for losses that exceed a certain limit. For example, a firm might self-insure all losses up to $2 million and then purchase insurance to cover losses over $2 million.

Internal Claim Departments

If the organization is large enough, it might establish a separate claim department. A smaller organization might decide to hire one or two claim representatives to handle its claims. In either case, the organization uses its own personnel to investigate and settle claims.

Regardless of the number of claim representatives an organization employs, the internal claim staff should have the skill and experience necessary to handle many different types of claims. However, the employees of internal claim departments might have little or no experience in handling certain types of complex cases, such as products liability claims or workers compensation injuries. Furthermore, in workers compensation cases, a problem could occur if the injured employee and the claim representative cannot agree on a settlement. In such situations, employees might feel that they must fight their own employers to reach a settlement. Because of the problems that can arise from the use of an internal claim department, many organizations with self-insurance plans have hired third-party administrators to handle the claims associated with self-insured exposures.

Third-Party Administrators

Third-party administrators (TPAs) are business firms that contract to provide administrative services to other businesses. Businesses that have self-insurance plans often hire TPAs to handle their claims.

The growth of self-insurance has created a need for **third-party administrators (TPAs)**. TPAs are business firms that contract to provide administrative services, including claim handling, to other businesses, particularly to businesses that have self-insurance plans. Large independent adjusting firms sometimes function as TPAs for self-insured businesses in addition to providing independent claim handling services to insurers. Many property and liability insurers have also established subsidiary companies that serve as third-party administrators. When a self-insuring organization hires a third-party administrator, that organization generally purchases more than claim handling expertise. Most TPAs offer claim record keeping and statistical analysis in addition to claim handling services.

Educational Objective 3

Identify the steps in the claim handling process.

The Claim Handling Process

Claim handling procedures can vary widely, depending on the type of claim involved. A minor, single-vehicle auto accident might require only verifying coverage, obtaining estimates of the damage to the automobile, and paying the claim. Little else is involved as long as the accident involves no bodily injuries and no other vehicles. Once the claim representative verifies that coverage applies and determines the cost of repairing the auto, the claim can be settled.

An auto accident involving two or more autos and several injured people can take months or even years to settle. In such cases, different persons might provide conflicting testimony concerning the events surrounding the accident, and difficult questions regarding legal responsibility can arise. The claim representative might need the perspective of a physician, a lawyer, an engineer, and a psychologist to understand all the issues involved.

Despite the unique challenges and variations from case to case, the same three steps are involved in the processing of most claims:

1. Investigation
2. Valuation
3. Negotiation and settlement

Although the claim handling process generally involves these three steps, the manner in which they are carried out is quite different for property insurance claims and for liability insurance claims.

Educational Objective 4

Describe the claim handling process for property insurance claims.

Property Insurance Claims

For several reasons, claim handling procedures are more defined for *property insurance claims* than for liability insurance claims. In property insurance claims, there are usually only two parties to the negotiation process: the insured and the insurer. In addition, many of the variables associated with liability claims are not a factor. Claim representatives usually do not have to determine who was at fault in a property insurance claim (unless the insured is suspected of an intentional act, such as arson). When handling a property insurance claim, the claim representative rarely has to worry about some unforeseen side effect manifesting months or years after the claim has occurred, which is often the case when bodily injury is involved. Finally, valuing property is usually easier than placing a dollar value on the income-earning ability or the life of a person who has been disabled or killed in an accident.

Step 1: Investigation

When the claim representative receives the initial report of a claim, he or she must investigate to gather further information relevant to the loss. This investigation is necessary to determine the cause of the loss, to assess the damage, and to verify coverage.

Determining the Cause of Loss and Assessing Damage

For a property insurance claim, investigation often involves visiting the site to inspect the damaged property. Whether it is real property, such as a house or an office building, or personal property, such as household furnishings or business inventory, the claim representative needs to inspect the property to determine the cause of the loss and to assess the damage.

Jargon Alert!

The term *property insurance claim* generally refers to a claim for property, usually property that belongs to an insured, that is covered for certain causes of loss under an insured's policy.

In contrast, a claim for property of someone other than an insured that is damaged due to the insured's alleged negligence is a type of liability claim (called a *property damage liability claim*). Liability claims are discussed later in this chapter.

The investigation must reveal sufficient information to verify whether coverage exists under the policy. One of the most important facts is the cause of the loss, such as fire, windstorm, vandalism, or some other cause. For some losses, the cause is obvious; in others, the cause is harder to determine. In all cases, determining the cause of loss is one of the most critical aspects of the investigation.

Another critical aspect of a loss, particularly with regard to real property, is the physical condition of the property before the loss occurred. This information is difficult to obtain when a building has been completely destroyed. The claim representative must consult with the insured, measure the building remains, study pictures that might be available, and examine blueprints showing the building's dimensions.

For personal property, the most critical information is what property was damaged or destroyed. Creating an inventory of damaged personal property can be a long and arduous task for some losses, such as serious fire losses. However, in order for the claim representative to determine the value of the loss, a detailed inventory is essential, and very specific information must be gathered. When the loss involves a business, historical valuation information often appears in the company's financial records. In addition, if a business income loss is involved, the financial records are useful in determining the proper valuation of the lost income.

The claim representative might also need to interview and take statements from witnesses to the loss, if any exist, to better understand how and why the loss occurred. When a building is totally destroyed, the best information concerning how the loss occurred often comes from witnesses. This information can help determine the cause of loss, which could be especially important in situations in which third parties might be responsible.

Verifying Coverage

In addition to determining the facts surrounding the loss, the claim representative must determine whether the coverage provided by the policy will pay any or all of the claim submitted. For a property insurance claim, the claim representative must seek the answers to several questions to verify that the claim is covered:

- Does the insured have an insurable interest in the property?
- Is the damaged property covered under the policy?
- Is the cause of loss covered under the policy?
- Do any additional coverages, endorsements, or limitations on coverage apply?

Does the Insured Have an Insurable Interest in the Property?
The person or organization making a claim for the damaged property must have an **insurable interest** in the property. In most property insurance losses, the insured is the owner of the property, so the question of insurable interest is easily answered. However, others might also have an insurable interest in the property. For example, a mortgagee has an insurable interest in real property to the extent of the outstanding mortgage. Under certain circumstances, the mortgagee has rights to collect under an insurance policy if the mortgaged property has been damaged or destroyed. It is important for the claim representative to identify who has an insurable interest in the property so that payment can be made according to the policy provisions.

In property insurance, **insurable interest** exists if a person or other entity has any right to or interest in the property such that a loss to that property would cause a direct *monetary* loss to that person or entity.

Is the Damaged Property Covered Under the Policy?
Another question that the claim representative must answer is whether the damaged property is covered by the policy. In the case of a damaged home or commercial building, the answer might seem obvious. The answer, however, might not be as simple as it appears.

For example, insurance coverage on a building usually includes any item permanently attached to the building and any outdoor equipment used to maintain the building. Although the building might be clearly insured, would a room air conditioner attached to a window frame be considered a part of the building? Would a toolshed connected to a dwelling by a fence be considered a part of the dwelling? These are the types of questions that the claim representative must answer according to the terms of the policy.

The question of whether the damaged property is covered by the policy is equally important for personal property. Most property insurance policies exclude losses to certain types of property. For example, the homeowners policy generally does not cover losses to property of tenants or to most motorized vehicles.

Is the Cause of Loss Covered Under the Policy?
Often, the cause of the loss, such as fire or lightning, is obviously covered under the policy and disputes between the insured and the insurer are not likely. However, disagreements might arise when the cause of loss is less obvious. Disputes could occur, for example, if there is more than one possible cause of loss, as in a hurricane when damage might have been caused either by wind or by flooding. Disputes might also arise about the meanings of terms used in the policy. In some cases, the burden of proving whether coverage exists under a particular property insurance policy lies with the insured. In other cases, the burden of establishing that the cause of loss is excluded rests with the insurer. Chapter 8 will discuss this burden of proof issue.

Do Any Additional Coverages, Endorsements, or Limitations on Coverage Apply? In many insurance policies, additional coverages and limitations modify the basic coverage provided. For example, under a homeowners policy, the definition of covered property does not include trees, shrubs, plants, or lawns. However, these items are covered under an additional coverage, which specifically states that trees, shrubs, plants, and lawns are covered up to a specific dollar amount if damaged by certain specified causes of loss.

The insured might have purchased an additional coverage, selected one or more optional coverages printed in the policy, or modified coverage through an endorsement (policy amendment). Such changes to the basic policy can eliminate or modify exclusions or limitations. The claim representative should recognize that such policy modifications might apply and must consider them when determining whether coverage exists.

There are also important limitations on coverage. Although a homeowners policy covers most types of personal property, certain types of property, such as jewelry and furs, are covered for only a specified dollar amount when the loss is due to theft. Similarly, a homeowners policy does not cover losses caused by vandalism if the dwelling has been vacant more than thirty consecutive days. Such policy limitations are critical in verifying coverage.

The claim representative must also check the policy to see whether a deductible applies to the loss, which would reduce the amount of the loss payment. Before determining whether a given loss is covered, the claim representative must confirm that the loss occurred during the period and within the territory described in the policy.

Step 2: Valuation

For claim representatives, the valuation of loss can be the most difficult aspect of settling property insurance claims. In order to indemnify the insured according to the policy provisions, the claim representative must be able to answer two questions:

1. How does the policy specify that the property be valued?
2. Based on that specification, what is the value of the damaged property?

How Does the Policy Specify That the Property Be Valued?

All property insurance policies include a valuation provision that specifies how to value covered property at the time of the loss. The most common property valuation methods are:

- Actual cash value
- Replacement cost
- Agreed value

Actual cash value (ACV) is the cost to replace the property minus an allowance for the property's **depreciation**. For example, assume a fire completely destroys a new television and a five-year-old sofa. The television has a **replacement cost** of $600 (its cost when it was purchased a week earlier), and the sofa would cost $800 to replace with a comparable new sofa. (A sofa that is five years old probably cannot be replaced with exactly the same sofa because styles change; therefore, its replacement cost would be the cost of a new sofa comparable to the one that was destroyed.) Under these circumstances, an ACV settlement includes $600 for the television because it has not yet had time to depreciate. For the sofa, however, the claim representative has to place a value on the used property.

The claim representative must determine the extent of depreciation that should be taken into account. This determination is usually made by estimating the property's expected useful life. If, under normal circumstances, a sofa might be used for ten years and it is now five years old, a good estimate of depreciation from normal wear and tear is 50 percent. Therefore, with a replacement cost of $800 and depreciation estimated at 50 percent, the ACV of the damaged sofa is $400. A payment of $400 would indemnify the insured for the loss of the sofa. Certain types of property, such as computers, become obsolete after a certain amount of time, so obsolescence must also be estimated.

Another valuation method specified in some property insurance policies allows for valuation on a replacement cost basis. In this case, deduction for depreciation is not a part of the valuation, and the insured in the previous example would be paid $800 for the sofa.

Still another method for valuing property losses is **agreed value**, which is used to insure property that is difficult to value, such as fine arts, antiques, and collections. The insurance company and the insured agree on the value of the property at the time the policy is written, often on the basis of an appraisal, and that amount is stated in the policy declarations. If a total loss to the property occurs, the insurer will pay the agreed value, without regard to the exact value of the property at the time of the loss.

What Is the Value of the Damaged Property?

Once the claim representative has verified coverage and identified the valuation method specified in the policy, the valuation process begins. Claim representatives must use some guidelines to determine both replacement cost and ACV. Personal property and real property present different valuation problems.

Personal Property   If the exact style and brand of the damaged personal property are available for purchase, obtaining the replacement cost is simple. If the particular item is no longer available, the claim representative identifies the closest substi-

Actual cash value (ACV) is the *replacement cost* of property minus *depreciation*.

Replacement cost is the cost to repair or replace property using new materials of like kind and quality with no deduction for depreciation.

Depreciation is an allowance for physical wear and tear or technological or economic obsolescence.

Agreed value is a method of valuing property in which the insurer and the insured agree on the value of the property at the time the policy is written, and that amount is stated in the policy declarations and is the amount the insurer will pay in the event of a total loss to the property.

In commercial lines insurance, various *agreed value* options exist for property insurance policies. In some policies, the term agreed value has a different meaning and relates to the amount of insurance that the insured must carry to avoid a penalty for underinsurance. Such agreed value options are discussed in more detail in INS 23—*Commercial Insurance*.

tute in style and quality and uses that substitute's value as the replacement cost.

For ACV, however, depreciation must be estimated. While claim representatives have attempted to develop straightforward methods, such as the "useful life" procedure described in the case of the damaged sofa, these procedures are not perfect and do not fit every circumstance. For example, if a sofa has an expected life of ten years, the claim representative makes a reasonable estimate in considering the five-year-old sofa to be 50 percent depreciated. But what if the sofa is fifteen years old? Is the sofa considered worthless? The fifteen-year-old sofa has some value as long as it is functional, so the depreciation procedure must make allowance for that fact. The claim representative might have guidelines stating that property still being used is no more than 75 percent depreciated, no matter how old it is. While such guidelines might be developed to treat most cases, it is impossible to anticipate every situation the claim representative might encounter. Therefore, good judgment on the part of the claim representative is essential to determining depreciation.

Real Property   The replacement cost of real property can usually be determined by using three factors:

- Square footage of the property
- Quality of construction
- Construction cost per square foot

The first factor is the square footage of the property. If the building has been badly damaged, its area can be determined from the original blueprints or by measuring the remains.

The second factor is the quality of construction. A one-family frame house with standard trim and fixtures costs far less to replace than the same size house built of stone with high-quality woodworking, skylights, and spiral staircases. The quality of the house or building is more apparent if part of the structure has escaped damage. Pictures of the house or building can be useful, particularly if the structure has been totally destroyed.

The final factor affecting replacement cost is the construction cost per square foot currently charged for the style and quality of the destroyed building. Contractors in the location of the damaged building can quote costs per square foot in various quality-of-construction categories, such as $60 per square foot for standard quality, $70 per square foot for medium quality, and $85 per square foot for superior quality. Multiplying the square footage by the appropriate cost per square foot yields the building's replacement cost.

If the building is only partially damaged, the claim representative usually prepares a repair estimate or obtains repair estimates from one or more contractors. Replacing the property when a partial loss has occurred involves restoring the property to its previous state, as closely as possible.

Some policies specify that the actual cash value method should be used to measure loss to real property. For policies specifying ACV valuation, claim representatives estimate depreciation of real property using methods similar to those used for estimating depreciation of personal property. Other policies state that the insured can collect the replacement cost of damaged real property under certain circumstances. Often, however, these policies provide for immediate payment of the ACV of the property, and payment of the remainder of the replacement cost is made when actual repair or replacement is completed. Either type of policy requires a claim representative to calculate the ACV of damaged real property.

Step 3: Negotiation and Settlement

After completing the investigation and valuation steps of the claim handling process for a property insurance claim, the claim representative must conclude the settlement with the insured. This step usually requires that the claim representative and the insured discuss the details of the loss and the valuation of the damage in order to agree on an amount for the insurer to pay in settlement of the loss. The negotiation phase of claim handling can be relatively simple, as in the case of the fire-damaged television in a previous example, or it can be complicated because of a large number of damaged items, property of high value, or disagreement between the insured and the claim representative regarding the value or circumstances of the loss. Successful negotiation requires an understanding of human nature and good interpersonal skills.

Whenever possible, questions of coverage, valuation, and other matters should be discussed and resolved as they arise. In addition, investigation and valuation often continue while the negotiation is in progress.

After the claim representative and the insured agree on the amount of the settlement, two other factors can affect the insurer's cost for property claims: subrogation and salvage rights.

Subrogation

Subrogation refers to the insurer's right to recover its claim payment to an insured from the party responsible for the loss. Subrogation often applies in claims involving auto accidents. Once the insurer pays the insured for the repair or replacement of the damaged auto, the policy provides that any rights to collect from another party responsible for the damage to the auto belong to the insurer (up to the amount the insurer paid the insured for

Subrogation is the insurer's right to recover payment from a negligent third party. When an insurer pays an insured for a loss, the insurer assumes the insured's right to collect damages from a third party responsible for the loss.

the claim). Subrogation prevents an insured from collecting from both the insurer and the party at fault for the same loss.

The claim representative investigates whether another party involved in the accident is legally responsible for the damage paid by the insurer. If another party is at fault, the insurer can attempt to collect the repair or replacement cost from that person or that person's insurer. Formal legal proceedings might be necessary to determine who is legally responsible for the damage.

Salvage Rights

Salvage rights are the rights of the insurer to recover and sell or otherwise dispose of insured property on which the insurer has paid a total loss or a *constructive total loss*.

A **constructive total loss** exists when a vehicle (or other property) cannot be repaired for less than its actual cash value minus the anticipated salvage value.

The insurer also has **salvage rights** to the property once it pays for a total loss. For example, if an auto damaged in an accident cannot be repaired for less than its ACV minus the anticipated salvage value, the auto is considered to be a **constructive total loss**. In this case, the insurer pays the auto's ACV to the insured (or finds an auto similar to the insured's auto before it was damaged). While the settlement with the insured is paid as a total loss, the insurance company might be able to collect some salvage value for the damaged auto. Depending on the actual condition of the vehicle, an auto salvage dealer might be willing to pay for the auto in order to obtain scrap metal and undamaged parts that could be resold as used parts. In this way, the salvage value can offset some of the insurer's claim cost. For example, assume the ACV of the insured's car at the time of an accident is $10,000, and the repairs will cost $9,000. If the car could be sold for $1,500 to a salvage dealer, the insurer would consider the car a constructive total loss because it would cost more for the insurer to pay the repair cost than to pay the insured the ACV of $10,000 and then sell the salvage for $1,500. ($10,000 ACV – $1,500 salvage value = $8,500, which is less than the $9,000 cost of repairing the car.)

Educational Objective 5

Describe the claim handling process for liability insurance claims.

Liability Insurance Claims

Liability claim handling can be complex for several reasons. For liability claims, the claimant is a third party who has been injured or whose property has been damaged by the insured. The claimant might perceive the claim representative as an adversary, and this perception could cause the claimant to act in a hostile or unfriendly manner. Another complicating factor is the possibility that a liability claim might involve bodily injury. While it is not always easy to determine the amount of the loss in property damage liability claims, the problem becomes even more complex when the loss involves bodily injury or death.

Liability claim settlement sometimes involves a claim for damage to the property of others that the insured has allegedly caused. The process for handling property damage liability claims need not be described in detail here because it resembles the claim handling process for property insurance claims with the added difficulty of determining whether the insured is legally responsible for the property damage that has occurred. The following discussion concentrates on the issue of legal responsibility, which lies at the heart of the liability claim handling process.

Step 1: Investigation

After receiving the first report of injury or damage, the claim representative must gather more detailed information relating to the liability claim. The question of how much damage occurred might be secondary because the amount of the loss is relevant only if the loss is covered under the insured's policy and if the insured is legally responsible for the loss. The claim representative's initial emphasis must be on determining how and why the loss occurred and whether it appears that the insured is responsible.

Determining How the Loss Occurred and Assessing the Situation

In investigating a liability claim, the claim representative often inspects the scene of the occurrence. This inspection is particularly useful if a traumatic event has occurred, such as an auto accident, a building collapse, or a fire. By studying the scene of the occurrence and by interviewing the insured, the claimant, and any witnesses, the claim representative attempts to reconstruct the events that led to the loss. This reconstruction helps to determine, as closely as possible, how the loss occurred and who is responsible. While additional details are needed to determine the size of the loss, at this point the claim representative must collect enough information to determine whether the liability policy covers the loss and, if so, whether the insured might be legally responsible.

As soon as possible, the claim representative usually speaks directly with the injured party or that party's legal representative to hear that side of the story and to assess what injury or other damage has been sustained. Many times the events surrounding an accident are difficult, if not impossible, to reconstruct, so the claim representative often receives different interpretations from the injured party and the insured as to how the loss occurred. The claim representative also gathers reports from witnesses, if available. All of this information helps the claim representative to determine whether the insured might be legally responsible.

The injured party has the option of suing the insured, and the ensuing legal process could end in a legal decision concerning who is responsible and to what extent. Because of the time, expense, and uncertainty involved in a trial, insurers often prefer to settle claims out of court. If the claim does go to court, the insurer is obligated to provide and pay for the insured's defense for a covered claim (until the insurer has paid the full policy limit for the occurrence involved).

Verifying Coverage

Liability policies usually cover the insured's liability arising from certain specified activities, such as owning or using an automobile or operating a business, subject to certain exclusions. Therefore, coverage verification depends on whether the activity leading to the claim comes within the scope of the policy's coverage and whether any exclusions in the policy apply to the specific case. Based on the information gathered, the claim representative must determine whether coverage exists.

If the claim representative's investigation establishes that no coverage applies, the insurer will deny the claim. For example, if the policy excludes injury intended by the insured and the insured purposely injures someone with a baseball bat, there would be no coverage unless the insured can establish that the injury was not intentional but merely a careless act. In that case, the claim representative would need to investigate further to determine whether the injury was indeed intentional on the part of the insured. If coverage does exist, the valuation aspect of liability claims settlement then becomes very important.

Step 2: Valuation

Damages refer to a monetary award that one party is required to pay to another who has suffered loss or injury for which the first party is legally responsible.

When bodily injury is involved, determining the amount of **damages** often depends on medical records and the reports and opinions of attending physicians. Properly evaluating medical information is critical in determining the amount of damages and is a distinguishing factor in the loss settlement process for bodily injury liability claims. This evaluation aspect of bodily injury claims requires experience and skill.

Legal liability cases might involve the following types of damages:

Compensatory damages are *damages*, which include both *special* and *general damages*, that are intended to compensate a victim for harm actually suffered.

- Compensatory damages (which include both special damages and general damages)
- Punitive damages

Compensatory Damages

Compensatory damages are intended to compensate a victim for harm actually suffered. Compensatory damages include *special damages* and *general damages*.

Special damages are compensatory damages allowed for specific, out-of-pocket expenses, such as doctor and hospital bills.

Special Damages Specific, out-of-pocket expenses are known as **special damages.** In bodily injury cases, these damages usually include hospital expenses, doctor and miscellaneous medical expenses, ambulance charges, prescriptions, and lost wages for time spent away from the job during recovery. Because they are specific and identifiable, special damages are easier to calculate than general damages.

General Damages   Examples of **general damages**, which do not have a specific economic value, include pain and suffering; disfigurement; loss of limbs, sight, or hearing; and loss of the ability to bear children. Because these losses do not involve specific measurable expenses, estimating their dollar value requires considerable experience and might still seem arbitrary to someone who is not experienced in injury evaluation. For the claim representative, the best guide is usually the analysis of past cases similar to the case at hand.

> **General damages** are compensatory damages awarded for losses, such as pain and suffering, that do not have a specific economic value.

There is usually no direct relationship between the amount of general damages and the amount of special damages. In some cases, such as when a claimant loses an eye, the amount of special damages might be relatively low, but the general damages might be quite high because of the pain and suffering involved and the change in the claimant's quality of life. In other cases, such as for whiplash injuries, general damages might be minimal, but special damages might be considerable because the claimant has extensive physical therapy or other medical treatment.

In recent years, courts have often made large awards for general damages, particularly for traumatic incidents like automobile accidents. Claim representatives must be aware of the awards for damages made in their jurisdictions, because these awards provide a guideline for negotiating with the injured party.

Punitive Damages

When a court finds the defendant's conduct particularly reprehensible, it might award a third type of damages known as **punitive damages**. The purpose of punitive damages is to punish the wrongdoer and to deter others from committing similar wrongs. In some states, the insurer's payment of an award for punitive damages is not permitted because such payment by an insurer would not punish the insured. Some policies expressly exclude the payment of punitive damages.

> **Punitive damages** are damages awarded by a court to punish wrongdoers who, through malicious or outrageous actions, cause injury or damage to others.

Step 3: Negotiation and Settlement

While the awards for damages described above might result from court decisions, a very large percentage of liability cases are settled out of court through negotiations between the claim representative and the claimant or the claimant's attorney. In most instances, neither party wishes to become involved in a formal legal action with the accompanying costs and delays. When negotiations do not bring about a settlement, however, the claimant has the option of suing for the alleged damages.

The court then decides who is responsible and determines the value of the injury or damage. Even after the claimant initiates a suit, however, the claim negotiation process usually continues. Many out-of-court settlements have resulted after some or all of the courtroom testimony has been given. Negotiating with the claimant while simultaneously preparing for proceedings in court requires a great deal of skill, patience, and understanding on the part of the claim representative.

Educational Objective 6

Describe the claim representative's role in establishing an insurer's loss reserves.

Establishing Loss Reserves

Claim representatives also play a vital role in establishing an insurance company's loss reserves. As stated in Chapter 3, loss reserves represent funds held by the insurance company to pay claims for losses that have occurred but have not yet been settled. Loss reserves are the largest and most important liabilities of property and liability insurers. They are liabilities because they represent an estimate of the amount of claim payments the insurer will make in the future.

After the claim representative receives notice of a loss, obtains initial information, and verifies coverage, a loss reserve for that claim is established. Assume, for example, that an insured had a minor auto accident in which her car hit a guardrail on a foggy night and that no injuries or other cars were involved. After obtaining initial information concerning the accident, verifying coverage, and receiving written estimates of the cost to repair the insured's car, the claim representative establishes a loss reserve of $1,500. This figure is probably a very accurate estimate because a single-car collision loss is relatively easy to evaluate. Two weeks later, the repairs are made to the insured's car, and the insurer issues a check for $1,500. Once the loss is paid, the reserve is reduced to zero because no future loss payment is contemplated. Therefore, the $1,500 claim paid by the insurer equals the initial loss reserve.

On the other hand, complex claims are often very difficult to estimate, especially liability claims. Assume that an insured was involved in a serious auto accident and that two persons in the other car are hospitalized with severe injuries. The cause of the accident is not immediately clear because of conflicting testimony of witnesses, and it is difficult to determine whether the insured is responsible for the accident. What loss reserve should be established? The amount eventually paid because of this accident could range from almost nothing (if the insured is not found to be legally responsible) to hundreds of thousands of dollars (if the insured is responsible and the injured victims die or are permanently disabled). The eventual payment on this particular claim, which might not be made for several years, might vary significantly from the original reserve.

The calculation of the loss reserves is always an estimate—no one knows exactly how much the insurer will pay in the future for an individual claim or all claims for a particular period. Although actuaries calculate an insurer's overall loss reserves for inclusion on the insurer's financial statements, claim representatives generally estimate loss reserves for individual claims based on their knowledge and experience. Actuaries then use individual claim reserves in determining the overall claim reserves to show on the insurer's financial statements. No system of estimating overall loss reserves can be accurate unless the underlying reserves on individual claims are reasonably accurate. A claim representative who properly estimates a loss reserve for a given claim provides a valuable service to the insurer, who in turn is better able to report appropriate loss reserves to legislators, investors, and others.

The process of setting individual claim reserves varies by company. Often, the claim representative's input, based on an analysis of the many factors associated with a particular claim, is combined with the knowledge and experience of a claim supervisor or manager. Reserving is not a one-time activity for any particular claim; the loss reserve must be constantly evaluated and re-evaluated as new information becomes available. A good claim representative should be able to set appropriate loss reserves that accurately reflect the ultimate expected claim payment.

Educational Objective 7

Describe and, in a given situation, analyze the practices prohibited by unfair claim practices laws.

Unfair Claim Practices Laws

Although most claim representatives strive to treat insureds and claimants as fairly as possible while adhering to the terms of the insurance policy, the claim handling process is far from perfect. The task of the claim representative is a difficult one. Not only is it difficult to master some of the skills, such as understanding complex policy conditions and determining the value of the loss, but the entire process depends on skillful interpersonal communication in a situation that might involve stress and disagreements.

If the claimant perceives the claim representative as an adversary, this perception can lead to problems. Unfortunately, the claimant might have the misconception that the claim representative's job is to pay as little as possible under the contract and that the only way to receive a proper recovery is through confrontational negotiation or by hiring a lawyer. A liability claim accentuates the adversarial aspect since the claimant, who has suffered a loss allegedly as a result of the insured's actions, views the claim representative as representing the "other side" (the insurer and the insured) and thus not being trustworthy.

Unfair claim practices laws are state laws that specify claim practices that are illegal.

Because of problems that have occurred in the claim process, most states have enacted **unfair claim practices laws**. These laws specify claim practices that are illegal. The prohibited claim practices usually include:

- Misrepresentation of pertinent facts or insurance policy provisions relating to coverage at issue in a claim
- Failure to acknowledge and promptly respond to communications with respect to claims arising under insurance policies
- Actions that compel an insured to sue to recover amounts due under insurance policies by offering amounts that are substantially lower than the amounts ultimately recovered in legal actions brought by such insureds
- Refusal to pay claims without first conducting a reasonable investigation based on all available information

Insurance regulators usually learn of unfair claim practices when they receive complaints from insureds and claimants. Claim representatives must be able to justify their actions and provide proper documentation when asked to do so by state insurance regulators. Some complaints are frivolous, often occurring because the claimant is annoyed that the policy does not cover a loss. On the other hand, some complaints are valid, and regulators might take action when a serious complaint occurs or when several complaints, especially of a similar nature, are registered against a claim representative or insurance company. The claim representative or insurance company must justify the practices that are under scrutiny or face a reprimand, a fine, a license suspension, or some other legal penalty.

Educational Objective 8

Define or describe each of the Key Words and Phrases for this assignment. (All Key Words and Phrases appear in bold print in the text and in the margins throughout this chapter.)

Summary

When an insurance company sells a policy, it promises to pay claims covered by that policy. The purpose of the claim handling process is to fulfill that promise. A claim representative, the person responsible for handling claims, has several responsibilities:

- To respond promptly when a claim is submitted
- To obtain adequate information
- To properly evaluate the claim
- To treat all parties fairly

Depending on the circumstances, different types of claim representatives may handle claims, including:

- *Staff claim representatives*, who are insurance company employees and include inside claim representatives and outside (field) claim representatives
- *Independent adjusters*, who are independent claim representatives who offer claim handling services to insurers for a fee
- *Agents*, who often have draft authority to settle certain small claims
- *Public adjusters*, who are hired by and represent the insured in the claim handling process

A self-insurance situation can also require claim handling services. In that situation, the self-insuring organization may use its own personnel to settle claims, or it may use the services of a third-party administrator.

Regardless of who handles claims, the claim handling process involves the same three steps

1. Investigation of the claim
2. Valuation (establishing the amount of the loss)
3. Negotiation and settlement of the claim

For property claims, the investigation usually means inspecting the damaged property to determine the cause of loss and to assess the damage. The investigation also involves verifying coverage by determining whether an insurable interest exists, whether the policy covers the damaged property, whether the policy covers the cause of loss involved, and whether any additional coverages, endorsements, or limitations on coverage apply. The procedure for the valuation of the loss depends on whether the policy specifies actual cash value, replacement cost, agreed value, or some other method for valuing losses.

In liability claims, the claim representative's investigation focuses on whether the activity leading to liability comes within the scope of the policy and whether the insured could be legally responsible for the loss. The valuation of a bodily injury loss involves the examination of medical records and physicians' reports. If the case goes to court, the total liability loss can result in compensatory damages (which include special damages and general damages) and, conceivably, punitive damages. Often, however, it is in the best interest of all parties to negotiate a settlement out of court rather than to incur the expense and delay of legal proceedings.

In addition to fulfilling the promise contained in the insurance contract, claim representatives play an important role in measuring the insurer's liabilities by establishing loss reserves for individual claims. A loss reserve for a particular claim is the best estimate of the amount the insurance company will eventually have to pay for that claim.

Many states have passed laws prohibiting unfair claim practices. Regulators also monitor complaints from insureds and claimants. A number of complaints about a particular insurance company or claim representative could lead to a reprimand, a fine, or some other legal penalty.

Segment C:

Insurance Contracts, Loss Exposures, and Risk Management

This final segment begins by discussing common characteristics of insurance contracts. It continues by presenting both property and liability loss exposures and policy provisions that cover those exposures. Finally, risk management is introduced as a means of managing loss exposures.

Chapter 7

Insurance Contracts

Educational Objectives

After studying this chapter, you should be able to:

1. Identify and explain the four essential elements of any valid contract. (pp. 7-4 to 7-6)

2. Identify and describe the special characteristics of insurance contracts. (pp. 7-6 to 7-12)

3. Explain and illustrate the principle of indemnity. (pp. 7-10 to 7-12)

4. Identify and describe the items usually found on the declarations page of an insurance policy. (pp. 7-12 to 7-14)

5. Explain the purpose in an insurance policy of each of the following: (pp. 7-13 to 7-18)
   a. Definitions
   b. Insuring agreements
   c. Exclusions
   d. Conditions
   e. Miscellaneous provisions

6. a. Describe and distinguish between manuscript policies and standard forms. (pp. 7-18 to 7-19)
   b. Describe the advantages of standard forms to (1) insurers and (2) insureds. (pp. 7-19 to 7-20)

7. Describe and distinguish between a self-contained and a modular policy. (pp. 7-20 to 7-23)

8. Describe the conditions commonly found in property and liability insurance policies. (pp. 7-23 to 7-28)
9. Explain how subrogation works. (pp. 7-27 to 7-28)
10. Define or describe each of the Key Words and Phrases for this assignment. (All Key Words and Phrases appear in bold print in the text and in the margins throughout this chapter.)

Chapter 7

Insurance Contracts

Purchasing an insurance policy differs from purchasing tangible goods. A car buyer, for example, can examine and even test drive a car before buying it. Although warranties and promises of reliable service might influence the decision to buy, the primary consideration is the car itself. The car's physical characteristics are readily apparent at the time of the sale. The buyer cannot blame the dealer if the car is too small or the wrong color. Insurance, on the other hand, is not something a person can test before buying. The essence of insurance is the insurance company's promise that it will pay claims in the future for losses that are covered under the policy.

The evidence of this promise is the insurance contract, or policy. The policy defines in detail the rights and duties of both parties to the contract: the insured and the insurer. A particular insurance policy meets a buyer's needs only if the terms of the policy obligate the insurer to provide the protection desired. Although it is possible to evaluate a car with a test drive, evaluating an insurance policy requires an analysis of its terms.

This chapter provides a foundation for such an analysis. The chapter first discusses contracts in general and then describes the special characteristics of insurance contracts, their content, and their structure; it concludes with a description of several conditions that are common to most property and liability insurance policies. The material in this chapter provides a basis for studying Chapters 8 and 9, which deal with property and liability loss exposures and specific provisions in policies that cover those exposures.

Elements of a Contract

A **policy** is a complete written *contract* of insurance. (As stated in Chapter 4, a *binder* is a temporary contract of insurance and can be either oral or written; a binder is usually replaced within a short period by a policy.)

A **contract** is a legally enforceable agreement between two or more parties.

An insurance contract, called a **policy**, is an agreement between the insurer and the insured. An insurance policy must meet the same requirements as any other valid **contract**, which is a legally enforceable agreement between two or more parties.

If a dispute arises between the parties to a contract, a court will enforce only those agreements that are valid contracts. The validity of a contract depends on four essential elements:

- Agreement (offer and acceptance)
- Competent parties
- Legal purpose
- Consideration

If a court cannot confirm the presence of all of these elements, it will not enforce the contract.

Agreement (Offer and Acceptance)

One essential element of a contract is that agreement must exist between the parties to the contract. One party must make a legitimate *offer* and another party must *accept* the offer. In other words, there must be mutual assent.

In the case of insurance, the process of achieving mutual assent generally begins when someone who wants to purchase insurance completes an insurance application—an offer to buy insurance. The details on the application describe the exposures to be insured and indicate the coverage the applicant requests.

In an uncomplicated case, an insurance company underwriter (or an agent, acting on behalf of an insurer) accepts the application and agrees to provide the coverage requested at a price acceptable to both the insurer and the applicant. At this point, agreement exists; the insurer has accepted the applicant's offer to buy insurance.

In a more complicated case, the underwriter might not be willing to meet all the requests of the applicant. As explained in Chapter 5, one of the underwriter's options is to accept the application with modification. In other words, the underwriter might be willing to provide coverage, but only on somewhat different terms. For example, the underwriter might insist on a higher deductible than the applicant had requested. When the underwriter communicates the proposed modifications to the applicant, these modifications constitute a *counteroffer*. Several offers and counteroffers might be made before both parties agree to an exact set of terms. If the other essential elements of a contract exist, the mutual assent of the insurer and the applicant forms a contract.

To be enforceable, the agreement cannot be the result of duress, coercion, fraud, or a mistake. If either party to the contract can prove any of these circumstances, a court could declare the contract to be void.

Competent Parties

For the contract to be enforceable, all parties must be legally competent. In other words, each party must have the legal capacity to make the agreement binding. Individuals are generally considered to be competent and able to enter into legally enforceable contracts, *unless* they are one or more of the following:

- Insane or otherwise mentally incompetent
- Under the influence of drugs or alcohol
- Minors (persons not yet of legal age)

However, minors are sometimes considered competent to purchase auto insurance, especially when auto insurance qualifies as a necessity. State laws vary in regard to issues involving minors.

Another aspect of legal capacity involves the fact that, in most states, an insurer must be licensed to do business in the state. If an insurer mistakenly writes a policy in a state where that insurer is not licensed, the insured might later argue that the contract is not valid and demand the return of the premium. This demand would be based on the fact that the insurer did not have the legal capacity to make the agreement.

Legal Purpose

An enforceable contract must also have a legal purpose. The courts might consider a contract to be illegal if its purpose is against the law or against public policy (as defined by the courts). For example, an agreement to pay a bribe to a government official in exchange for receiving a government job would not be enforced by the courts because such activities are against public policy.

Although most insurance policies do not involve a question of legality, certain situations do exist that might invalidate an insurance policy. Courts will refuse to enforce any insurance policy that is illegal or that tends to injure the public welfare.

Insurance contracts must involve a legal subject matter. Property insurance on illegally owned or possessed goods is invalid. For example, property insurance covering illegal drugs would be illegal and therefore unenforceable. If fireworks are illegal in a particular state, then an insurance policy covering fireworks would be illegal in that state. In addition, no insurance contract will remain valid if the wrongful conduct of the insured causes the operation of the contract to violate public policy. Thus, arson by an insured would render a property insurance policy unenforceable and would preclude recovery by the insured under the policy for a building the insured intentionally burned.

Consideration

Consideration is an exchange of something of value that is required in any valid contract. In insurance, consideration given by the insured is the payment of (or the agreement to pay) the premium. Consideration on the part of the insurer is the promise to pay covered losses. Even though someone purchasing insurance receives only a document containing a promise, that promise has value because it is a legal obligation.

Consideration is something of value given by each party to a contract. For example, when an auto is purchased, the buyer gives money (consideration) to the seller who, in turn, provides the car (which is also consideration).

Some contracts do not involve the exchange of one tangible item for another, but instead involve *performance*. For example, an author might sign a contract agreeing to write a book in exchange for payment by the publisher.

Performance can also involve a promise to perform some act in the future that is dependent on a certain event occurring. In the case of an insurance contract, the insurer's consideration is its promise to pay a claim in the future *if* a covered loss occurs. If no loss occurs, the insurer is still fulfilling its promise to provide financial protection even though it does not pay a claim. In insurance contracts, two types of consideration are involved:

- The *insured's* consideration is the payment of (or the promise to pay) the premium.
- The *insurer's* consideration is its promise to pay claims as specified in the contract, conditioned on the occurrence of covered losses.

Insurance Contracts

In addition to having the four essential elements of all contracts, insurance contracts have certain special characteristics.

Educational Objective 2

Identify and describe the special characteristics of insurance contracts.

Special Characteristics of Insurance Contracts

The wording of an insurance policy reflects certain fundamental principles of insurance. An insurance policy is a contract that generally has certain distinct characteristics:

- A personal contract
- A conditional contract
- A contract involving the exchange of unequal amounts
- A contract of the utmost good faith
- A contract of adhesion
- A contract of indemnity

Personal Contract

The identities of the people insured are extremely relevant to the insurance company, which has the right to select the insureds with whom it is willing to enter into contractual agreements. Once an insurance policy is in effect, an insured may not freely transfer the policy to some other party. If such a transfer were allowed to take place, the insurance company would be legally bound to a contract with a party it might not wish to insure. Most insurance policies contain a provision (called *assignment*) that states that the insurer's written permission is required before an insured can transfer a policy to another party.

Conditional Contract

An insurance policy is a **conditional contract** because the parties have to perform only under certain *conditions*. Whether the insurer pays a claim depends on whether an insured loss occurs. In addition, the insured must fulfill certain duties before a claim is paid, such as giving prompt notice to the insurance company when a loss occurs.

A **conditional contract** is a contract in which one or more parties must perform only under certain conditions.

An insured loss might not occur during a particular policy period, but that fact does not mean the insurance contract has been worthless. In buying an insurance policy, the insured acquires a valuable promise—the promise of the insurer to make payments if a covered loss occurs. The promise exists, even if the insurer's performance is not required during the policy period.

Contract Involving the Exchange of Unequal Amounts

In addition to being conditional, insurance contracts involve an exchange of unequal amounts. Sometimes, the premium paid by the insured for a particular policy is more than the amount paid by the insurer to, or on behalf of, the insured because no losses occur. If a large loss occurs, on the other hand, the insurer's claim payment might be much more than the premium paid by the insured. It is the additional factor that the insurer's obligation *might* be much greater than the insured's (if covered losses occur) that makes the insurance transaction a fair trade.

For example, suppose an insurance company charges a $1,000 annual premium to provide property coverage (known as auto "physical damage" coverage) on a car with an actual cash value of $20,000.

- If the car is not damaged while the policy is in force, the insurance company pays nothing.
- If the car is partially damaged, the insurance company pays the cost of repairs, after subtracting a deductible.
- If the car is a total loss, the insurance company pays $20,000 (minus any deductible) to the insured.

Unless by chance the insurer's obligations in a minor accident come to exactly $1,000, unequal amounts are involved in all three cases. However, it does not follow that insureds who have no losses—or only very minor losses—do not get their money's worth or that insureds involved in major accidents profit from the insurance.

As stated in Chapter 2, the premium for a particular policy should reflect the insured's share of estimated losses that the insurer must pay. Many insureds have no losses, but some have very large losses. The policy premium reflects the insured's proportionate share of the total amount the insurer expects to pay to honor its agreements with *all insureds* with similar policies.

Contract of Utmost Good Faith

Utmost good faith is an obligation to act in complete honesty.

Because insurance involves an intangible promise, it requires complete honesty and disclosure of all relevant facts from both parties. For this reason, insurance contracts are considered contracts of **utmost good faith**. Both parties to an insurance contract—the insurer and the insured—are expected to be ethical in their dealings with each other.

The insured has a right to rely on the insurance company to fulfill its promises. Therefore, the insurance company is expected to treat the insured with utmost good faith. An insurance company that acts in bad faith, such as denying coverage for a claim that is clearly covered, could face serious penalties under the law.

The insurer also has a right to expect that the insured will act in good faith. An insurance buyer who intentionally conceals certain information or misrepresents certain facts does not act in good faith. Because an insurance contract requires utmost good faith from both parties, an insurance company could be released from a contract because of *concealment* or *misrepresentation* by the insured.

Concealment

Courts have held that the insurer must prove two things in order to establish that **concealment** has occurred. First, it must establish that the failure to disclose information was *intentional*, which is often difficult. The insurer must usually show that the insured knew that the information should have been given and then intentionally withheld it.

Second, the insurer must establish that the information withheld was a **material fact**—information that would affect an insurer's underwriting or claim settlement decision. For an auto insurance applicant, for example, material facts include how the autos are used, who drives the autos, and the ages and driving records of the drivers. If an insured intentionally conceals the material fact that her 16-year-old son lives in the household and is the principal driver of one of her cars, that concealment of a material fact could *void* the policy.

Insurance companies carefully design applications for insurance to include questions regarding facts material to the underwriting process. The application includes questions on specific subjects to which the applicant must respond. These questions are designed to encourage the applicant to reveal any pertinent information.

Misrepresentation

In normal usage, a misrepresentation is a false statement. As used in insurance, a **misrepresentation** is a false statement of a material fact on which the insurer relies. Unlike a concealment, the insurer does not have to prove that the misrepresentation is intentional.

For example, assume an applicant for auto insurance has had two speeding tickets during the eighteen months immediately before he submitted his application for insurance. When asked if any driving violations have occurred within the past three years (a question found on most auto application forms), an applicant giving either of the following answers would be making a misrepresentation:

- "I remember having one speeding ticket about two years ago."
- "I've never been cited for a moving violation—only a few parking tickets."

The first response provides incorrect information, and this false statement might or might not be intentional. The false statement made in the second response is probably intentional. The direct question posed in the application requires a full and honest response from the applicant because the insurer relies on the information. Anything less is a misrepresentation, whether intentional or not.

Concealment is an intentional failure to disclose a *material fact.*

For insurance purposes, a **material fact** is any information that would affect the insurer's underwriting decision to provide or maintain insurance or that would affect a claim settlement.

Jargon Alert!

There is a difference among the terms used in regard to the termination of an insurance policy: void, canceled, and nonrenewed.

When a policy is *void*, it never had any legal existence.

When a policy is *canceled*, it is terminated (by either the insurer or the insured) during the policy period.

When a policy is *nonrenewed*, it is terminated (by either the insurer or the insured) at the end of the policy period.

In insurance, a **misrepresentation** is a false statement of a material fact.

As with a concealment, if a material fact is misrepresented, the insurer could choose to void the policy because of the violation of utmost good faith.

Contract of Adhesion

A **contract of adhesion** is a contract in which one party (the insured, in insurance) must adhere to the agreement as written by the other party (the insurer).

The wording in insurance contracts is usually drafted by the insurance company (or an insurance advisory organization), enabling the insurer to use preprinted forms for many different insureds. Since the insurance company determines the exact wording of the policy, the insured has little choice but to "take it or leave it." That is, the insured must adhere to the contract drafted by the insurer. Therefore, insurance policies are considered to be **contracts of adhesion**, and that characteristic significantly influences their enforcement.

If a dispute arises between the insurance company and the insured about the meaning of certain words or phrases in the policy, the insured and the insurer are *not* on an equal basis. The insurer designed the policy wording, and the insured did not have a chance to select the wording. For that reason, if the policy wording is ambiguous, a court will generally apply the interpretation that favors the insured.

Educational Objective 3

Explain and illustrate the principle of indemnity.

Contract of Indemnity

In a **contract of indemnity**, the insurer agrees, in the event of a covered loss, to pay an amount directly related to the amount of the loss. Property insurance policies contain a valuation provision that explains how the value of the insured property is to be established at the time of the loss. Liability insurance policies agree to pay, on behalf of the insured, amounts that the insured becomes legally obligated to pay to others.

The purpose of insurance is to provide indemnification—that is, to *indemnify* an insured who suffers a loss. As stated in Chapter 1, to indemnify is to restore a party who has had a loss to the same financial position that party held before the loss occurred. Most property and liability insurance policies are contracts of indemnity. With a **contract of indemnity**, the amount paid by the insurer depends on the amount of loss the insured has suffered, as follows:

- Property insurance generally pays the amount of money necessary to repair covered property that has been damaged or to replace it with similar property. The policy specifies the method for computing the amount of the loss. For example, most auto policies, both personal and commercial, specify that vehicles are to be valued at their actual cash value (ACV) at the time of a loss. If a covered accident occurs that causes a covered vehicle to be a total loss, the insurer will normally pay the ACV of the vehicle less any applicable deductible.

- Liability insurance generally pays to a third-party claimant, on behalf of the insured, any amounts (up to the policy limit) that the insured becomes legally obligated to pay as damages due to a covered liability claim, as well as the legal costs associated with that claim. For example, if an insured with a liability limit of $300,000 is ordered by the court to pay $100,000 for bodily injury incurred by the claimant in a covered accident, the insurer will pay $100,000 to the claimant and will also pay the cost to defend the insured in court.

A contract of indemnity does not necessarily pay the *full* amount necessary to restore an insured who has suffered a covered loss. However, the amount the insurer pays is directly related to the amount of the insured's loss. Most policies contain a policy limit that specifies the maximum amount the insurer will pay for a single claim. Many policies also contain limitations and other provisions that could reduce the amount of recovery. For example, a homeowners policy is not designed to cover large amounts of cash. Therefore, most homeowners policies contain a special limit, such as $200, for all covered losses to money owned by the insured. If a covered fire destroys $1,000 in cash belonging to the insured, the homeowners insurer will pay only $200 for the money that was destroyed.

According to the **principle of indemnity**, the insured is not supposed to profit from the insured loss. That is, the insured should not be better off financially after the loss than before. Insurance policies usually include certain provisions that reinforce the principle of indemnity. For example, policies generally contain an "other insurance" provision to prevent an insured from receiving full payment from two different insurance policies for the same claim. Insurance contracts usually protect the insurer's subrogation rights, as discussed in Chapter 6. "Other insurance" provisions and subrogation provisions clarify that the insured cannot collect more than the amount of the loss.

Another factor enforcing the principle of indemnity is that a person usually cannot buy insurance unless that person is in a position to suffer a financial loss. In other words, as discussed in Chapter 6, the insured must have an insurable interest in the subject of the insurance. For example, property insurance contracts cover losses only to the extent of the insured's insurable interest in the property. This restriction prevents an insured from collecting more from the insurance than the amount of the loss he or she suffered. A person cannot buy life insurance on the life of a stranger, hoping to gain if the stranger dies. Insurance companies normally sell life insurance when there is a reasonable expectation of a financial loss from the death of the insured person, such as dependents of the insured person losing that person's future income. Insurable interest is not a problem in liability insurance because a liability claim against an insured causes that insured to suffer a financial loss if the insured is legally responsible; even if the insured is not responsible, the insured could incur defense costs.

The **principle of indemnity** states that the insured should not be better off financially after a loss than before. In other words, the insured should not profit from an insured loss.

A **valued policy** is one in which the insurer pays a stated amount in the event of a specified loss (usually a total loss), regardless of the actual value of the loss.

Some insurance contracts are not contracts of indemnity but **valued policies**. When a loss occurs, a valued policy pays a specified sum that might bear no direct relationship to the amount that is actually lost. For example, an accident insurance policy might specify that it will pay "$10,000 for loss of one arm." The amputee might have medical bills much smaller or much greater than $10,000, but the policy will pay $10,000 in either case. Life insurance policies are also valued policies because they state that the insurer will pay a fixed sum when the insured person dies rather than attempting to measure the financial consequences of the death.

Content of Insurance Policies

Because they must provide for contingencies, insurance policies must be drafted carefully. The parties must agree on how to handle many situations that could arise even if these situations are not likely to occur. The resulting documents are far from simple. Although insurance contracts can be complex, a framework of knowledge helps enormously in understanding them. Some familiarity with both the content and the structure of insurance policies in general helps in analyzing the terms of a particular policy.

An insurance policy specifically describes the coverage it provides. Since no insurance policy can cover every contingency, the policy must describe its limitations, restrictions, and exclusions as clearly as possible. For example, most insurance policies do not cover losses caused by acts of war or nuclear contamination. If the insurer does not intend to cover such losses, the policy must clearly state that fact. The best way to determine the coverage provided by a particular policy is to examine its provisions, which are generally included in the following sections of the policy:

- Declarations
- Definitions
- Insuring agreements
- Exclusions
- Conditions
- Miscellaneous provisions

Educational Objective 4

Identify and describe the items usually found on the declarations page of an insurance policy.

Declarations

An insurance policy must first identify the parties to the contract. Information such as the name and location of the insurer and the name and address of the insured is usually shown on the first page of the policy. This information page is called the **declarations page,** or simply the **declarations** or **dec**. As its name implies, a declarations page declares important information about the specific policy of which it is a part. The name of the insurance company is almost always preprinted on the declarations page; the name and address of the insured are entered when the policy is issued. Exhibit 7-1 shows the declarations page of a personal auto policy.

Insurance policies usually provide coverage for a specified period. The inception date of the policy is stated in the declarations. The expiration date might also appear in the declarations, or the policy period might be clarified elsewhere in the policy, usually as part of the conditions.

The insurance policy must describe the consideration involved. As stated previously, the insured's consideration is the premium, and the insurer's consideration is its promise to pay if an insured loss occurs. The premium amount is normally shown in the policy declarations. Other statements regarding when the premium should be paid, to whom it should be paid, and the consequences if it is not paid might appear elsewhere in the policy.

The policy limits are also shown in the declarations. A *limit* is the maximum amount of coverage the insurer will pay for a given type of loss. In some situations, however, the insurer might ultimately pay an amount greater than a policy limit. For example, under some liability policies, defense costs might be paid in addition to the amount of damages. Some property policies include additional coverages, such as debris removal, which might be paid in addition to a policy limit.

In addition, a declarations page usually includes any information that specifically describes the covered property or locations, specific coverages, deductibles, policy forms, endorsements, and other important details about the insured, the subject of the insurance, and the coverages provided by the policy.

The **declarations page** (also simply called the **declarations** or **dec**) of an insurance policy is an information page that provides specific details about the insured and the subject of the insurance, such as:

- Name and location of the insurer
- Name and address of the insured
- Policy number
- Policy period (inception and expiration dates)
- Description of covered property or locations
- Schedule of coverages and limits
- Deductibles
- Premium(s)
- Policy forms
- List of endorsements, if any
- Agent's name
- Other important details

Educational Objective 5

Explain the purpose in an insurance policy of each of the following:
a. Definitions
b. Insuring agreements
c. Exclusions
d. Conditions
e. Miscellaneous provisions

Exhibit 7-1

Declarations Page of a Personal Auto Policy

INS Insurance Company, Malvern, PA

Personal Auto Policy Declarations

POLICYHOLDER:　　David M. and Joan G. Smith
(Named Insured)　　216 Brookside Drive
　　　　　　　　　　Anytown, USA 40000

POLICY NUMBER:　　296 S 468211

POLICY PERIOD:　　FROM:　December 25, 1999
　　　　　　　　　　TO:　　June 25, 2000

But only if the required premium for this period has been paid, and for six-month renewal periods if renewal premiums are paid as required. Each period begins and ends after 12:01 A.M. standard time at the address of the policyholder.

INSURED VEHICLES AND
SCHEDULE OF COVERAGES

VEHICLE COVERAGES	LIMITS OF INSURANCE		PREMIUM
1.　1990 Toyota Tercel	ID #JT2AL21E0B3306553		
Coverage A—Liability	$300,000	Each Occurrence	$102.00
Coverage B—Medical Payments	$ 5,000	Each Person	$ 18.00
Coverage C—Uninsured Motorists	$300,000	Each Occurrence	$ 31.00
		TOTAL	$151.00
2.　1998 Ford Taurus	ID #1FABP3OU8GG212619		
Coverage A—Liability	$300,000	Each Occurrence	$102.00
Coverage B—Medical Payments	$ 5,000	Each Person	$ 18.00
Coverage C—Uninsured Motorists	$300,000	Each Occurrence	$ 31.00
Coverage D—Other Than Collision	Actual Cash Value Less $100		$ 51.00
—Collision	Actual Cash Value Less $250		$136.00
		TOTAL	$338.00
		TOTAL PREMIUM	$489.00

POLICY FORM AND ENDORSEMENTS:　　PP 00 01 PP 03 06

COUNTERSIGNATURE DATE:　　December 1, 1999

AGENT:　　A. M. Abel

Definitions

Since insurance policies often contain technical terms or words that are used in a very specific way, most policies define terms that have a specific meaning with regard to the coverage provided. These definitions might be in a separate section of the policy, or the terms might be defined where they first appear in the policy. If a policy definition differs from normal usage for a term, the definition in the policy prevails. Unless the contract provides specific definitions, the words in insurance policies and other contracts are generally interpreted according to their ordinary meanings or dictionary definitions. If ambiguity exists, the words could be interpreted by the courts.

Insurance policies sometimes distinguish defined terms by placing quotation marks around the terms or by printing them in boldface type each time they appear in the policy. Exhibit 7-2 shows the definitions section of a typical homeowners policy.

Insuring Agreements

An insurance policy contains at least one **insuring agreement**, which is a specific statement regarding the nature of the insurer's promises. For example, the personal auto policy developed by Insurance Services Office (ISO) has one broad insuring agreement, which simply states that "In return for payment of the premium and subject to all the terms of this policy, . . .", the insurer agrees with the insured to the policy provisions. The policy then provides a separate insuring agreement for each of the four coverages provided by the policy: liability, medical payments, uninsured motorists, and coverage for damage to the insured's auto.

An **insuring agreement** in an insurance policy is a statement that the insurer will, under certain circumstances, make a payment or provide a service.

For example, the insuring agreement in the ISO personal auto policy for Part D—Coverage for Damage to Your Auto reads, in part, as follows:

> We will pay for direct and accidental loss to "your covered auto" or any "non-owned auto," including their equipment, minus any applicable deductible shown in the Declarations.

The words in quotation marks in the above insuring agreement are defined in the definitions section of the policy.

Exclusions

The **exclusions** in an insurance policy indicate the exposures the insurer does not cover. While the insuring agreement makes a broad promise to provide coverage, the exclusions eliminate some of the coverage that would otherwise be provided. No insurance policy can reasonably cover *all* possible losses. Insurance policies contain exclusions for several reasons:

Exclusions are policy provisions that eliminate coverage for specified exposures.

Exhibit 7-2
Definitions Section of a Homeowners Policy

DEFINITIONS

In this policy, "you" and "your" refer to the "named insured" shown in the Declarations and the spouse if a resident of the same household. "We," "us" and "our" refer to the Company providing this insurance. In addition, certain words and phrases are defined as follows:

1. "Bodily injury" means bodily harm, sickness or disease, including required care, loss of services and death that results.

2. "Business" includes trade, profession or occupation.

3. "Insured" means you and residents of your household who are:

   a. Your relatives; or

   b. Other persons under the age of 21 and in the care of any person named above.

   Under Section II, "insured" also means:

   c. With respect to animals or watercraft to which this policy applies, any person or organization legally responsible for these animals or watercraft which are owned by you or any person included in **3.a.** or **3.b.** above. A person or organization using or having custody of these animals or watercraft in the course of any "business" or without consent of the owner is not an "insured";

   d. With respect to any vehicle to which this policy applies:

      (1) Persons while engaged in your employ or that of any person included in **3.a.** or **3.b.** above; or

      (2) Other persons using the vehicle on an "insured location" with your consent.

4. "Insured location" means:

   a. The "residence premises";

   b. The part of other premises, other structures and grounds used by you as a residence and:

      (1) Which is shown in the Declarations; or

      (2) Which is acquired by you during the policy period for your use as a residence;

c. Any premises used by you in connection with a premises in **4.a.** and **4.b.** above;

d. Any part of a premises:

   (1) Not owned by an "insured"; and

   (2) Where an "insured" is temporarily residing;

e. Vacant land, other than farm land, owned by or rented to an "insured";

f. Land owned by or rented to an "insured" on which a one or two family dwelling is being built as a residence for an "insured";

g. Individual or family cemetery plots or burial vaults of an "insured"; or

h. Any part of a premises occasionally rented to an "insured" for other than "business" use.

5. "Occurrence" means an accident, including continuous or repeated exposure to substantially the same general harmful conditions, which results, during the policy period, in:

   a. "Bodily injury"; or

   b. "Property damage."

6. "Property damage" means physical injury to, destruction of, or loss of use of tangible property.

7. "Residence employee" means:

   a. An employee of an "insured" whose duties are related to the maintenance or use of the "residence premises," including household or domestic services; or

   b. One who performs similar duties elsewhere not related to the "business" of an "insured."

8. "Residence premises" means:

   a. The one family dwelling, other structures, and grounds; or

   b. That part of any other building;
   where you reside and which is shown as the "residence premises" in the Declarations.

   "Residence premises" also means a two family dwelling where you reside in at least one of the family units and which is shown as the "residence premises" in the Declarations.

- *To avoid covering "uninsurable" losses.* Some losses cannot reasonably be insured by private insurers. For example, war and nuclear losses involve a potential for catastrophic losses that are not economically feasible to insure.

- *To avoid insuring losses that could be prevented.* Some losses are within the control of the insured. For example, many policies exclude coverage for damage intentionally caused by the insured.

- *To eliminate duplicate coverage.* Some losses are best covered by one type of insurance and are thus excluded by other types of policies. For example, most motor vehicle exposures are excluded from homeowners policies because they should be covered under automobile insurance policies.

- *To eliminate coverage that most insureds do not need.* For example, since the average homeowner does not own a private airplane, coverage for destruction of aircraft is not needed by most homeowners and is not provided under the homeowners policy.

- *To eliminate coverage for exposures that require special handling by the insurer.* For example, most commercial property policies exclude coverage for steam boiler explosions because boilers require special inspections and coverage that many insurance companies do not have the expertise to handle.

- *To keep premiums reasonable.* For example, auto insurance policies exclude coverage for mechanical breakdown of the auto. If auto insurers were to provide coverage for all regular maintenance of insured autos, premiums would probably become unreasonable because of the large number of expected losses.

Many exclusions, including those given as examples above, fit into more than one of the above reasons. Any exclusion can serve more than one purpose. To a certain extent, all exclusions fit the last purpose of keeping premiums reasonable. Logically, it would require a higher premium to pay for the additional losses that might be covered whenever a policy is broadened by eliminating an exclusion.

Although exclusions often appear in a separate section or sections labeled "Exclusions," they can also appear in various places throughout the policy. The term "exclusion" can accurately apply to any policy provision whose function is to eliminate coverage for specified loss exposures—whether or not the provision is labeled as an exclusion. For example, in the ISO homeowners policies, exclusions appear in various parts of the policy, labeled in different ways, including:

- "Property Not Covered," which lists specific types of uninsured property

- "Section I—Perils Insured Against," which lists both covered causes of loss and specific causes of loss that are not covered
- "Section I—Exclusions," which specially lists exclusions that apply to covered property

Conditions

Insurance policies contain several conditions relating to the coverage provided. The insured must generally comply with these conditions if coverage is to apply to a loss. Some of the more common conditions included in insurance policies are discussed later in this chapter.

Miscellaneous Provisions

Insurance policies often contain provisions that do not qualify as one of the policy components described above. These miscellaneous provisions sometimes deal with the relationship between the insured and the insurer, or they might help to establish procedures for carrying out the terms of the contract. However, actions by the insured that depart from the procedures in the miscellaneous provisions normally do not affect the insurer's duty to provide coverage.

Some miscellaneous provisions are unique to particular types of insurers. For example, a policy issued by a mutual insurance company is likely to describe the right of each insured to vote in the election of the board of directors.

Educational Objective 6

a. Describe and distinguish between manuscript policies and standard forms.
b. Describe the advantages of standard forms to (1) insurers and (2) insureds.

Manuscript Policies and Standard Forms

A **manuscript policy** is an insurance policy that is specifically drafted according to terms negotiated between a specific insured (or group of insureds) and an insurer.

Although insurance contracts, like all other contracts, represent freely negotiated agreements between the parties, most insurance policies use standard, preprinted forms. The parties do not normally negotiate all the terms of the contract each time someone purchases an insurance policy. Only in a special situation, usually involving a large amount of insurance, might such negotiation happen. When it does, the result is a **manuscript policy**, specifically drafted for the purpose.

As mentioned in Chapter 5, insurance advisory organizations such as Insurance Services Office (ISO) and the American Association of Insurance Services (AAIS) develop industrywide standardized forms for different types of insurance, and many insurers use these *standard forms* for any insured accepted for a particular coverage. Similarly, an insurer might develop its own standard forms that meet the coverage needs of most insureds. A standard policy form has no specific reference to the insured's name, address, policy limits, premiums, and so forth. Instead, the standard form is attached to a declarations page that contains all of the specific information relating to the insured.

The use of standard forms has many advantages for insurers and is an efficient way to provide contracts to thousands of insureds. Not only do standard forms save considerable time and expense in issuing the policy, but they also promote consistency in the insurance company's operations. When a prospective insured applies for a specific insurance policy, the underwriter knows the scope of the coverage provided by that policy, including the applicable restrictions and exclusions. If the underwriter had to develop a manuscript policy for each individual case, underwriting efficiency and consistency would be seriously hampered. With standardized forms, the underwriter can choose from among applicants for the same coverage and can determine appropriate premiums on a consistent basis. Similarly, claim representatives know the extent of coverage provided by standardized forms and can more quickly and easily decide whether the policy covers a particular loss.

Standard policies benefit insureds as well as the insurance companies that use these policies. For example, a person in the process of selecting an insurer does not need to compare differences in policy provisions and language if the various insurers use the same standard form. In addition, if a loss is covered by two or more insurers, the likelihood of claim disputes is reduced if all insurers involved have provided coverage under the same standardized form.

Standardized wording also leads to a more consistent interpretation of insurance policies. When disagreements arise between the insured and the insurer concerning the interpretation of a particular insurance contract, a court ruling might be necessary to determine the appropriate legal interpretation of the contested policy language. If the identical language appears in many other policies of the same type, the insurer knows how the court is likely to interpret this language in the future and can properly underwrite and price the policy based on that interpretation. If the language were constantly changing or were different for each insured, more disputes would occur, and there would be no standard legal interpretation on which the insurer and the insured could rely. Therefore, insurance policies often repeat terms and clauses used elsewhere in the same policy or in different policies to diminish the possibility of a disputed interpretation.

After the policy wording has been drafted by the insurer or advisory organization and approved by state regulators, the insurance company prints thousands of copies of each standardized form. When insurance is purchased, the appropriate preprinted documents are combined with a declarations page to create the policy for that particular insured. The documents can be combined in many different ways to create policies that meet the needs of many different insureds.

Educational Objective 7

Describe and distinguish between a self-contained and a modular policy.

Structure of Insurance Policies

Insurance companies use two approaches to structuring an insurance policy, whether manuscript or standardized. A policy can be either *self-contained* or *modular*.

Self-Contained Policies

A **self-contained policy** is a single document that contains all the agreements between the insurer and the insured and that forms a complete policy by itself.

One example of a **self-contained policy** is the personal auto policy. Probably the most widely used auto insurance policy, this policy includes both property and liability insurance coverage in a single document.

The cover of a personal auto policy might be a multicolor wrapper or "jacket" containing the name and logo of the insurance company. Like the wrappers on most products, the purpose of the cover is to enhance the appearance of the product, to highlight the provider's name, and to protect the contents.

Inside the cover of a personal auto policy is the declarations page. Although the preprinted personal auto policy form is the same for all insureds, the declarations page and any attached endorsements personalize it for a particular insured. As described earlier, the policy contains a broad insuring agreement and separate insuring agreements that relate specifically to the four coverages provided. Exclusions and conditions that relate to each coverage are presented as well. The personal auto policy contains a definitions section that defines certain terms as they are used in the policy. The policy also includes a section that states the duties of the insured after a loss occurs. A separate section called "General Provisions" provides conditions that apply to the policy as a whole.

An **endorsement** is a document that amends an insurance policy in some way. Endorsements might add or delete coverage, include state-specific changes, show a change in the insured's exposures, or otherwise modify the policy.

The personal auto policy, with the declarations page added to the standard form, is a complete contract of insurance. However, it is often modified by the addition of one or more endorsements. An **endorsement** might add coverage—such as coverage for towing and labor on a car that breaks down. An endorsement might modify the policy in some way to conform to the requirements of the state where the insured lives. For example, an endorsement might change the termination provision in the policy by placing some state-specific restrictions on cancellation of the policy by the insurer. An endorsement might also deal with a change in the insured's exposures, such as the purchase of an additional car or the addition of a new driver in the insured's household.

Modular Policies

Modular policies combine coverage forms and other documents to tailor a policy to the insured's needs. Commercial package policies (CPPs), for example, are modular policies.

A **modular policy** consists of several different documents, none of which by itself forms a complete contract.

CPPs can provide many different coverages to businesses and other organizations. Unlike the personal auto policy, which contains four coverages in one form, a CPP combines different forms, depending on the coverages a particular insured purchases. Modular policies contain a combination of coverages, some of which might not be purchased by a given insured. An insured elects coverages by having a limit and premium shown in the declarations and declines other coverages by leaving the limit and premium blank.

The components that can be used to compile a CPP are illustrated in Exhibit 7-3.

All CPPs must contain common policy declarations and common policy conditions. The *common policy declarations* contain information that applies to the entire policy, such as the name and address of the insured, the policy period, and the coverage(s) for which a premium has been or will be paid. The *common policy conditions* are standard provisions that apply to all CPPs, regardless of the coverages included.

The remaining components of a CPP vary, depending on the coverage needed by the insured. In most cases, a separate declarations page is included for each coverage provided in the CPP. As illustrated in Exhibit 7-3, a CPP can be used to provide many types of coverage that a commercial enterprise might need. Unlike a self-contained policy such as the personal auto policy, however, a CPP includes several different documents. For example, if a business owner wanted to purchase property and liability insurance, the CPP would include the following documents:

- Common policy declarations
- Common policy conditions
- Commercial property declarations
- One or more commercial property coverage forms
- Commercial property conditions
- One or more causes of loss forms
- Commercial general liability declarations
- Commercial general liability coverage form

Exhibit 7-3

Components of a Commercial Package Policy

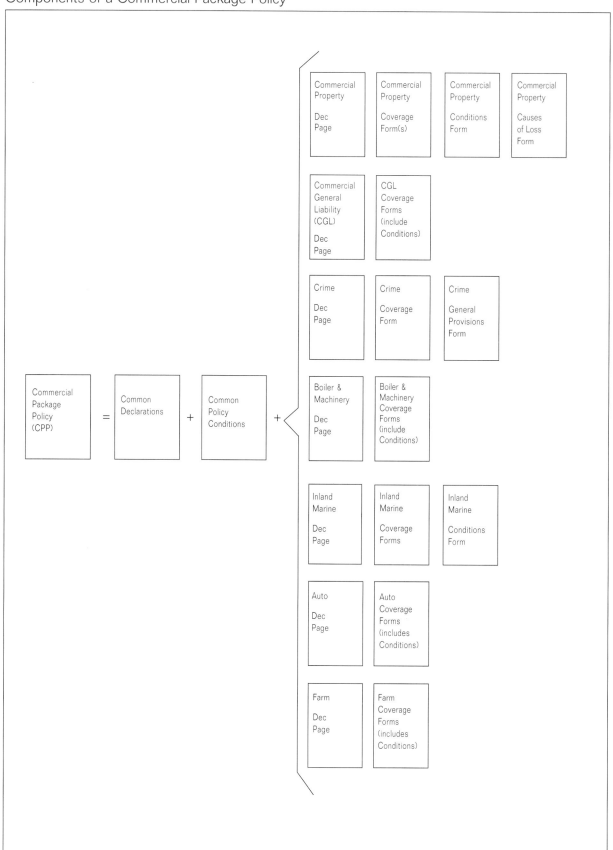

If the business owner wanted other coverages, such as coverage for autos used in the business, additional documents would be added to the CPP. Detailed information about the various CPP documents is provided in INS 23—*Commercial Insurance*.

Educational Objective 8

Describe the conditions commonly found in property and liability insurance policies.

Conditions Commonly Found in Property and Liability Insurance Policies

An insurance policy describes the coverage the insurance company provides and also stipulates the conditions under which the coverage is provided. These conditions provide the rules for the relationship between the insurance company and the insured. Without such rules, insurers would find it difficult to operate efficiently. Some conditions relate to a specific coverage and appear only in policies providing that coverage. Other conditions typically appear in most property and liability insurance policies. Similarly, some conditions appear in both personal and commercial insurance policies, while others are in only one or the other type of policy. Conditions common to most property and liability insurance policies, both personal and commercial, include:

- Cancellation
- Changes
- Duties of the insured after a loss
- Assignment
- Subrogation

The descriptions of policy conditions in this section are based on policies developed by ISO. Policies developed by other advisory organizations, such as AAIS, and by individual insurance companies might have different names for these conditions, or the provisions themselves might differ from those presented here.

Cancellation

Cancellation occurs when either the insurer or the insured terminates a policy during the policy term. The cancellation provision states the procedures that must be followed when cancellation is initiated by the insured or by the insurer. This

Cancellation refers to the termination of a policy, by either the insurer or the insured, during the policy period.

provision also states any limitations on the rights of either party to cancel the policy midterm and explains how any premium refunds will be computed.

Cancellation by the Insured

The insured may usually cancel the policy at any time. To do this, the insured may either:

- Return the policy to the insurer
- Provide the insurer with advance written notice of the date the policy is to be canceled

Written notice obviously eliminates the possibility of a dispute over an oral cancellation request. The reason for requiring advance notice is also fairly obvious. Suppose an insured were permitted to request that an insurance company cancel insurance on a given building as of six months earlier and return the premium for those six months. The insurer would have been obligated to pay a claim if the building had been damaged during that six-month period because there was a policy in force. Now that the time has passed and no loss has occurred, the insurer has a right to keep the premium for that period during which claims would have been paid if they had occurred.

Cancellation by the Insurance Company

The insurance company may also cancel most insurance policies. However, the procedures described in the policy provide the insured with some safeguards, such as a given number of days' written notice before the cancellation takes effect. Many policies also prohibit the insurer from canceling, except for certain stated reasons. State law might require a longer notification period or limit the reasons for which an insurer may cancel. If the law is more favorable to the insured than are the policy provisions, the law prevails.

When a policy is canceled, the insured might be entitled to a refund. If the insurance company cancels the policy, the return premium is calculated on a pro rata basis. Therefore, if the insurer cancels a one-year policy and the cancellation is effective exactly six months after the policy's inception date, the insurer will return to the insured a **pro rata refund** of exactly half the premium.

Some policies state that if the insured requests the cancellation, the premium refund will be less than pro rata. For example, the insurance company might return only 45 percent of the premium on a policy that is canceled at exactly the halfway point of the policy term. This cancellation penalty (also known as a short-rate charge) reflects the fact that the insurer incurred some expense in issuing the policy and will not be able to keep the full premium. The **short-rate refund** also serves to discourage insurance buyers from canceling their insurance before the end of the policy period.

A **pro rata refund** is the unused premium (based on the pro rata portion of the premium for the number of days remaining in the policy) returned to the insured when a policy is canceled.

A pro rata refund of a one-year policy is calculated by dividing the premium by 365 days of the year and multiplying the resulting number by the number of days that would have remained in the policy period. For example, if the one-year policy premium is $365, and the policy is canceled after 200 days, the pro rata refund to the insured would be $165:

($365/365 = $1; $1 × 165 days remaining = $165).

A **short rate refund**, which is sometimes used when the insured cancels a policy midterm, is a refund of premium that is less than the pro rata refund would be. A short rate refund includes a penalty for the insured's cancellation of the policy before the end of the policy period.

Changes

Many policies contain a policy changes provision stating that the written insurance policy contains all the agreements between the insurer and the insured and that the terms of the policy can be changed only by a written endorsement issued by the insurer. Other policies state that changes to the policy are valid if the insurer agrees to the change in writing.

A **liberalization clause** in most policies addresses a different situation. Some insurers revise their policies fairly frequently, perhaps to clarify policy language or to broaden or restrict coverage. If a revision broadens coverage with no additional premium charge to insureds, the liberalization clause makes it clear that the revision automatically applies to all similar policies in force at the time of the revision. The liberalization clause is a benefit to insurers as well as insureds because it precludes the need for such a change to be endorsed on every similar policy already in force.

A **liberalization clause** is a policy condition that provides that if a policy form is broadened at no additional premium, the broadened coverage automatically applies to all existing policies of the same type.

Duties of the Insured After a Loss

If a covered loss is to be paid, the insurer must be informed that the loss occurred. Therefore, under property and liability insurance policies, the insured must immediately notify the insurer of the loss; most policies state that notice be given "promptly" or "as soon as is practical." Insureds are also required to cooperate with the insurer and to perform certain other duties in settling a loss. The type of cooperation and the duties required depend on the type of coverage. For example, property insurance policies generally require that the insured prepare an inventory of damaged and undamaged property and protect the property from further damage. Liability insurance policies usually require that the insured promptly forward all papers regarding a claim or suit to the insurer. Other specific duties of the insured are determined by the type of coverage provided and by the wording of the policy.

Exhibit 7-4 shows the section of the ISO personal auto policy that lists the duties of the insured after an accident or loss.

Assignment

As previously stated, an insurance policy is a personal contract between the insurance company and the insured. Insurance companies select their insureds carefully. The selection process would be bypassed if an insured were permitted to transfer the insurance coverage to some other person. The other person might be someone with whom the insurer would prefer not to do business.

The assignment provision, which is sometimes labeled "Transfer of Your Rights and Duties Under This Policy," makes it clear

Exhibit 7-4
Part E of the ISO Personal Auto Policy: Duties of the Insured After an Accident or Loss

---

PART E—DUTIES AFTER AN ACCIDENT OR LOSS

We have no duty to provide coverage under this policy unless there has been full compliance with the following duties:

A. We must be notified promptly of how, when and where the accident or loss happened. Notice should also include the names and addresses of any injured persons and of any witnesses.

B. A person seeking any coverage must:

1. Cooperate with us in the investigation, settlement or defense of any claim or suit.

2. Promptly send us copies of any notices or legal papers received in connection with the accident or loss.

3. Submit, as often as we reasonably require:

   a. To physical exams by physicians we select. We will pay for these exams.

   b. To examination under oath and subscribe the same.

4. Authorize us to obtain:

   a. Medical reports; and

   b. Other pertinent records.

5. Submit a proof of loss when required by us.

C. A person seeking Uninsured Motorists Coverage must also:

1. Promptly notify the police if a hit-and-run driver is involved.

2. Promptly send us copies of the legal papers if a suit is brought.

D. A person seeking Coverage For Damage to Your Auto must also:

1. Take reasonable steps after loss to protect "your covered auto" or any "non-owned auto" and their equipment from further loss. We will pay reasonable expenses incurred to do this.

2. Promptly notify the police if "your covered auto" or any "non-owned auto" is stolen.

3. Permit us to inspect and appraise the damaged property before its repair or disposal.

Copyright, Insurance Services Office, Inc., 1997 (Form PP 00 01 06 98).

Assignment is the transfer of rights or interest in a policy to another party by the insured. Most policies cannot be assigned without written permission of the insurer.

that **assignment** is not permitted without the written consent of the insurer. For example, a homeowner cannot transfer his or her homeowners policy to a new owner when the house is sold unless the insurer agrees in writing to the transfer, which is seldom the case. Insurers rarely agree to such policy transfers because they want the right to reunderwrite the policy based on the exposures presented by the new owner.

The assignment provision could present a problem when an insured dies, because coverage would cease at the time of death. Property that is now part of the insured's estate could be damaged or destroyed, and liability claims could be brought against the estate. Because of this problem, insurance policies usually state that the rights and responsibilities of an insured who has died pass to the insured's legal representative (such as the executor of an insured's estate).

Educational Objective 9

Explain how subrogation works.

Subrogation

Most property and liability insurance policies contain a *subrogation* provision. This provision is sometimes labeled "Our Right to Recover Payment" or "Transfer of Rights of Recovery Against Others to Us." Insurance practitioners, however, often use the term subrogation even when that word is not used in the policy.

When the insurer pays an insured for a loss, the insurer takes over the insured's right to collect damages from any other person responsible for the loss. The insurer is subrogated to the insured's rights of recovery, and the insurer's process of recovering is called subrogation. In short, subrogation shifts the ultimate cost of a loss to the party responsible for causing the loss.

For example, suppose Michael drives his car too fast for the existing road conditions and slides off the road into Joanne's building. Joanne would have a right to recover damages from Michael. However, Joanne might also file a claim with the insurer providing her property coverage, and her insurer would pay for the damage to her building. After paying the property insurance claim, Joanne's insurer has the right of subrogation against Michael.

In the above example, Joanne has no further rights of recovery if she has been fully indemnified for her loss. If she could *also* recover from Michael, the principle of indemnity would be violated. Joanne's insurer now has any rights of recovery Joanne had before the insurer paid for the loss, including the right to file a claim against Michael. If Michael has liability insurance, his insurance company is obligated to defend him and to pay damages on his behalf.

However, if Joanne has not been fully indemnified, she could recover the portion of her loss that her insurer did not cover. For example, if Joanne had a deductible of $1,000 on her property insurance policy, she could recover the $1,000 from Michael that her insurer deducted from its payment to her. Usually, insurers will help insureds recover deductibles as part of the subrogation process.

Most subrogation provisions require that the insured do nothing *after* a loss to impair the insurer's subrogation rights. Therefore, in the above example, Joanne may not tell Michael, "Don't worry about the damage—you won't have to pay anything because my property insurance will cover it." If Joanne were to

Reminder

As discussed in Chapter 6, *subrogation* is the insurer's right to recover payment from a negligent third party for losses the insurer has paid to an insured. When an insurer pays an insured for a loss, the insurer takes over the insured's right to collect damages from a third party responsible for the loss.

make such a statement, her property insurer could refuse to pay for the loss because Joanne has no authority to waive the insurer's rights.

Some insurance policies, however, permit an insured to waive rights of recovery *before* a loss. For example, in a property lease that states the tenant will not be held responsible for accidental damage to property owned by the insured, the insurer will have no right to recover from the tenant if the tenant accidentally causes a fire that damages the insured's property.

Educational Objective 10

Define or describe each of the Key Words and Phrases for this assignment. (All Key Words and Phrases appear in bold print in the text and in the margins throughout this chapter.)

Summary

When someone buys an insurance policy, the value he or she receives is the insurance company's binding promise to pay for specified kinds of losses. The promise is binding because the policy is a contract that can be enforced in a court of law. To be legally valid, any contract must have certain essential elements:

- It must represent an *agreement* between the parties.
- Each party must be legally *competent* to make the agreement.
- The purpose of the agreement must be *legal*.
- Each party must give some form of *consideration* to the other party.

Although all of the rules of contract law apply to insurance policies, certain special characteristics distinguish insurance policies from other contracts:

- An insurance policy is a *personal contract*.
- An insurance contract is a *conditional contract*.
- The insurance contract involves an *exchange of unequal amounts*.
- The policy is a *contract of utmost good faith*.
- The policy is a *contract of adhesion*.
- Most insurance policies are *contracts of indemnity*.

All insurance policies contain certain components, and the insured should review the provisions in each of these components in order to determine the coverage provided. Most policies include the following:

- The declarations page
- Definitions

- One or more insuring agreements
- Exclusions
- Conditions
- Miscellaneous provisions

In general, insurance policies consist of standard forms to which only the specific details regarding a particular insured must be added. Occasionally, a manuscript policy is drafted according to terms specially negotiated between the insured and the insurer. An insurance policy can be either self-contained or modular. A self-contained policy (such as a personal auto policy) is a single document that, when combined with a declarations page, forms a complete policy. A modular policy (such as a commercial package policy) comprises several different documents, none of which forms a complete contract by itself.

Insurance policies stipulate certain conditions under which the policy is issued. The insured accepts those conditions as part of the transaction. Typical conditions found in most property and liability insurance policies include:

- A cancellation provision
- A policy changes provision
- Duties of the insured after a loss
- A assignment provision
- A subrogation provision

This chapter provides a basis for studying the material in the next two chapters. Those chapters deal with property and liability loss exposures and specific provisions in policies that insure many of those exposures.

Chapter 8

Property Loss Exposures and Policy Provisions

Educational Objectives

After studying this chapter, you should be able to:

1. Describe the types of property that might be exposed to loss and that are typically covered by property insurance. (pp. 8-5 to 8-8)

2. Explain the ways in which causes of loss are treated in various types of property insurance policies. (pp. 8-8 to 8-9)

3. Identify and describe the potential financial consequences of property losses. (pp. 8-10 to 8-12)

4. Identify and describe the parties that might be affected by property losses. (pp. 8-12 to 8-13)

5. Explain how covered property and locations are specified in property insurance policies. (pp. 8-14 to 8-18)

6. Explain how covered causes of loss are typically described in various property insurance policies. (pp. 8-18 to 8-25)

7. Identify and describe the causes of loss that are usually excluded in property insurance policies. (pp. 8-25 to 8-26)

8. Identify and describe the financial consequences of loss that might be covered by property insurance policies. (pp. 8-27 to 8-28)

9. a. Identify the parties that can be covered by property insurance policies. (pp. 8-28 to 8-31)

   b. Explain how property insurance policies provide coverage for various parties. (pp. 8-28 to 8-31)

10. Explain how various policy limits and other provisions affect the amounts of recovery under a property insurance policy. (pp. 8-31 to 8-34)

11. Define or describe each of the Key Words and Phrases for this assignment. (All Key Words and Phrases appear in bold print in the text and in the margins throughout this chapter.)

Chapter 8

Property Loss Exposures and Policy Provisions

Everything seemed normal when Mr. Brown closed the supermarket for the night. Therefore, he was shocked when he was later awakened by a telephone call from someone exclaiming, "Get down to the shopping center. Your store is on fire!"

The fire apparently started in the market's storage area. A problem in an electrical fixture probably caused some sparks that ignited trash in a nearby bin. Paper goods, bags of charcoal, and other combustible materials in the storage area were apparently ablaze long before the fire was visible from outside the building. The fire spread rapidly through the sprawling open spaces of the store. (Exhibit 8-1 shows a fire-gutted supermarket, similar to Mr. Brown's.)

A few months after the fire, Mr. Brown cut the ribbon for the store's grand reopening sale, and it was soon business as usual. Thanks to his property insurance, Mr. Brown was in almost the same financial condition he would have been in had the fire not occurred. The building had been rebuilt, and the food, freezers, and other contents had been replaced. Business income insurance also reimbursed Mr. Brown for the income lost while the store was closed, as well as for the extra expenses he incurred due to the fire.

Exhibit 8-1
Fire-Gutted Supermarket

It was not by chance that Mr. Brown's insurance enabled him to reopen quickly. He had planned ahead. With the help of his insurance agent, he had identified his property loss exposures and made sure that he was insured against the financial consequences of damage from fire and other causes. This was no simple task. Mr. Brown had to identify the various items of property that could be lost or damaged, and he had to determine what could occur to cause loss or damage. In addition, he had to estimate the dollar amount that he could lose. Having done these things well, he was aware of his property loss exposures and had taken steps to properly insure the property.

To help you understand how Mr. Brown was able to successfully handle the consequences of the fire, this chapter explores the various aspects of *property loss exposures* and then describes various policy provisions that cover those exposures.

Reminder

As stated in Chapter 1, a *property loss exposure* is any condition or situation that presents the possibility that a property loss will happen.

Property Loss Exposures

This chapter begins the study of property loss exposures by examining three important aspects of those exposures:

- *Types of property* that might be exposed to loss, damage, or destruction

- *Causes of loss* that might result in property being lost, damaged, or destroyed
- *Financial consequences* that might result from a property loss

In addition to describing the above aspects of property loss exposures, this chapter discusses the parties that might be affected when property is lost, damaged, or destroyed.

Educational Objective 1

Describe the types of property that might be exposed to loss and that are typically covered by property insurance.

Types of Property

Property is any item with value. Individuals, families, and business organizations own and use property, depend on it as a source of income or services, and rely on its value. Property can decline in value—or even become worthless—if it is lost, damaged, or destroyed. Different kinds of property have different qualities that affect the owner's or user's exposure to loss.

Property can be classified in a number of different ways. One common approach is to distinguish between *real property* and *personal property*. Insurance practitioners use categories that relate to the insurance treatment of property, such as:

- Buildings
- Personal property ("contents") contained in buildings
- Money and securities
- Motor vehicles and trailers
- Property in transit
- Ships and their cargo
- Boilers and machinery

These categories overlap to some extent. Consider, for example, money and waterborne cargo. Money is personal property and can therefore be included in the contents of buildings; it can also be property in transit. Cargo on a ship is also a form of property in transit. These categories are listed separately here because they represent types of property for which specific forms of insurance have been developed.

Buildings

Buildings include more than bricks and mortar and other building materials. Most buildings also include plumbing, wiring, and heating and air conditioning equipment, which can lead to leaks, electrical fires, and explosions. Most buildings contain some basic portable equipment—fire extinguishers, snow shovels, lawn mowers, and so forth—required to service the building and surrounding land, and this equipment is

Reminder

Real property consists of land as well as buildings and other structures attached to the land or embedded in it. The term "real estate" is commonly used to refer to real property.

Personal property consists of all tangible or intangible property that is not real property.

considered part of the building. A high-rise building usually has elevators and might have specially designed portable platforms, hoists, and tracks for use by window washers. This equipment is also considered to be part of the building. Property that is permanently attached to the structure, such as wall-to-wall carpeting, built-in appliances, or paneling, is generally considered part of the building as well.

Personal Property (Contents) Contained in Buildings

The contents of a typical home include personal property such as furniture, clothing, televisions, jewelry, paintings, and other personal possessions. The contents of a commercial building might include the following:

- *Furniture and fixtures*, such as the desks in an office or portable shelves in Mr. Brown's store.
- *Machinery and equipment*, such as cash registers in Mr. Brown's supermarket.
- *Stock*, such as the groceries in Mr. Brown's store or the raw materials and completed products in the inventory of a shoe factory. A shoe factory's "stock" includes leather (raw materials), partly finished shoes (goods in process), and shoes (finished goods).

Although most policies use the term "personal property" to refer to the contents of a building, many insurance practitioners and policyholders use the term "contents" as a matter of convenience and common practice. Property insurance policies refer to personal property, rather than contents, because the property is often covered even when it is not literally contained in the building. When the contents of a commercial building are involved, policies generally use the term "business personal property."

Money and Securities

Money means currency, coins, and bank notes. Traveler's checks, credit card slips, and money orders held for sale to the public are also considered money in some cases.

Securities are written instruments representing either money or other property. Stocks and bonds, for example, are securities.

For insurance purposes, **money** and **securities** are classified separately from other types of contents because their characteristics present special problems. Money and securities are highly susceptible to loss by theft. Cash is particularly difficult to trace, since it can be readily spent. In contrast, other types of property must be "fenced," or sold for cash, before the thief can make a profit. Money and securities are also light in weight, easily concealed, and easy to transport.

Besides being susceptible to theft, money and securities are easily destroyed by fire. Unless Mr. Brown made a bank deposit every night when the store closed, he probably lost a considerable amount of currency and checks during the fire in his store.

Motor Vehicles and Trailers

The primary purpose of most vehicles is to move people or property, and this movement exposes vehicles to several causes of loss. It is difficult to classify motor vehicles. No matter what categories are used, some vehicles (such as snowmobiles) fit into more than one category, depending on the purpose for which they are owned and used. To identify property loss exposures, however, it helps to think of the following three broad vehicle categories:

- Autos and other highway vehicles
- Mobile equipment
- Recreational vehicles

In insurance terminology, the meaning of the word **auto** is very broad. It includes vehicles, such as cars, trucks, trailers, and buses, designed for road use and can also include such diverse vehicles as fire engines, ambulances, motorcycles, and camping trailers. **Mobile equipment** such as tractors, bulldozers, road graders, front-end loaders, forklifts, backhoes, and power shovels, might be damaged in a highway collision, but the most frequent exposures to loss involve off-road situations. **Recreational vehicles** include a wide range of vehicles used in a variety of sports and recreational activities. Examples include dune buggies, all-terrain vehicles, and dirt bikes. Most snowmobiles also fall into this category. In some cases, the owners of these recreational vehicles face exposures to loss both on and off the road.

Property in Transit

A great deal of property is transported by truck, but property is also moved in cars, buses, trains, airplanes, and ships. When a conveyance containing cargo overturns or is involved in a collision, the cargo could also be damaged. In addition, cargo might be destroyed without damage to the transporting vehicle. Liquids can leak out of a truck, fragile articles can be tossed around during transit, and heat-sensitive objects can melt or spoil in a conveyance with a defective refrigeration system.

When property is damaged or lost in transit, it must be replaced. Delays often result, since replacement property might have to be shipped from the place where the first shipment originated. The property owner might also incur expense to move the lost or damaged property.

Ships and Their Cargo

Ships and their cargo are exposed to special perils not encountered in other means of transit. For example, ships that operate along coastal waters can run aground, leaving the cargo stranded. Even more than other property, ocean cargoes fluctuate in value according to their location. If the ship cannot reach

In insurance, **auto** is a broad term that includes cars, trucks, buses, and other motorized vehicles designed for use on public roads.

Mobile equipment, which is specifically defined in most commercial insurance policies, includes many types of land vehicles—usually designed for use principally off public roads—including equipment attached to them. Examples include bulldozers, farm machinery, and forklifts.

Recreational vehicles are vehicles used for sports and recreational activities. Examples include dune buggies and all-terrain vehicles.

its intended destination and the cargo must be sold in a different port, the price received for the cargo might be less than the price expected at the original destination.

Boilers and Machinery

Many businesses have objects that can be classified as boilers or machinery. For example, many buildings use steam boilers to provide heat. A steam boiler is a large water tank heated by burning gas, oil, or coal to produce steam. Dry cleaners and laundries invariably have boilers. Public utilities, refineries, and steel mills often use boilers to generate power. Other objects that can be classified as boilers or machinery include unfired pressure vessels, such as air tanks; refrigerating and air conditioning systems; mechanical equipment, such as compressors and turbines; production equipment; and electrical equipment. Machinery such as transformers and other electrical apparatus is found in most factories and power stations. Boilers and machinery share two characteristics:

- They are susceptible to explosion or breakdown that can result in serious financial losses.

- They are less likely to have explosions or breakdowns if they are periodically inspected and properly maintained.

Educational Objective 2

Explain the ways in which causes of loss are treated in various types of property insurance policies.

A **cause of loss** (or **peril**) is the actual means by which property is damaged or destroyed. Examples include fire, lightning, windstorm, hail, and theft.

Named perils are listed and described in the policy. Only losses caused by those listed perils are covered.

Special form coverage (also called **open perils**) provides coverage for "risk of direct loss" to property; in other words, coverage is provided for any direct loss to property unless the loss is caused by a peril specifically excluded by the policy.

Causes of Loss to Property

Most **causes of loss**, or **perils**, adversely affect property and leave it in an altered state. A fire can change a building to a heap of rubble. A collision can change a car to twisted scrap. Some causes of loss do not alter the property itself, but they do affect a person's ability to possess or use the property. For example, when property is lost or stolen, it is still usable, but it is no longer usable by its proper owner.

Many property insurance policies list the covered causes of loss. Such policies are commonly known as **named perils** policies because they "name" or list the covered perils. Usually, these policies also list the causes of loss that are excluded from coverage. Other policies cover all causes of loss except those that are specifically excluded. These policies are known by several different terms, including **open perils** policies; in this text we refer to them as **special form coverage** policies.

Perils and Hazards

The terms "peril" and "hazard" are often confused.

As stated earlier, a *peril* is a cause of loss. Fire, theft, collision, and flood are examples of perils that cause property losses. (Many property insurance policies use the term "cause of loss" instead of "peril." This text uses these terms interchangeably.)

As explained in Chapter 5, a *hazard* is anything that increases the likelihood of a loss or the possible severity of a loss. Examples include the following:

- Careless smoking practices are a fire hazard because they increase the likelihood of a fire.
- Paint cans and oily rags are fire hazards because they enable a fire to spread and cause severe damage.
- Keeping large amounts of money in a cash register overnight is a theft hazard affecting both the likelihood of loss and the severity of loss. This practice would attract thieves if they became aware of it. The amount that would be stolen—the severity of the loss—is also affected by the amount of cash in the register.

Burden of Proof

An important difference between named perils and special form ("all-risks") coverage involves the burden of proof.

- With a named perils policy, for coverage to apply, the insured must prove that the loss was caused by a *covered* cause of loss.
- With a special form coverage policy, if a loss to covered property occurs, it is initially assumed that coverage applies. However, coverage may be denied if the *insurer* can prove that the loss was caused by an *excluded* cause of loss.

In the first case, the burden of proof is on the insured; in the second, it is on the insurer.

By shifting the burden of proof, special form coverage can provide an important advantage to the insured who suffers a property loss by an unknown cause. For example, suppose that after a flood strikes the community, the insured's wrought-iron patio furniture is missing. Assume also that the patio furniture is clearly covered property. It is possible that the furniture was swept away in the flood, but it is also possible that the furniture was stolen following the flood. If a named perils policy covered theft but not flood, the *insured* would have to prove that the property had been stolen. Under a special form coverage policy, the insurer would have to pay the claim (even if the policy excluded flood losses) unless the *insurer* could prove that the property was swept away in the flood.

Jargon Alert!

"All-risks" is a term used by many insurance professionals to indicate policies that cover all causes of loss that are not specifically excluded. This term was used in previous editions of property insurance policies, and many insurance practitioners continue to use it for the sake of simplicity. However, this term is misleading because the policies do not cover *all* risks of loss; some exclusions always apply. For this reason, the term is not used in current policy forms. Therefore, insurance professionals should avoid the term "all-risks" when talking to customers and others who might misunderstand its meaning. A better term to describe "all-risks" policies is "special form coverage" or "open perils" (meaning that perils are left "open" rather than being "named" in the policy). Other terms used to describe the coverage provided by "all-risks" policies are "risk of direct loss," "risks of direct physical loss," and "accidental direct physical loss," all subject to policy exclusions.

Educational Objective 3

Identify and describe the potential financial consequences of property losses.

Potential Financial Consequences of Property Losses

The loss of or damage to property can have undesirable financial consequences. The adverse financial effects of a property loss might occur in one or more ways:

- Reduction in the value of the property
- Lost income
- Increased expenses

Reduction in Value of Property

When a property loss occurs, the property is reduced in value. The reduction in value can be measured in different ways, sometimes with differing results. If the property can be repaired or restored, the reduction in value can be measured by the cost of the repair or restoration. Property that must be replaced has no remaining worth, unless some salvageable items can be sold as junk. Consider the following examples:

- A fence worth $5,000 is damaged by a car, and the owner of the fence will have to pay $1,000 to have the damage repaired. The accident—a *partial loss*—has reduced the value of the fence by $1,000.
- A camera worth $200 was run over by a truck. The value of the now worthless camera has been reduced by $200. The camera is a *total loss*.

If an item is lost, is stolen, or otherwise disappears, its value *to the owner* is reduced just as though it had been destroyed and retained no salvage value.

A further reduction in value might occur if repaired property is worth less than it would be if it had never been damaged. This is true for items such as fine paintings and other art objects. Many collectibles are valuable largely because they are in "mint condition" or "original condition." An object that has been repaired after damage from a tear, scratch, or fire is no longer in that unspoiled condition, and its value will decline. The owner faces loss in the form of the cost to repair the object, as well as a further reduction in value because of the altered condition.

Property might have a few different "values," depending on the method by which the value is determined. As discussed in Chapter 6, the most common valuation measures used in insurance policies are *replacement cost* and *actual cash value*

Reminder

Replacement cost is the cost to repair or replace property using new materials of like kind and quality with no deduction for depreciation.

Actual cash value (ACV) is the replacement cost of property minus depreciation.

Depreciation is an allowance for wear and tear, or technological or economic obsolescence.

(ACV). In certain situations, however, other valuation measures (such as *agreed value*) are used.

Lost Income

When property is damaged, income might be lost because the income-producing capacity of the property is reduced or terminated until the property is repaired, restored, or replaced. Mr. Brown temporarily lost the income from his store because the building and contents were damaged by fire.

Determining the amount of business income that might be lost due to a property loss requires estimating the future level of activity of an organization and doing a "what if" analysis: "What if the business could not operate for six months because it would take six months to rebuild after a fire? How much income would be lost?" This analysis involves projections of the organization's revenues and expenses in normal circumstances to determine the amount of income that would be lost in the event of a property loss that disrupts normal operations. The comparison of projected revenues and expenses reveals the potential loss of income.

The owner of rental property faces a similar situation because rental income would be lost if the property were damaged and temporarily could not be rented. The owner would probably continue to incur some expenses, such as mortgage payments and taxes, but would not receive the rent that helped to pay those expenses.

Increased Expenses

When property is damaged, the property itself declines in value, and the owner or other affected party suffers a corresponding loss. In addition, the owner or other user of that property might incur increased expenses in acquiring a temporary substitute or in temporarily maintaining the property in usable condition. Consider the following examples:

- A family whose house is damaged might have to live in a hotel temporarily at considerably greater expense than living at home.
- When a newspaper's printing presses are damaged, it might spend extra money to have the newspaper printed on another newspaper company's presses.
- When a car is damaged in a collision, the owner might need to rent a temporary substitute auto until the damage has been repaired.
- If a bank building is damaged, the bank might have to hire additional guards until the building can be made secure.

Because so many variables are involved, it is difficult to estimate the extra expenses that might be required to stay in business

Reminder

Agreed value is a method of valuing property in which the insurer and the insured agree on the value of the property at the time the policy is written, and that amount is stated in the policy declarations and is the amount the insurer will pay in the event of a total loss to the property.

following damage to business property or to keep a family together and maintain its standard of living after a home is damaged. Determining the extent of a property loss exposure involves considering the extra expenses required in the event of the loss of property.

Educational Objective 4

Identify and describe the parties that might be affected by property losses.

Parties Affected by Property Losses

Parties that might be affected by a property loss include the following:

- The property owner
- Secured lenders of money to the property owner
- Users of the property
- Other holders of the property

The Property Owner

The party most affected when property is lost, damaged, or destroyed is usually the owner of the property. If property has some value and is lost, damaged, or destroyed, the owner of the property incurs a financial loss because of the cost of repairing or replacing the property. In the earlier example, Mr. Brown incurred a considerable financial loss because he had to rebuild his store and restock the shelves.

Secured Lenders

A **mortgagee** (or **mortgage holder**) is a lender that loans money on a home, building, or other real property.

A **mortgagor** is the person or organization that borrows money from a mortgagee to finance the purchase of real property.

When money is borrowed to finance the purchase of a car, the lender usually acquires some conditional rights to the car, such as the right to repossess the car if the car's owner (the borrower) fails to make loan payments. This right gives the lender security. Such a lender is therefore called a secured lender or a secured creditor. When a person or business borrows money to buy a home or a building and the property serves as security for the loan, the secured lender is called a **mortgagee** (or **mortgage holder**), and the borrower is a **mortgagor**.

When property is used to secure a loan, both the property owner and the lender are exposed to loss. If, for example, Mr. Brown had a mortgage on his supermarket building, the mortgagee would lose the security for the mortgage loan when the building burned. Similarly, if a financed car is destroyed in an accident and the owner has no money to repay the loan, there would be no car for the lender to repossess. Property insurance policies generally protect the secured lender's interest in the financed property by naming the lender on the insurance policy and by giving the lender certain rights under the policy.

Users of Property

Some events result in losses to users of the damaged property, even though the users do not own the property. Consider the following example: Fish Store's twenty-year lease, signed eight years ago, specifies a rental rate much lower than the cost to rent similar space today. If the building is destroyed, the lease will be canceled, and Fish Store will probably have to pay higher rent, either for the rebuilt building or another location.

Other Holders of Property

Some parties are responsible for the safekeeping of property they do not own. Dry cleaners, TV repair shops, common carriers, and many other businesses temporarily hold property belonging to others. Holders of property entrusted to them by others are called **bailees**.

A **bailee** is a person or business that holds the property of others for some specific purpose.

For example, assume that Mr. Brown's supermarket offered a film-processing service. He would be the bailee of the rolls of film his customers left for developing. In estimating his property loss exposures, Mr. Brown would have to consider not only the property he owned, but also the property (such as film) that he held for others.

Property Insurance Policy Provisions

Property insurance policies must specify exactly which property loss exposures are covered—that is, the types and locations of property, causes of loss, and financial consequences that are covered. Policies must also state what parties are covered and how the value of insured property will be determined.

Property insurance is any type of insurance that indemnifies an insured who suffers a financial loss because property has been lost, stolen, damaged, or destroyed.

This section examines characteristics common to policies that provide property insurance. Property insurance includes many different types of coverages, including those coverages that are classified as "boiler and machinery," "auto physical damage," and "crime" insurance. Property insurance is sometimes written alone and sometimes as a part of a policy that also provides liability coverage. In this chapter, the discussion focuses on illustrating certain principles rather than on the content of specific policies. (For those who are interested in specific policy details, INS 22—*Personal Insurance* discusses personal insurance policies, and INS 23—*Commercial Insurance* discusses commercial insurance policies.)

> **Educational Objective 5**
>
> Explain how covered property and locations are specified in property insurance policies.

Covered Property and Locations

An insurance policy must carefully specify the property that is covered and where the property is covered. For example, a typical auto insurance policy covers collision damage to an auto described in the declarations, provided the collision occurs in the United States, its territories and possessions, Puerto Rico, or Canada.

Many types of property insurance are designed primarily to cover buildings and personal property. The identification of a covered building is generally not a problem because its location is fixed. However, stating the location of covered property might not be as simple as it seems. One challenge lies in describing *precisely* what is and is not covered under an insurance policy that provides building coverage. Another challenge lies in the fact that buildings and personal property do not necessarily remain at a fixed location. Portions of a building might be removed from the premises for repair or storage. For example, screen windows might be removed from the building and placed in storage during the winter while storm windows are being used. Furniture might be found not only inside buildings but also on outdoor patios and decks. Items usually kept in a building might be temporarily located in a car or truck.

Floaters are policies that are designed to cover property that "floats," or moves from location to location.

Other types of property insurance policies are designed to cover personal property that often moves from place to place. Such policies are called **floaters** because they provide coverage that "floats," or moves, with the property as it changes location. Examples of policies that cover movable personal property are floaters that cover jewelry, furs, cameras, and other types of property owned by individuals and families; transportation policies that cover property transported on trucks or other conveyances; and contractors equipment floaters that cover earthmovers and other construction equipment. Policies covering movable property might have territorial limits, or they might provide coverage anywhere in the world.

Dwellings, Buildings, and Other Structures

A property insurance policy generally stipulates that the policy covers only the building or buildings at the specific location listed in the declarations. The policy also defines exactly what items qualify as part of the building and are therefore covered by insurance.

Dwellings and Other Structures

In personal insurance, a residential structure is generally called a dwelling and is usually covered under a homeowners or dwelling policy. A typical policy on a dwelling covers the "residence premises," which is defined as the location shown in the policy declarations. Usually, the policy definition of residence premises also includes structures attached to the dwelling and materials and supplies located on or next to the dwelling used to construct, alter, or repair the dwelling or other structures on the premises. The coverage for a residence premises does not apply to land.

"Structures attached to the dwelling" include an attached garage or carport. A free-standing, detached garage is not part of the dwelling. A separate insuring agreement for "other structures" covers such detached items. What difference does it make whether a garage is part of the dwelling or qualifies as an "other structure," since it seems to be covered either way? The answer is that different policy limits (dollar amounts of insurance) apply for the dwelling and for other structures. When determining how much insurance the insured should purchase to adequately insure real property—and how much the insurer must pay when a claim occurs—it is necessary to know whether the garage is considered part of the dwelling or a separate structure.

Buildings and Other Structures

In commercial insurance, a permanent structure with walls and a roof is usually called a building. Other outdoor structures, such as carports, antenna towers, and swimming pools, might not be buildings, but they also need insurance coverage.

A typical commercial property policy covers the building or structure described in the declarations. The policy definition of "building" might include additions that are either completed or under construction as well as materials and supplies used for constructing the additions.

Permanently installed fixtures, machinery, and equipment are also included as part of the building. Thus, items such as a pipe organ in a church or equipment installed in a manufacturing plant would be considered part of the insured building.

The building coverage of a commercial property policy also includes some items that might seem to be personal property, such as fire extinguishing equipment, outdoor furniture, wall-to-wall carpeting, and refrigerators.

Personal Property

Although buildings and personal property can be insured in the same policy, they are treated as separate coverage items. When a building sustains damage by fire or some other peril, the personal property in that building is often damaged. Likewise, a fire that starts in a wastebasket, for example, is likely to spread and damage the building. Therefore, it is not surprising that buildings and personal property are often covered in the same policy.

On the other hand, because personal property can be moved more easily than buildings, it is exposed to additional perils, such as theft. In addition, property such as valuable papers, computer programs, accounts receivable records, fine arts, stamp collections, money, and securities give rise to loss exposures that require special handling.

Dwelling Personal Property

The personal property coverage of a homeowners policy typically covers personal property owned or used by an insured while it is anywhere in the world. The homeowners insuring agreement for personal property is a very broad statement of coverage, but such broad coverage is restricted by a number of *exclusions* and *limitations*.

Exclusions and Limitations

Exclusions and limitations are not the same thing. While *exclusions* eliminate all coverage for excluded property or causes of loss, *limitations* place a specific dollar limit on specific property that is covered. Consider these examples:

- Commercial property insurance policies usually contain *exclusions* for money. A business needing insurance on money should buy an appropriate crime insurance policy or endorsement for the amount exposed to loss.

- Homeowners policies usually have a *limitation* for money of $200 or some other relatively small amount. Homeowners who need coverage for larger amounts of cash might be able to increase the limitation by purchasing an endorsement to the homeowners policy.

Business Personal Property

As stated, commercial property insurance policies usually refer to the contents of buildings as "business personal property," which includes personal property of the insured located in or on the building described in the declarations. Business personal property also includes personal property in the open (or in a vehicle) within 100 feet of the described premises.

Regarding locations where coverage applies, the usual 100-foot limitation in commercial policies is obviously narrower than the worldwide coverage of most homeowners policies. Commercial property policies often include an additional coverage (known as a "coverage extension") that provides a certain limit, such as

$10,000, of coverage for property off-premises; this extension, however, applies only to losses that occur in the specified policy territory.

Further definitions in commercial property policies make it clear that coverage for business personal property applies to such items as furniture, machinery and equipment that is not part of the building, and stock.

Property Other Than the Insured's Buildings and Contents

Property insurance policies usually clarify coverage by listing "property not covered." Policies that cover buildings and personal property typically show autos in such a listing because autos are more appropriately covered under auto insurance policies. Some policies exclude money and securities because these items should be insured under crime insurance policies.

Autos

The declarations page of an auto insurance policy, either personal or commercial, describes the specific autos that are covered, including the vehicle identification number (serial number) unique to each vehicle. The declarations also state where each vehicle is normally kept (or "garaged") because this information is necessary to establish the proper premium. However, the location where coverage applies is not limited to the garage but includes anywhere in the specified coverage territory.

Most auto insurance policies do not cover personal property while transported in autos, but some provide a minimal amount of coverage for "personal effects." Such personal property owned by individuals or families can be covered by homeowners policies. When businesses need coverage, business personal property in transit can be covered by a transportation policy.

Nonowned Property

As noted previously, property insurance policies often provide coverage for property that is owned by someone other than the insured. Homeowners policies provide coverage for the personal property of others, such as guests or residence employees, while the property is in the insured's home. Commercial property policies generally extend a limited amount of coverage to the personal effects of officers, partners, and employees as well as to the personal property of others while it is in the care, custody, or control of the insured. The personal auto policy provides coverage for damage to a borrowed auto if the owner of the borrowed auto does not have physical damage coverage.

Movable Property

As mentioned, some property insurance policies cover personal property that does not remain at a fixed location. For example, homeowners policies cover personal property of the insured while it is anywhere in the world. Auto insurance policies provide coverage while the insured auto is in the United States, its territories and possessions, Puerto Rico, or Canada. Commercial property insurance policies are more restrictive; they provide coverage for the insured's business personal property while it is in the insured building or within 100 feet of the building. Commercial policies also provide limited coverage for property away from the insured premises under certain circumstances. Many floaters provide coverage for movable property anywhere in the world.

Educational Objective 6

Explain how covered causes of loss are typically described in various property insurance policies.

Covered Causes of Loss

The causes of loss examined in this section are commonly covered by property insurance policies and create the majority of property losses. In named perils policies, these causes of loss are specifically listed and defined. In special form coverage policies, the causes of loss are not specifically listed because they are covered unless excluded.

Most property insurance policies today cover many causes of loss, which was not always the case. Property insurance policies once covered only fire losses. Over time, however, policies evolved and expanded, and most now cover many different perils in addition to fire. The various types of crime losses, such as burglary and robbery, are covered by crime insurance policies as well as by some package policies; losses from earthquake and flood can be covered by special types of policies or endorsements.

Most property insurance policies group several causes of loss and offer coverage for them in one policy form. Insureds can obtain the coverage they need by selecting among the forms covering various causes of loss.

Personal and commercial property insurance policies on buildings and personal property are available with three different degrees of coverage:

1. *Basic form coverage*—the lowest-cost version that provides coverage for approximately a dozen named perils.
2. *Broad form coverage*—a higher-cost version of coverage that adds several perils to those covered by basic coverage.
3. *Special form (open perils) coverage*—the version that covers all causes of loss that are not specifically excluded. Special form coverage covers all the perils of broad form coverage, as well as other perils.

Most homeowners policies currently in use provide either broad or special form coverage. Homeowners policies providing basic form coverage are not available in most states.

Basic Form Coverage

Property insurance policies define many causes of loss in some detail. The precise definitions vary by policy. The causes of loss discussed below are generally included in policies, both personal and commercial, that provide basic form coverage.

Fire and Lightning

Fire is one of the most serious causes of loss, but not every fire causes a loss. A gas fire in a kitchen oven, an oil fire in a furnace, and a wood fire in a fireplace serve a specific purpose and cause no loss—unless they blaze out of control.

The term **friendly fire** refers to fires that remain in their intended places. Such fires are generally *not* covered by property insurance policies. A fire that leaves its intended place is called a **hostile fire** and *is* generally covered by property insurance. If a person's wig accidentally fell into a fireplace and was burned, many property insurance policies would not cover the loss because the fire did not leave its intended place. However, if sparks flying from the fireplace set the house on fire, a hostile fire would have occurred and the damage would be covered.

A **friendly fire** is a fire that stays in its intended place. For example, a fire in a fireplace is a friendly fire as long as it remains contained in the fireplace.

A **hostile fire** is a fire that leaves its intended place. For example, if a spark escapes the fireplace and sets the carpet on fire, the fire becomes a hostile fire.

Some fires ensue from another peril. Lightning might strike a house and set it on fire. It is standard practice that policies covering fire also cover loss caused by lightning.

In property policies, "damage caused by fire" includes damage resulting from those conditions accompanying the fire (such as heat and smoke) and those events that can be linked to the fire in an unbroken chain of causation (such as collapse resulting from the fire or water damage caused by firefighters). When these conditions occur because of a fire, the fire is considered the **proximate cause** of the entire loss. It does not matter that the fire itself was caused by some other peril, such as an earthquake. If property insurance covers loss from fire but not from earthquake, damage from *fire* would be covered even if the fire resulted directly from the earthquake. The insurance policy would cover the portion of the loss caused by fire but not the portion caused exclusively by earthquake.

The proximate cause of a loss is the event that sets in motion an uninterrupted chain of events contributing to the loss. For example, if property is damaged by firefighters spraying water to control a fire, the proximate cause of the water damage is the fire.

Windstorm

Like fire, windstorm can cause serious damage to buildings and their contents, as well as to other property. Windstorm includes hurricanes and tornadoes but is not confined to those disturbances. Less severe winds can also cause damage.

Water damage due to flood, waves, or spray sometimes accompanies a windstorm. Many insurance policies cover windstorm damage but not water damage, unless wind causes an opening in the structure through which water enters. When a loss occurs, it is not always easy to determine which damage was done by wind and which by water. Exhibit 8-2 shows coastal property destroyed by a hurricane.

Exhibit 8-2
Coastal Property Destroyed by Hurricane

Hail

Hail consists of ice particles created by freezing atmospheric conditions. Hailstones the size of marbles, golfballs, or baseballs can cause substantial damage to autos, buildings, and other property in the open. Aluminum siding and metal roofs are susceptible to "dimpling" caused by hail. Light hail that is not capable of damaging most property can cause serious crop damage by knocking kernels out of standing grain or by destroying blossoms on fruit trees, for example.

Aircraft

Aircraft damage occurs when all or part of an airplane or satellite strikes property on the ground. Although such incidents are rare, the damage can be severe. For example, if debris from an airplane crash damages Anita's home, Anita could collect from her homeowners insurer for the damage to her house. (Her homeowners insurer could then subrogate against the airline and thus attempt to recover its payment to Anita.)

Vehicle Damage

Vehicle damage refers to damage caused by a motor vehicle to some other kind of property, such as a building. When a car runs into a house, the house suffers vehicle damage and the car suffers collision damage. The homeowner could submit a claim for the vehicle damage to his or her homeowners insurer, and the insurer could in turn subrogate against the driver for the claim paid under the homeowners policy.

Riot and Civil Commotion

While legal distinctions might exist between riot and civil commotion, both terms refer to approximately the same kind of unruly mob behavior, and insurance covering riot invariably covers civil commotion. Although losses from these perils do not occur very often, they can be quite large. For example, insured losses from the 1992 riots in Los Angeles totaled almost $800 million.

Explosion

An explosion is a violent expansion or bursting accompanied by noise. Explosions include combustion explosions resulting from the ignition of gases, dust, or other explosive materials; combustion explosions are often followed by fire. Explosions can also occur when a pressurized object bursts, such as when a tank containing compressed air bursts. An explosion can destroy an entire building, as illustrated in Exhibit 8-3.

Vehicle damage is damage done by a motor vehicle to some other kind of property.

Exhibit 8-3
Building Destroyed by Explosion

Smoke

The sudden or accidental release of large amounts of smoke can result in considerable damage to walls and other objects. When damaging smoke comes from a fire, the fire is generally considered to be the proximate cause of the loss. However, the sudden malfunction of an oil-burning furnace might result in the discharge of clouds of grimy, sooty smoke. In that case, the resulting damage is not caused by fire but by a peril independent of fire. Property insurance policies that cover loss from fire almost always include smoke as a covered cause of loss as well. However, coverage for smoke damage does not include smoke produced by many industrial operations.

Some property is particularly susceptible to smoke damage. In a clothing or grocery store, a relatively small amount of smoke can cause considerable damage. Clothes must be cleaned to remove the smell and might be permanently stained. Foods such as fresh vegetables might be a total loss. Other property—such as a stack of plumbing pipes—might be essentially undamaged by a large volume of smoke.

Vandalism

Vandalism is willful and malicious damage to or destruction of property.

Vandalism losses are not accidental; they are intentionally caused, usually by an unknown person or persons. However, since they are not intentionally caused *by the insured*, they can be covered in insurance policies. Examples of vandalism include graffiti spray painted onto building walls, defacement of statues or other objects of art, and the multiple incidents of mischief that often occur on Halloween. Some insurance policies refer to "vandalism and malicious mischief"; others simply use the term "vandalism." The meaning is the same in either case.

Sprinkler Leakage

Sprinkler leakage is the accidental leakage or discharge of water or other substance from an automatic sprinkler system.

Many commercial and institutional buildings, as well as some private residences, are equipped with automatic sprinkler systems. An automatic sprinkler system is designed to discharge water (or a chemical or gas) when a fire occurs, thus extinguishing or containing the fire. When a fire sets off a sprinkler, the fire is considered the proximate cause of any water damage from the operation of the sprinkler. However, sometimes an automatic sprinkler system discharges accidentally. The system's pipes can freeze and burst, or a buildup of heat from some cause other than fire can cause the system to discharge. Maintenance workers might accidentally bang a ladder against a sprinkler head and cause it to discharge. The peril of **sprinkler leakage** includes such accidental discharges. Compared to fire, sprinkler leakage in most cases is not a serious threat to a building. The vulnerability of a building's contents could be another matter, however. With some occupancies, such as dealers in paper products, sprinkler leakage losses can be devastating.

Sinkhole Collapse and Mine Subsidence

The action of underground water on limestone or similar rock formations can create empty spaces underground. A **sinkhole collapse** occurs when land suddenly sinks or collapses into one of these empty spaces, as illustrated in Exhibit 8-4. This problem occurs most often in Florida, but other states are also susceptible to sinkhole losses.

A similar problem exists in states such as Pennsylvania and West Virginia because of underground mining. The **mine subsidence** peril is present when the ground surface sinks as underground open spaces, caused by mining operations, are gradually filled in by rock and earth from above.

Volcanic Action

Losses caused by **volcanic action** occur primarily in the Pacific coastal states, Alaska, and Hawaii. Volcanic action encompasses loss resulting from the eruption of a volcano, such as Mount St. Helens in 1980 and Kilauea and Redoubt in 1992.

Many property insurance policies used to specifically exclude losses caused by volcanic eruption. However, since there were no volcanoes considered active in the continental United States, specific reference to volcanoes began to disappear from insurance policies as they were revised and simplified. When Mount St. Helens erupted in 1980, many policies did not

Sinkhole collapse is a cause of loss involving damage by the sudden sinking or collapse of land into underground empty spaces created by the action of water on limestone or dolomite.

Mine subsidence is a cause of loss involving the sinking of ground surface when underground open spaces, resulting from the extraction of coal or other minerals, are gradually filled in by rock and earth from above.

Volcanic action is a cause of loss by lava flow, ash, dust, particulate matter, airborne volcanic blast, or airborne shock waves resulting from a volcanic eruption.

Exhibit 8-4
Sinkhole Collapse

specifically provide or exclude coverage for volcanic action but did cover the peril of "explosion." There was considerable debate over whether a volcanic eruption constitutes an explosion. Insureds, seeing explosion as a covered cause of loss and noting no policy definition of the term, requested coverage for damage from the eruption. The outcome was that many losses were treated as explosion losses, and claims were paid. Now, most property insurance policies specifically include coverage for volcanic action, but some specifically exclude such coverage.

Broad Form Coverage

While property insurance policies that cover basic form causes of loss cover the perils discussed above, other property insurance policies add coverage against additional causes of loss that are commonly referred to as "broad form coverage" or "broad form perils":

- Breakage of glass—Glass can break as a result of causes other than basic causes of loss.
- Falling objects—Trees or other objects might fall onto a building.
- Weight of snow, ice, or sleet—The weight of accumulations of any of these might damage or destroy buildings and their contents.
- Sudden and accidental water damage—Sudden leaks might, for example, damage carpets, floors, or ceilings.

Collapse

Although collapse is usually not listed as either a basic or a broad form peril, many property insurance policies provide an additional coverage for loss or damage involving collapse of all or part of a building, but only if the collapse is caused by one or more of the basic or broad causes of loss described above. Other covered causes of collapse are hidden decay; hidden damage by insects or vermin; weight of people or contents; weight of rain that collects on a roof; and use of defective material or methods in construction, remodeling, or renovation if the collapse occurs during the construction, remodeling, or renovation.

Crime Perils

Coverage for various crime perils can be included in insurance policies. The definitions of these causes of loss as used in crime insurance might differ somewhat from the usual definitions of these terms. For example, **burglary** is a type of crime committed by someone who breaks into a building and illegally removes property. The definition of burglary in insurance policies also includes breaking *out* of a building because thieves might hide inside a building before it is closed for the night and make a forcible exit after stealing some of the contents. **Robbery** is a type of theft committed by someone who takes property from a

Burglary is the taking of property from inside a building by someone who unlawfully enters or exits the building.

Robbery is the taking of property from a person by someone who has caused or threatened to cause the person harm.

Theft is a broad term that means any act of stealing; theft includes burglary and robbery.

A break-in is a burglary; a purse snatching or a holdup is a robbery; and both are thefts.

person in the presence of that person through use of intimidation or force. **Theft** is a general term meaning any act of stealing. It includes robbery, burglary, and other forms of stealing. Some insurance policies cover the peril of theft, but others cover only a specific type of theft, such as burglary or robbery.

Auto Physical Damage

Insurance policies that provide auto physical damage coverage (property coverage for autos) offer the following types of coverage:

- **Collision**
- **Other than collision** (also called **comprehensive**)
- **Specified causes of loss** (used primarily in commercial auto policies)

Like other property, cars and trucks are subject to fire, theft, vandalism, and other perils. However, the most serious cause of loss to autos is collision. Insurance against collision costs considerably more than insurance against all other perils combined. Collision coverage is not included with either of the other coverages and must be purchased as a separate coverage.

Educational Objective 7

Identify and describe the causes of loss that are usually excluded in property insurance policies.

Causes of Loss Often Excluded

Discussion to this point has focused on causes of loss covered by most property insurance policies. Numerous other perils can also cause loss to property but are usually excluded from insurance policies.

Catastrophe Perils

Insurance functions best when many insureds pay relatively small premiums in order to provide a fund for paying large losses incurred by relatively few insureds. Some perils that affect a great many people at the same time are generally considered to be uninsurable by insurance companies, since the resulting losses would be so widespread that the funds of the entire insurance business might be inadequate to pay all of the claims.

For this reason, almost all property insurance policies exclude coverage for losses from catastrophes such as war and nuclear reaction. However, there are policies that provide so-called war risks coverage on oceangoing vessels and cargo. Insurance against losses to property from nuclear reaction is available for nuclear power plants and transporters of nuclear materials. Most property insurance policies also exclude property losses resulting

Collision covers damage to an insured motor vehicle caused by its impact with another vehicle or object or by its upset or overturn.

Other than collision (or **comprehensive**) covers losses to a covered auto by fire, theft, vandalism, falling objects, flood, and various other perils. Other than collision is a type of open perils ("all-risks") coverage because it covers any "direct and accidental loss" that is not caused by collision and is not specifically excluded.

Specified causes of loss is a less expensive alternative to comprehensive coverage in commercial auto policies. This coverage is a named perils coverage that covers loss to a covered vehicle caused by fire, lightning, theft, windstorm, hail, earthquake, flood, vandalism, and other specifically listed perils.

Reminder

As discussed in Chapter 7, insurance policies contain exclusions for several reasons:

- To avoid covering "uninsurable" losses
- To avoid insuring losses that could be prevented
- To eliminate duplicate coverage
- To eliminate coverage that most insureds do not need
- To eliminate coverage for exposures that require special handling by the insurer
- To keep premiums reasonable

from governmental action, such as governmental seizure of property.

Most policies providing coverage on buildings and personal property at fixed locations exclude coverage for earthquake and flood losses. An earthquake can be a catastrophe affecting many different properties in the same geographic area at the same time. Also, the extent of earthquake damage depends in part on the type of construction of the property. A building that is susceptible to fire damage might be less susceptible to earthquake damage, and vice versa. For these and other reasons, insurers prefer to handle earthquake coverage separately, making a specific decision on how to handle each application for insurance.

Flood damage can also be catastrophic. However, floods are much more predictable than earthquakes. For property in low-lying areas near rivers, creeks, or streams, the question is not whether floods will occur, but when. Insurance companies are generally not willing to provide coverage for a loss that is certain to occur. However, flood insurance on buildings and personal property is available through the National Flood Insurance Program sponsored by the federal government. Auto insurance policies and other policies covering movable personal property generally include coverage against flood losses.

Maintenance Perils

Property insurance policies also typically exclude loss from wear and tear, inherent vice, latent defect, and other "maintenance perils." Such losses are generally uninsurable because they either are certain to occur, over time, or are avoidable through regular maintenance and care. Maintenance perils that are excluded from most policies include:

- Wear and tear
- Marring and scratching
- Rust
- Gradual seepage of water
- Damage by insects, birds, rodents, or other animals

These maintenance perils are usually not covered even in the broadest property insurance policies. As stated in Chapter 1, insurance works well only for definite and accidental losses. Some of these excluded perils (wear and tear, marring and scratching, or rust) involve the results of ordinary use and aging rather than unexpected damage. Damage from the other perils (water seepage, insects, or rodents) is preventable through proper care and maintenance.

Educational Objective 8

Identify and describe the financial consequences of loss that might be covered by property insurance policies.

Covered Financial Consequences

As stated, property losses can lead to any or all of the following financial consequences:

- Reduction in the value of the property
- Lost income
- Extra expenses

Property insurance policies must specify which financial consequences of a property loss are covered and which are not.

Reduction in Property Value (Direct Loss)

A reduction in the value of property is often referred to as **direct loss**. The loss occurs directly and often immediately when a covered cause of loss affects covered property. It costs money to replace or restore a home, a commercial building, or the personal property in either to its pre-loss condition. If the property is not restored, it is not worth as much after the loss as before.

Direct loss is a reduction in the value of property that results directly and often immediately from damage to that property.

Time Element (Indirect) Loss

Discussion to this point has described insurance that covers the reduction in value of property that has been damaged or destroyed. However, lost income and increased expenses can also be insured.

The insurance coverages that apply to loss of income and increased expenses are often called **time element loss** coverages. The longer the property is unusable, the greater the time element loss. If a building cannot be occupied for six months, the financial loss for the insured is much more severe than if the building cannot be occupied for only a few days. Sometimes the term **indirect loss** is used to distinguish the effect of the loss on future income and expenses from the direct property loss, but that term is not as precise as "time element loss," which indicates that the extent of loss is directly related to the passage of time. Time element losses include lost income, extra expenses, or both.

Time element loss (or **indirect loss**) includes loss of income or extra expenses resulting from direct loss to property. This type of loss is called "time element" because it takes place over days, weeks, months, or even years following a direct loss.

Lost Income

Business income insurance protects a business from income lost because of a covered direct loss to its building or personal property. Covered business income includes the organization's net profit (income minus expenses) that *would have been earned* if the insured property had not been damaged. It also includes the operating expenses that continue while the business is interrupted. By replacing lost profits and reimbursing expenses, business income insurance can put the business in the same financial position it would have experienced if no direct loss had occurred.

Coverage for loss of income is also provided by homeowners policies. When a covered cause of loss damages the part of the residence that the insured rents, or holds for rental, to others, "fair rental value" coverage in the homeowners policy indemnifies the insured for the loss of rental income while the rented portion of the residence undergoes repair.

Extra Expenses

Extra expenses are expenses that reduce the length of a business interruption or enable a business to continue some operations when the property has been damaged by a covered cause of loss.

Additional living expense is a coverage in homeowners policies that indemnifies the insured for the *additional* expenses that are incurred following a covered property loss so that the household can maintain its normal standard of living while the dwelling is uninhabitable.

With regard to business income losses, **extra expenses** include additional expenses that reduce the length of the business interruption or enable a business to continue some operations despite damage to its property. For example, Iris Arnold, an insurance agent, might rent office space to conduct her business at a temporary location during the repairs to her office building following a fire. Ms. Arnold's rental expense would be covered as an extra expense, as would as any extra expenses (over and above her normal expenses) such as installing telephone service and notifying her clients of the temporary location.

The **additional living expense** coverage in homeowners and other policies covering dwellings is also an example of extra expense coverage. If a direct loss to the dwelling makes the dwelling uninhabitable, this coverage indemnifies the insured for the *additional* expenses that are incurred so that the household can maintain its normal standard of living while the dwelling is being restored.

Another example of coverage for extra expenses is the optional rental reimbursement coverage available by endorsement to personal auto policies. This coverage pays up to a certain amount per day toward the cost of renting a substitute vehicle because the covered auto has been damaged by collision or some other covered cause of loss.

Educational Objective 9

a. Identify the parties that can be covered by property insurance policies.

b. Explain how property insurance policies provide coverage for various parties.

Parties Covered by Property Insurance

Although a property insurance policy reflects an agreement between the insurance company and the insured, the insured is not always the only party who can recover in the event of an insured loss. Depending on the policy terms and conditions, property insurance can protect the insured and sometimes other parties that have an insurable interest in the property and that suffer a financial loss because covered property is lost, damaged, or destroyed.

As mentioned, persons or organizations with an insurable interest in property can include property owners, secured lenders, users of property, and other holders of property. How do property insurance policies handle these various interests? Generally, policies are written to cover these interests as follows:

- The owner of a building is the named insured on a property insurance policy covering the building.
- A party that owns and occupies a building is the named insured on a policy covering both building and personal property.
- The tenant of a building is the named insured on a property insurance policy covering the tenant's personal property in that building.
- A secured lender, although usually *not* a named insured, is listed by name in the declarations (or in an endorsement) as a mortgagee or a loss payee.
- A bailee, such as Warehouse, Inc., is the named insured on a bailee policy.

Named Insured(s)

The declarations page of a policy has a space labeled **named insured(s)**. Only parties whose names appear *in that space* (or on an attached endorsement listing "additional named insureds") are, in fact, named insureds. In personal insurance, the named insured's spouse usually receives the same coverage as the named insured, even if the spouse is not named on the declarations page. Coverage for the spouse of a named insured depends on the policy definition of "named insured" and generally requires that the spouse live in the same household as the named insured. For example, a homeowners policy states:

> In this policy, "you" and "your" refer to the "named insured" shown in the Declarations and the spouse if a resident of the same household.

Therefore, if Larry Maple's name is the only name that appears on the declarations page of his homeowners policy as a "named insured," the policy also provides coverage for his wife, Mary, who lives in the house with Larry. The wording in the pre-printed portion of the policy, following the declarations page, does not refer to them as "Larry" and "Mary" but uses the word "you" (or "your") to include both Larry and Mary.

The **named insured** is the policy-holder whose name(s) appears on the declarations page of an insurance policy.

The **first named insured** is the person or organization whose name appears *first* as the named insured on a commercial insurance policy and who, depending on the policy conditions, might be the one responsible for paying premiums and the one who has the right to receive any return premiums, to cancel the policy, and to receive the notice of cancellation or nonrenewal.

The situation is somewhat different with commercial insurance. For one thing, several different individuals and business organizations may be listed as named insureds. Do all receive the same protection? Which one of these named insureds should the insurance company deal with? Commercial insurance policies often resolve these issues by stating that the **first named insured** is, in effect, the contact person. The first named insured is responsible for paying premiums and has the right to receive any return premiums and to cancel the policy. If the insurance company decides to cancel or not renew a policy, the first named insured receives the notice of cancellation or nonrenewal.

Secured Lenders

Although secured lenders are generally not named insureds on insurance policies covering property for which they have loaned money, the insurable interests of such lenders are protected when they are listed in the policy.

Mortgagee or Mortgage Holder

Until the loan is paid in full, the lender has an insurable interest in the property because destruction of the property could cause a financial loss to the lender. To protect its interest in real property, a lender usually requires the borrower to purchase property insurance covering the building and to have the lender listed by name as mortgagee on the policy's declarations page.

The **mortgage clause** (or **mortgage holders clause**) of a property insurance policy protects the insurable interest of the mortgagee by giving it certain rights, such as the right to be named on claim drafts for losses to insured property and the right to be notified of policy cancellation.

The mortgagee has the following rights under the **mortgage clause** (or **mortgage holders clause**) of the building owner's insurance policy:

1. The insurer promises to pay covered claims to both the named insured and the mortgagee as their interests appear (that is, to the extent of each party's insurable interest).
2. The insurer promises to notify the mortgagee before any policy cancellation or nonrenewal. This notice enables the mortgagee to replace the policy with other insurance.
3. If the insurer cancels the policy and neglects to inform the mortgagee, the mortgagee's interest is still protected, even if the named insured no longer has coverage.
4. So that the policy will remain in effect, the mortgagee has the right to pay the premium to the insurer if the insured fails to pay the premium.
5. In case of loss, the mortgagee may file a claim if the insured does not.
6. If a claim is denied because the insured did not comply with the terms of the policy, the mortgagee may still collect under the policy.

Loss Payee

While a mortgage clause is used in a policy covering *real property*, a **loss payable clause** is used when a secured lender has an insurable interest in *personal property*. The secured lender is listed as a **loss payee**. A loss payable clause provides that a loss will be paid to both the insured and the loss payee as their interests appear. In addition, a loss payee is entitled to the same advance notice of cancellation as is the named insured. Therefore, to the extent of its insurable interest, a loss payee has the right to participate in the recovery whenever any covered claim entitles the insured to payment. However, a loss payee does not have any right to recover in cases where the insured cannot recover. In this regard, a loss payee does not have the same level of protection that a mortgagee has.

A **loss payee** is a lender, named on an insurance policy, who has loaned money on personal property, such as a car.

A **loss payable clause** provides that a loss will be paid to both the insured and the loss payee as their interests appear and gives the loss payee certain rights. However, a loss payable clause does not extend as many rights to the lender as does a mortgage clause.

Other Parties Whose Property Is Covered

Many property insurance policies provide coverage to parties who are neither named insureds nor secured lenders. The following examples illustrate this point:

- A homeowners policy can provide coverage for property owned by relatives and other persons under the age of twenty-one who reside in the named insured's household.

- A homeowners policy can provide coverage for property belonging to guests, residence employees, and others while it is in the named insured's home.

- A commercial property policy providing coverage on the named insured's personal property can also provide limited coverage for (1) the personal effects of officers, partners, or employees and (2) personal property of others in the care, custody, or control of the insured.

- A personal auto policy can provide coverage for collision damage if the named insured borrows a car belonging to somebody else, the car sustains collision damage, and the owner of the borrowed car has no insurance.

The typical property policy provides that property of others is covered only if the named insured requests that the insurer cover a loss. In the above examples, the other parties do not enter into the insurance contract with the insurer, and they have no specific rights to collect under someone else's policy. However, the named insured can request that the insurer pay claims of this type.

Educational Objective 10

Explain how various policy limits and other provisions affect the amounts of recovery under a property insurance policy.

Amounts of Recovery

When covered property is damaged by a covered cause of loss, how much will an insurer pay to a covered party with an insurable interest? That question must be clearly addressed in any insurance policy providing property coverage. The answer depends on policy provisions in the following categories:

- Policy limits
- Valuation provisions
- Settlement options
- Deductibles
- Insurance-to-value provisions
- "Other insurance" provisions

Policy Limits

When buying property insurance, the applicant usually requests a certain dollar amount of coverage. If the insurer agrees to provide that amount of coverage, the policy limit is established and the applicable policy limit is entered in the policy declarations. If a policy provides more than one coverage, different limits are shown for each coverage.

A policy limit plays several roles. It tells the insured the *maximum* amount of money that can be recovered from the insurance company after a loss. By comparing the policy limit to the value that might be lost, the insured can determine whether the amount of insurance is adequate.

The policy limit tells the insurer the maximum amount it may have to pay for a covered loss. This limit is important, because insurance companies must keep track of their overall obligations in any one geographic area. Otherwise, a fire or windstorm that affected several insured properties on, for example, one city block could have an unexpected effect on the insurer who relied on a spread of risk.

The policy limit is important to both the insurer and the insured for another reason. For most property insurance coverages, the premium charged is directly related to the policy limit.

Valuation Provisions

Several approaches may be used to set a value on a single item. As previously discussed, the two most common valuation approaches in property insurance policies are *replacement cost* and *actual cash value*. A third approach, used for certain types of property, involves *agreed value*.

Settlement Options

The presence of valuation provisions might create the impression that all insured losses are paid in money. Actually, property insurance policies usually give the insurer the choice of different ways to settle a loss.

The insurer generally has the option of:

1. Paying the value (as determined by the valuation provision) of the lost or damaged property
2. Paying the cost to repair or replace the property (if repair or replacement is possible)
3. Repairing, rebuilding, or replacing the property with other property of like kind and quality

These options for settling property losses can often reduce the insurer's costs of settling claims without diminishing the insured's actual indemnification. For example, the insurer might choose the second option and pay the cost to repair a partially burned garage if the cost of repair is less than an appraiser's estimate of the garage's decrease in value as a result of the fire.

The third option would allow an insurance company to replace a stolen watch, for example, with one of the same kind. An insurer might exercise that option because it is able to obtain the watch at a wholesale price that is less than the retail value of the watch.

Deductibles

Property insurance policies usually contain a **deductible** provision, which states that a portion of every insured loss will be subtracted (deducted) from the amount the insurer would otherwise pay. Property insurance deductibles serve several functions. Because the insured bears a part of any loss, deductibles encourage the insured to try to prevent losses. Shifting the cost of small claims to the insured also enables the insurer to reduce premiums. Handling claims for small amounts often costs more than the dollar amount of the claim. Thus, deductibles enable people to purchase coverage *for serious losses* at a reasonable price without unnecessarily involving the insurer in small losses.

> A **deductible** is a portion of a covered loss that is not paid by the insurer. The deductible is subtracted from the amount the insurer would otherwise be obligated to pay the insured.

Insurance-to-Value Provisions

Many property insurance policies include **insurance-to-value provisions**, which encourage insureds to purchase an amount of insurance that is equal to, or close to, the value of the covered property. Few losses are total. Unless all insureds purchase an amount of insurance close to the full value of their property, some insureds will pay considerably less for what provides, in most cases, the same recovery for a loss.

> **Insurance-to-value provisions** are provisions in property insurance policies that encourage insureds to purchase an amount of insurance that is equal to, or close to, the value of the covered property.

Assume, for example, that Jane and Jack both own buildings worth $100,000. Jane insures her building for $100,000, but Jack believes that the largest amount of loss he will suffer is $25,000 and insures his building for that amount. If their policies do not contain insurance-to-value provisions and each building suffers $25,000 damage, Jane and Jack will each receive $25,000 from their insurers to pay for the damage. However, because Jane's policy limit is four times higher than Jack's, her premium was considerably higher. Jack took a chance that his loss would be no more than $25,000 (a fairly safe assumption in most cases) and paid much less for his coverage. This result is not only unfair to policyholders, but it could also result in the insurance company receiving inadequate premiums to cover losses.

Insurers could solve this problem by charging a higher rate for those insureds who insure to less than the property's value. That solution is complicated, however (although it is used in some rare cases). Consequently, insurance companies have encouraged their insureds to buy "insurance to value" or to insure to a high percentage of the property's value. The traditional approach to encouraging insurance to value is to include a **coinsurance** provision in the policy. Insurers also offer alternatives to coinsurance, although their goal is still to have property insured to its full value.

Coinsurance is an insurance-to-value provision in many property insurance policies. If the property is underinsured, the coinsurance provision reduces the amount that an insurer will pay for a covered loss.

"Other Insurance" Provisions

In some cases, more than one insurance policy provides coverage for the same item of property. If two or more insurance companies paid in full for the same loss, the insured could profit from the loss, violating the principle of indemnity. Most policies contain an "other insurance" provision to deal with this problem. Several approaches are possible. The applicable approach depends on the wording of the particular policy and on the situation.

Educational Objective 11

Define or describe each of the Key Words and Phrases for this assignment. (All Key Words and Phrases appear in bold print in the text and in the margins throughout this chapter.)

Summary

This chapter begins by exploring various aspects of property loss exposures, with emphasis on the major types of property exposed to loss, potential causes of loss, and financial consequences that might result from a property loss, as well as parties that might be affected by a property loss.

Types of property discussed include:

- Buildings
- Personal property ("contents") contained in buildings

- Money and securities
- Motor vehicles and trailers
- Property in transit
- Ships and their cargo
- Boilers and machinery

These categories are useful for insurance purposes because they emphasize the characteristics that affect property loss exposures.

Causes of loss, or perils, that can damage or destroy property are sometimes listed in insurance policies, called "named perils" policies. Other policies, called "special form coverage" or "open perils" policies, provide coverage for any direct loss to property unless the loss is covered by a peril that is specifically excluded by the policy.

The financial consequences of a property loss can include:

- A reduction in the value of the property
- Lost income because the property cannot be used
- Increased expenses

Property can be valued in several different ways. The two valuation approaches most commonly used in property insurance policies are replacement cost and actual cash value. In certain situations, other valuation approaches (such as agreed value) are used.

Parties in addition to the property owner might be affected by a property loss. These parties include secured lenders, users of property, and other holders of property.

After exploring property loss exposures, this chapter discusses property insurance policy provisions that clarify which property loss exposures are covered. These provisions specify the specific property and locations covered, the causes of loss covered and those excluded, the financial consequences covered, and the parties covered.

Several factors can affect the amount of recovery in the event of a loss. Policy limits stipulate the maximum amount the insurance company will pay in the event of a loss. Policy valuation provisions explain how the amount of a loss payment will be determined, that is, according to replacement cost, actual cash value, or some other valuation method. Settlement options give the insurer a choice of several ways to settle a loss. Property insurance policies often specify a deductible to be subtracted from the amount of the loss payment. Some policies also include an insurance-to-value provision that encourages insureds to purchase insurance equal or close to the value of the property. When more than one policy covers a loss, the amount paid by each policy depends on the allocation procedure specified in the "other insurance" provisions of the policies.

Chapter 9

Liability Loss Exposures and Policy Provisions

Educational Objectives

After studying this chapter, you should be able to:

1. Distinguish among the following: (pp. 9-5 to 9-6)

    a. Constitutional law

    b. Statutory law

    c. Common law

2. Distinguish between criminal law and civil law. (pp. 9-6 to 9-8)

3. Explain how each of the following can create the legal basis for a claim by one party against another for damages: (pp. 9-8 to 9-14)

    a. Torts

    b. Contracts

    c. Statutes

4. Identify and describe the four elements of negligence. (pp. 9-9 to 9-10)

5. Describe the potential financial consequences of liability loss exposures. (pp. 9-14 to 9-15)

6. Identify and describe activities and situations that create liability loss exposures. (pp. 9-15 to 9-18)

7. Identify and describe the parties that might be insured by a liability insurance policy. (pp. 9-19 to 9-20)

8. Identify and describe the various types of injury or damage that are typically covered in liability insurance policies. (pp. 9-21 to 9-23)

9. Describe the costs typically covered in liability insurance policies. (pp. 9-23 to 9-27)

10. Demonstrate an understanding of the difference between occurrence basis and claims-made coverage. (pp. 9-27 to 9-29)

11. Explain how claim payments are affected by various limits and provisions in liability insurance policies. (pp. 9-29 to 9-31)

12. Define or describe each of the Key Words and Phrases for this assignment. (All Key Words and Phrases appear in bold print in the text and in the margins throughout this chapter.)

Chapter 9

Liability Loss Exposures and Policy Provisions

The day seemed like any other at the Alpha Insulation Company (AIC). Trucks entered and left the plant, and the chemical processing operations ran at 100 percent of capacity to keep up with demand. The only unusual event in the day's schedule was a tour by chemical engineering students who were impressed by the plant's efficiency.

However, disaster struck at 11:08 A.M. when the No. 2 storage tank exploded. Minor explosions had occurred before but had done little damage. Things turned out differently this time.

Apparently the No. 2 storage tank had been filled beyond its listed capacity, leaving inadequate space for expansion as the temperature of the contents increased. A pressure relief device failed to function, and the tank wall finally popped at a seam, causing the contents of the tank to spread into the plant yard. A large amount of the contents went into a drain leading to a nearby river. Some of the fluid flowed into one of AIC's buildings, where a furnace ignited the fluid. The fire spread quickly and burned for two days. Fumes from the fire injured 150 of AIC's employees, killed 15 other employees, and injured 10 of the visiting engineering students. Six more employees were injured in an auto accident as they attempted to escape from the fire and fumes. The accident injured three occupants in another vehicle and caused $5,000 damage to that car.

Reminder

As discussed in Chapter 1, a *liability loss* is a claim for monetary damages because of injury caused by a person or organization to another party or because of damage done to another party's property.

A *liability loss exposure* is any condition or situation that presents the possibility that a liability loss will happen.

The neighborhoods around the plant had to be evacuated, and some businesses near the plant were closed for two weeks. Over the next six months, a series of customer complaints and claims led AIC to conclude that the spillage and fire had caused impurities in its products from several production runs.

In addition to the losses that AIC suffered to its own property because of the explosion and ensuing fire, AIC could suffer devastating financial consequences because of the harm suffered by others. AIC could be legally liable to a number of persons and businesses, and it could suffer large *liability losses* as a result of the explosion and ensuing fire. This chapter explores *liability loss exposures*, based on the concept of legal liability, and the insurance policy provisions that deal with those exposures.

Liability Loss Exposures

In the AIC case, various liability loss exposures led to an occurrence that will inevitably result in claims for monetary damages. These claims arise from AIC's legal obligations to those people and organizations that were injured or suffered property damage caused by the explosion and its aftermath. The explosion at the AIC plant could lead to at least one court case, which might last for many months or even years. If the court rules against AIC and the ruling is upheld despite any appeals made by AIC's attorneys, the company will have no choice but to pay the amount stipulated by the court. AIC's liability losses might not be as obvious on the day after the explosion as its property losses, but the financial consequences of AIC's legal liability could be much greater than the financial consequences of its property losses.

Legal Liability

Legal liability means that a person or organization is legally responsible, or liable, for injury or damage suffered by another person or organization.

An understanding of **legal liability** is essential to recognizing liability loss exposures. Although complex legal questions require the professional expertise of an attorney, knowledge of some fundamental legal terms and concepts is essential for anyone dealing with liability loss exposures or liability insurance.

Laws exist in a civilized society to enforce certain standards of conduct. Although laws generally make the world safer and more secure, they also impose certain duties. Where there are rights, there are also responsibilities. People must accept the constraints of the law in order to enjoy its benefits. The law accomplishes its objectives by holding people responsible for their actions.

Educational Objective 1

Distinguish among the following:

a. Constitutional law

b. Statutory law

c. Common law

Sources of Law

The legal system in the United States derives essentially from the following:

- The Constitution, which is the source of *constitutional law*
- Legislative bodies, which is the source of *statutory law*
- Court decisions, which is the source of *common law*

Constitutional Law

The supreme law in the United States is the Constitution, which specifies the structure of the federal government and outlines the respective powers of the legislative, executive, and judicial branches of the government. The Constitution provides for a federal system of government in which powers not specifically granted to the federal government are reserved for the individual states. With its amendments, the Constitution also guarantees to all citizens certain fundamental rights, such as freedom of speech, freedom of religion, freedom from unreasonable searches and seizures, the right to a trial by jury, and the right to due process of law.

All other laws must conform to **constitutional law**. The courts interpret the Constitution to decide constitutional issues. If the U.S. Supreme Court decides that a particular law conflicts with the Constitution, that law is invalidated. The Supreme Court is the highest court of appeal, and lower courts must follow the Supreme Court's decision in judging future cases involving the same issue.

Constitutional law consists of the Constitution itself and all the decisions of the Supreme Court that involve the Constitution.

Each of the states also has a constitution establishing the powers of the state government. Each state has some type of supreme court to resolve legal conflicts in the state government and to hear appeals on matters of state law. States must ultimately follow the Constitution of the United States.

Statutory Law

Legislatures at national, state, and local levels enact laws, or statutes, to deal with perceived general problems. At the national level, Congress considers many proposed new laws each year. Any member of the U.S. Senate or House of Representatives may introduce a bill. After its introduction, a bill may be referred to a committee for study or perhaps for hearings before it is debated on the floor of the Senate or the House. If

Statutory law consists of the formal laws, or statutes, enacted by federal, state, or local legislative bodies.

the bill receives a majority vote in both the Senate and the House and the President signs it, the bill becomes law. State legislatures also make new laws in similar fashion. Laws made by local governments are often called ordinances. Collectively, these formal enactments of legislative bodies are referred to as **statutory law**.

Numerous federal, state, and local government agencies have regulatory powers derived from authority granted by legislative bodies. Examples of such agencies include the Federal Trade Commission, the Environmental Protection Agency, state public utility commissions, and local zoning boards. These regulatory bodies issue detailed rules and regulations covering a particular public concern or relating to a particular industry. They also render decisions on the application of these rules and regulations in certain cases.

Common Law

Common law, or **case law**, consists of a body of principles and rules established over time by courts on a case-by-case basis.

In contrast to statutory law, common law has evolved in the courts. When the king's judges began hearing disputes in medieval England, they had little basis for their decisions except common sense and the prevailing notions of justice. Each decision, however, became a precedent for similar cases in the future. Gradually, certain principles evolved that the judges applied consistently to all the cases they heard. These principles became known as **common law**, or **case law**.

These common law principles guided judges not only in England but also in the English colonies in America. Thus, the English common law heavily influenced the American legal system. When neither constitutional nor statutory law applies, judges still rely on precedents of previous cases in reaching their decisions. In many areas, laws have been passed that modify or replace common law principles, but common law is still important in matters of legal liability.

Educational Objective 2

Distinguish between criminal law and civil law.

Criminal Law Versus Civil Law

An important distinction exists in the U.S. legal system between criminal law and civil law. While criminal law cases generally receive more headlines, legal cases related to insurance usually involve civil law.

Criminal Law

Criminal law is the category of law that applies to wrongful acts that society deems so harmful to the public welfare that government takes the responsibility for prosecuting and punishing the wrongdoers.

Certain kinds of conduct so endanger the public welfare that society, through its legislative bodies, makes laws to prohibit them and to punish those who engage in such conduct. To cite only a few examples, **criminal laws** prohibit murder, rape, robbery, arson, fraud, theft, and driving while intoxicated. Such offenses are crimes (wrongs against society).

Crimes are punishable by fines, imprisonment, or, in some states, even death. The government uses its power to punish in order to enforce criminal laws. When a crime occurs, the police investigate and, if sufficient evidence is found, criminal charges are brought on behalf of the state against the accused wrongdoer. For example, if Jesse James were arrested for robbing the City Bank of Sedalia, the case would go to court as "The State versus Jesse James." The district attorney presenting the evidence against Jesse James would represent society as a whole, not just the City Bank of Sedalia. If the jury were to find Jesse James guilty of the bank robbery, he would probably go to jail. Such a punishment is meant to protect the public, to punish Jesse, and to deter other people from committing the same crime.

Civil Law

Actions that are not necessarily crimes can still cause considerable harm to other people. In the absence of laws, a dispute between neighbors can turn into a never-ending feud. **Civil law** proceedings provide a forum for hearing disputes between private parties and rendering a decision binding on all parties. This procedure enables individuals to protect themselves against infringement of their rights by others.

Civil law is the category of law that deals with the rights and responsibilities of citizens with respect to one another. Civil law applies to legal matters not governed by criminal law.

Civil law protects personal and property rights. If someone invades the privacy or property of another person or harms another's reputation, the injured person may seek amends in court. By protecting such personal and property rights, civil law contributes to the welfare and safety of society.

Civil law also protects contract rights. People and businesses are more willing to make agreements or contracts with one another when they know that those contracts are enforceable. If two parties make a contract that one party does not honor, the other party can ask the court to compel adherence to the contract or to assess damages. **Contract law** promotes commerce by making contracts more reliable.

Contract law is the branch of civil law that deals with contracts and settles contract disputes.

Criminal and Civil Consequences of the Same Act

Criminal and civil law do not necessarily deal with entirely different matters. A particular act can often have both criminal and civil law consequences. Consider, for example, the following two incidents in the life of Karen Smith.

Because she is an executive who travels frequently, Karen usually has large amounts of cash in her purse. Once when she was walking down the street, a stranger grabbed her purse and ran off. The police later found the stranger. He still had Karen's purse, but the money was gone. The stranger was arrested, tried, and convicted of the crime of robbery. Karen might also have started civil law proceedings against the robber to recover her money, but that would have accomplished little since the robber had no money and was going to jail.

Another time Karen put her purse on the conveyor belt for an airport security check and then retrieved it on the other side of the X-ray machine. When she stopped to buy coffee on her way to the plane, she discovered that the money was missing from her purse. Since Karen suspected that one of the guards had taken the money from her purse, she called the police. Although the police investigated, they did not find the missing money, nor was there sufficient evidence to bring criminal charges against any of the guards. However, Karen did bring a civil suit against the airport authority that employed the guards, and the court ordered the airport authority to repay the money Karen had lost.

In each incident, someone apparently took money from Karen's purse; and in each incident, both criminal and civil law proceedings could have resulted. The differing circumstances influenced the practical effectiveness of each type of legal action.

Elements of a Liability Loss Exposure

A liability loss exposure involves the possibility of one party becoming legally responsible for injury or harm to another party. This section examines the following elements of a liability loss exposure:

- The legal basis of a claim by one party against another for damages
- The financial consequences that might occur from a liability loss

---

Educational Objective 3

Explain how each of the following can create the legal basis for a claim by one party against another for damages:

- Torts
- Contracts
- Statutes

Legal Basis of a Liability Claim

For an injured party to have a right of recovery from another party, some principle of law must create a link between the two parties. This link can appear in tort law, in contract law, or in statutory law. Any law or legal principle that establishes a relationship between the two parties can be the basis for a claim of liability, but this discussion is confined to the most common types of recovery. Exhibit 9-1 illustrates the different aspects of civil law that can give an injured party the legal basis for recovering damages from another party.

Exhibit 9-1
Legal Basis of a Liability Claim

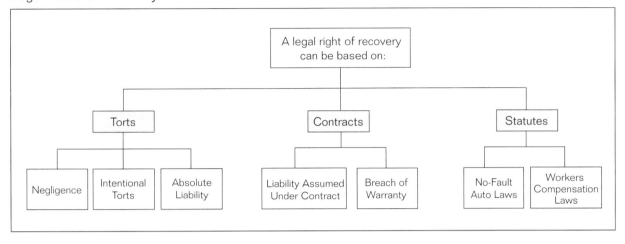

Torts

A **tort** is any wrongful act other than a crime or breach of contract. Crimes differ from torts, because criminal law allows the state to prosecute and civil law does not. The central concern of **tort law** is determining responsibility for injury or damage. Although largely modified or restated in statutes, tort law is still based mainly on common law.

Regardless of how much sympathy might be felt for the victim of an injury, the victim can be compensated by someone legally responsible for the injury only if there is some standard for assigning that responsibility. Under tort law, an individual or organization can face a claim for legal liability on the basis of any of the following:

- Negligence
- Intentional torts
- Absolute liability

Exhibit 9-2 presents a summary of the types of torts that might give rise to a liability loss.

Educational Objective 4

Identify and describe the four elements of negligence.

Negligence   The greatest number of liability cases arise from negligence. **Negligence** occurs when a person or other entity fails to exercise the appropriate degree of care. It usually in-

A **tort** is a wrongful act, other than a crime or breach of contract, committed by one party against another.

Tort law is the branch of civil law that deals with civil wrongs other than breaches of contract.

Negligence is failure to act in a manner that is reasonably prudent. Negligence occurs when a person or organization fails to exercise the appropriate degree of care under given circumstances.

volves acting differently from the way a reasonably prudent person would act under similar circumstances. Tort law gives injured parties the right to seek compensation if they can demonstrate that someone else's negligence led to their injuries.

Exhibit 9-2
Types of Torts

Negligence (Failure to act in a prudent manner)	Intentional Torts (Deliberate acts that cause harm)	Absolute Liability (Inherently dangerous activities)
Elements:	Examples:	Examples:
Duty owed to another	Assault	Owning a wild animal
Breach of that duty	Battery	Blasting operations
Injury or damage	Libel	
Unbroken chain of events from breach of duty to injury or damage	Slander	
	False arrest	
	Invasion of privacy	

A liability judgment based on negligence depends on the following four elements:

1. *A duty owed to another.* The first element of negligence is that a person or organization must have a duty to act (or not to act) that constitutes a responsibility to another party. For example, the driver of an automobile has a duty to operate the car safely. In the AIC case, AIC had a duty to provide safe conditions at its plant.

2. *A breach of that duty.* In order for a person or organization to be held negligent, a breach of the duty owed to another party must occur. A breach of duty is the failure to exercise a reasonable degree of care expected in a particular situation. In AIC's case, the fact that a storage tank had been filled beyond its listed capacity could indicate that AIC had failed to act reasonably and had breached its duty to provide safe conditions. However, if no breach of duty can be proved, no negligence can be found.

3. *Injury or damage.* The third element of negligence requires that the claimant must suffer definite injury or harm. Although a legal duty to act and a breach of that duty may exist, no recovery can be made based on negligence unless someone suffers injury or damage to property. For example, AIC could be accused of causing injury to the visiting students by breaching its duty to provide safe conditions.

4. *Unbroken chain of events between the breach of duty and the injury or damage.* A finding of negligence also requires that the breach of duty initiate an unbroken chain of events leading to the injury. The breach of the duty must be the *proximate cause* of the injury. In the AIC example, the injured students would have to prove that AIC's breach of its duty to provide safe conditions was the proximate cause of their injuries.

Reminder

The *proximate cause* of a loss is the event that sets in motion an uninterrupted chain of events contributing to the loss.

A person, a business, or another party whose conduct is proved to be negligent is generally responsible for the consequences. This party is called the **tortfeasor**, the wrongdoer, or the negligent party. All three terms refer to a party who does something that a reasonable person would not do (or fails to do something that a reasonable person would do) under similar circumstances. Besides the person who actually commits the act, other persons or organizations might be held responsible for the tortfeasor's action. This responsibility is called **vicarious liability**. Vicarious liability often arises in business situations from the relationship between employer and employee. An employee performing work-related activities is generally acting on behalf of the employer. Therefore, the employer can be vicariously liable for the actions of the employee. If, for example, an employee drives a customer to a meeting and negligently causes an accident in which the customer is injured, both the employee and the employer could be held liable for the customer's injuries. Responsibility would not *shift* from the employee to the employer but rather could *extend* to include the employer.

Intentional Torts   A deliberate act (other than a breach of contract) that causes harm to another person, regardless of whether the *harm* is intended, is called an **intentional tort**. Assault and battery are probably the most common intentional torts. **Assault** is an intentional *threat* of bodily harm under circumstances that create a fear of imminent harm. **Battery** is any unlawful and unprivileged *touching* of another person. Assault and battery often happen together at approximately the same time, but either can happen without the other.

Another common example of an intentional tort is defamation, which includes both libel and slander. **Libel** occurs when someone prints and distributes an untrue defamatory statement about another person. **Slander** is a spoken, untrue defamatory statement about another person. As a rule, the law affords public figures less protection against libel and slander than ordinary persons except when a false statement is also malicious. For defamation to occur, someone other than the defamed person must read or hear the false statement. Even if others read or hear the statement, the truth is a complete defense against a defamation claim.

False arrest or detainment is any unlawful physical restraint of another's freedom. This intentional tort presents a potential problem for retail stores. False arrest can occur when a store employee detains a customer suspected of shoplifting. If it is later determined that the customer had not stolen any merchandise, the detainment is a false arrest that inconveniences and embarrasses the customer.

Still another intentional tort is **invasion of privacy**, which is an encroachment on another person's right to be left alone. Legal liability for invasion of privacy can arise from the unauthorized release of confidential information, the illegal use of hidden

A **tortfeasor** is a person, a business, or another party who has committed a tort.

Vicarious liability is legal responsibility that occurs when one party is held liable for the actions of another party. For example, parents might be found vicariously liable for the actions of their minor children.

Intentional Torts

An **intentional tort** is a deliberate act (other than a breach of contract) that causes harm to another person. Intentional torts include:

- **Assault**—the intentional *threat* of bodily harm
- **Battery**—the unlawful *physical contact* with another person
- **Libel**—a *written or printed* untrue statement that damages a person's reputation
- **Slander**—an *oral* untrue statement that damages a person's reputation
- **False arrest**—an unlawful physical restraint of another's freedom
- **Invasion of privacy**—an encroachment on another person's right to be left alone

microphones or other surveillance equipment, an unauthorized search, or the public disclosure of private facts.

Absolute Liability Although most liability cases arise from negligence and some arise from intentional torts, liability under tort law is not entirely limited to cases of injury caused by negligent or deliberate conduct. In situations involving inherently dangerous activities, tort law can give an injured person a right of recovery without having to prove negligence or intent. Inherently dangerous activities can give rise to **absolute liability** (sometimes called **strict liability**) for any injury regardless of the intent or the carefulness of the person held liable. The situation itself, rather than the person's conduct, becomes the standard for determining liability.

For example, the owner of a wild animal, such as a pet rattlesnake or a circus lion, is liable for any injury the animal inflicts, regardless of the precautions the owner might have taken. Blasting operations present an exposure to absolute liability for business organizations. The mere fact that the business conducts blasting operations is enough to make the owners of the business liable for any injuries or damage that results.

Contracts

Contract law enables an injured party to seek recovery because another party has breached a duty voluntarily accepted in a contract. As discussed in Chapter 7, a contract is a legally enforceable agreement between two or more parties. If one party fails to honor the contract, the other may go to court to enforce it. In such a case, it is the specific contract, rather than the law in general, that the court interprets. Two areas of contract law important to insurance are liability assumed under a contract and breach of warranty.

Liability Assumed Under Contract Parties to a contract sometimes find it convenient for one party to assume the financial consequences of certain types of liability faced by the other. The party assuming the liability might be closer to the scene, exercise more control over operations, or have the ability to respond to claims more efficiently. For example, James Smith, the owner of a building, and Jane Jones, a contractor, make a contract in which Jones accepts responsibility for certain actions of Bob White, a subcontractor. If one of the specified actions of White injures a customer, Bonita Brown, and Brown sues Smith, then Jones will pay any damages owed to Brown because of White's specified action. Such arrangements, called **hold harmless agreements**, are common in construction and service businesses. They are called hold harmless agreements because they require one party to "hold harmless and indemnify" the other party against liability arising from the activity (or product) that is specified in the contract.

Absolute liability (sometimes called **strict liability**) is legal liability that arises from inherently dangerous activities or dangerously defective products that result in injury or harm to another, regardless of how much care was used in the activity. Absolute liability does not require proof of negligence. ("Strict liability" is also used to describe the liability imposed by certain statutes, such as workers compensation laws.)

A **hold harmless agreement** is a contractual provision that obligates one party to assume the legal liability of another party.

Businesses can transfer the financial consequences of certain types of liability to other persons and organizations through contracts, but, as a matter of public policy, not all types of liability can be transferred. Normally, one party cannot transfer to another party its liability for gross negligence, willful or wanton misconduct, or criminal actions.

Breach of Warranty   The law of contracts also governs claims arising from breach of warranty. Contracts for sales of goods include **warranties**, or promises made by the seller. The law also implies certain warranties. A seller warrants, for example, that an item is fit for a particular purpose. If Juanita buys the hair conditioner recommended and sold by her beautician, she relies on the warranty that the conditioner will be good for her hair. If the conditioner damages her hair instead, the beautician (as well as the manufacturer) could be held liable for a breach of warranty. The buyer does not have to prove negligence on the part of the seller. The fact that the product did not work shows that the contract was not fulfilled.

Warranties are promises, either written or implied, such as a promise by a seller to a buyer that a product is fit for a particular purpose.

Statutes

Statutory liability exists because of specific statutes. Although common law may cover a particular situation, statutory law may extend, restrict, or clarify the rights of injured parties in that situation or similar ones. One reason for such legislation is the attempt to ensure adequate compensation for injuries without lengthy disputes over who is at fault. Prominent examples of this kind of statutory liability involve no-fault auto laws and workers compensation laws. In these legal areas, a specific statute (rather than the common law principles of torts) gives one party the right of recovery from another or restricts that right of recovery.

Statutory liability is legal liability imposed by a specific statute or law.

No-Fault Auto Laws   Automobile accidents are among the leading causes of injury in the United States. Because of this fact, state legislatures seek ways to improve the system for distributing the generally high costs of those accidents. Specific statutes now modify many of the common law principles of negligence that apply to automobile accidents. Since these laws are enacted by state legislatures, the provisions vary considerably by state.

In an effort to reduce the number of lawsuits resulting from auto accidents, some states have enacted "no-fault" laws. These laws recognize the inevitability of auto accidents and restrict or eliminate the right to sue the other party in an accident, except in the more serious cases defined by the law. Victims with less serious injuries collect their out-of-pocket expenses from their own insurance companies without the need for expensive legal proceedings.

Workers Compensation Laws   A similar concept of liability without regard to fault applies to workplace injuries. Each of the fifty states has a workers compensation statute. Such a statute eliminates an employee's right to sue the employer for most work-related injuries and also imposes on the employer automatic (strict) liability to pay specified benefits. In place of the common law principle of negligence, workers compensation laws create a system in which injured employees receive benefits specified in these laws. As long as the injury is work-related, the employer pays the specified benefits regardless of who is at fault. In the AIC case, the workers compensation law in AIC's state would require that AIC provide benefits (such as medical, disability, and rehabilitation benefits) to the injured employees as well as death benefits to the survivors of the employees who were killed.

Educational Objective 5

Describe the potential financial consequences of liability loss exposures.

Potential Financial Consequences of Liability Loss Exposures

A person must sustain some definite harm for a liability loss to result in a valid claim. For the visiting engineering students to collect damages from AIC, for example, they must prove that they actually suffered some harm as a result of the explosion. Perhaps they had to be treated in the hospital emergency room, their clothing was ruined, or they could not go to their jobs and thus lost a day's pay. To those who can show that actual harm or injury was suffered because of AIC's negligence, the court may award *damages* that AIC will have to pay. In addition, AIC might incur *defense costs* to defend itself in court. Exhibit 9-3 shows the various types of damages and defense costs that might have to be paid as the result of a liability claim.

Damages

As explained in Chapter 6, *compensatory damages* are intended to compensate the victim for the harm actually suffered. An award of compensatory damages is the amount of money that has been judged to equal the victim's loss, and it is the amount the party responsible for the loss will have to pay. Compensatory damages include both *special damages* and *general damages*. In addition, the court could award *punitive damages*.

Defense Costs

In addition to the damages that might have to be paid because of liability for injury or damage, a liability loss might also include the costs to defend the alleged wrongdoer in court. These defense costs include not only the fees paid to lawyers but also all the other expenses associated with defending a liability claim. Such expenses can include investigation expenses, expert

Reminder

As discussed in Chapter 6, *damages* refer to a monetary award that the law requires one party to pay to another who has suffered loss or injury for which the first party is legally responsible.

Legal liability cases might involve various types of damages:

- *Compensatory damages*—damages that are intended to compensate a victim for harm actually suffered. Compensatory damages can include *special damages* (for specific out-of-pocket expenses) and *general damages* (for losses, such as pain and suffering, that do not have a specific economic value).

- *Punitive damages*—damages awarded by a court to punish wrongdoers who, through malicious or outrageous actions, cause injury or damage to others.

Exhibit 9-3
Potential Financial Consequences of Liability Exposures

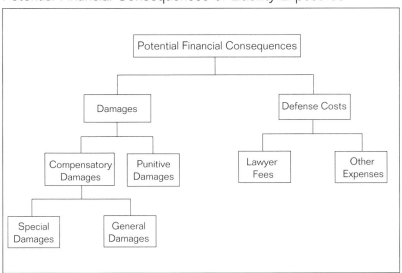

witness fees, the premiums for necessary bonds, and other expenses incurred to prepare for and conduct a trial. Even in the unlikely event that all the possible lawsuits against AIC are ultimately found groundless, AIC and its liability insurer will probably incur substantial defense costs.

Educational Objective 6

Identify and describe activities and situations that create liability loss exposures.

Activities and Situations Leading to Liability Loss Exposures

The potential for a liability loss exists whenever some activity or relationship can create liability to others. Numerous activities and situations have this potential. Although the following list is far from exhaustive, liability can arise from any of the following exposures:

- Automobiles and other conveyances
- Premises
- Business operations
- Completed operations
- Products
- Advertising
- Pollution
- Liquor
- Professional activities

Automobiles and Other Conveyances

A significant liability exposure that faces almost all persons and businesses comes from the ownership and operation of automobiles. In the United States, auto accidents produce the greatest number of liability claims. Even people or businesses that do not own an auto can be held vicariously liable for the operation of an auto by others. As shown in the AIC case, AIC could be held liable for the auto accident caused by its employee fleeing the fire, whether the employee was driving his own vehicle or one owned by AIC.

Liability loss exposures are also created by owning and operating other conveyances such as watercraft, aircraft, recreational vehicles, and the like.

Premises

Anyone who owns or occupies property has a premises liability exposure. If a visitor slips on an icy front porch, the homeowner might be held liable for the injury. A business has a similar loss exposure arising from its premises. As seen in the AIC case, the engineering students were injured while on AIC's premises, and AIC will probably be held liable for their injuries.

Business Operations

Businesses must be concerned not only about the condition of the premises but also about their business operations. As AIC discovered, whatever activity the business performs has the potential to go wrong and cause harm to someone else. When employees of a furniture store deliver a sofa, they must take care not to damage the customer's door or door frame. Damage caused by employees while delivering furniture, installing appliances, or repairing air conditioning, for example, is the responsibility of the employer.

Completed Operations

Even after a plumber, an electrician, a painter, or another contractor completes a job and leaves the work site, a liability exposure remains. If faulty wiring or toxic paint leads to an injury, the person or business who did the work might be liable. Considerable time could pass in the interim, but the person or business might still be held liable if faulty workmanship created the condition that eventually caused the injury. If, for example, AIC could prove that the explosion was caused by the negligence of the contractor who installed the pressure relief device on the storage tank, the contractor might be liable for some or all of the resulting damage and injury.

Products

Liability resulting from products that cause bodily injury or property damage is a significant exposure for manufacturing companies. This exposure begins with the design of the product and might not cease until the product is properly disposed of by the ultimate consumer. Mass-produced products are used by millions of people, and foods and pharmaceutical products are consumed by customers. A prescription drug might be dangerous, but the danger might not be known for several years, when it is too late to help the people who have taken the drug. AIC's customers complained of impurities in its products; if these impurities caused injury to one or more of its customers, AIC could be held liable for damages. If the manufacturer of the pressure relief device was found to be negligent, the manufacturer might also incur some liability.

Advertising

In their advertisements, businesses often include pictures of people using their products. If a local retailer cannot afford professional models, it might use pictures of people using its products or shopping in its store. Unless the retailer obtains proper permission, publishing the pictures could lead to a lawsuit alleging invasion of privacy. Using another company's trademarked slogan or advertisement can also give rise to a liability claim.

Pollution

Many types of products pollute the environment when they are discarded. In addition, the manufacture of some products creates contaminants that, if not disposed of properly, cause environmental impairment, or pollution. If the explosion at AIC's plant polluted the nearby river, AIC might have yet another liability loss. As illustrated by the Love Canal case in New York State some years ago, industrial products or wastes can have a tremendous effect on the environment. Toxic wastes in the Love Canal area polluted the ground water and made the surrounding community a dangerous place in which to live. Cleanup costs and expenses to relocate the residents can be enormous in such cases.

Liquor

Very serious dangers exist when people consume too much alcohol. Intoxicated persons threaten themselves as well as others. Providers of alcohol can be responsible for customers or guests who become intoxicated and injure someone while driving drunk. Both the drunk driver and the person who served the alcohol can be held legally liable. A business that sells or serves alcoholic beverages, therefore, has a significant liability loss exposure.

Professional Activities

As mentioned, negligence involves a failure to exercise the degree of care that is reasonable under the circumstances. It is reasonable to expect that professionals with special competence in a particular field or occupation will exercise great care in performing their duties. Attorneys, physicians, architects, engineers, and other professionals are considered experts in their field and are expected to perform accordingly. Professional liability arises if injury or damage can be attributed to a professional's failure to exercise the appropriate standard of care. For insurance professionals and others, that failure is sometimes called *errors and omissions* (*E&O*). For medical professionals, that failure is often called malpractice. For example, a physician who ignores the possible side effects of a drug when prescribing it might be held liable for any resulting harm to the patient, because accepted medical practice requires the doctor to consider possible side effects. Professionals can make errors, and when they do, the injured party often expects to be compensated.

Reminder

Errors and omissions (*E&O*) are negligent acts (errors) or failures to act (omissions) committed by a professional (such as an insurance agent) in the conduct of business that give rise to legal liability for damages.

Liability Insurance Policy Provisions

Liability insurance covers losses resulting from bodily injury to others or damage to the property of others for which the insured is legally liable and to which the coverage applies.

As discussed in Chapter 8, *property insurance* indemnifies an insured who suffers a financial loss because property has been lost, stolen, damaged, or destroyed.

Because of differences between the nature of liability loss exposures and property loss exposures, **liability insurance** differs from *property insurance* in several ways:

- Property insurance claims usually involve only *two parties*—the insurer and the insured. Liability insurance claims involve *three parties*: the insurer, the insured, and a "third party"—the claimant who brings a legal complaint against the insured for injury or damage allegedly caused by the insured. Although the claimant is not a party to the insurance contract, he or she is a party to the claim settlement.

- In property insurance, insurers pay claims *to an insured* when covered property is damaged by a covered cause of loss during the policy period. In liability insurance, on the other hand, insurers pay *a third party on behalf of an insured* against whom a claim has been made, provided the claim is covered by the policy.

- Property insurance policies must clarify which *property and causes of loss* the policy covers. In contrast, liability insurance policies must indicate the *activities and types of injury or damage* that are covered.

The insuring agreements of most liability insurance policies make essentially the same broad promise: to pay damages (usually for bodily injury or property damage) for which an insured becomes legally liable and to which the coverage applies. The insurer also promises to pay related defense costs. In order to clarify the intent of the insuring agreement, which is usually a relatively brief statement, the provisions of a liability insurance policy must answer the following questions:

- What parties are insured?
- What activities are covered?
- What types of injury or damage are covered?
- What costs are covered?
- What time period is covered?
- What factors affect the amount of claim payments?

Educational Objective 7

Identify and describe the parties that might be insured by a liability insurance policy.

What Parties Are Insured?

Liability insurance policies provide coverage for the *named insured* as well as others. A liability policy generally gives the broadest protection to the named insured. Coverage for others is generally based on their family or business relationship with the named insured. Therefore, liability insurance policy provisions must define the relationships that determine coverage. For example, the policy declarations page lists the named insured, and many policies provide the spouse of a named insured with the same coverage that is provided to the named insured if they live in the same household. If several named insureds are listed in the declarations of a commercial liability policy, a policy provision usually stipulates that the *first named insured* is the insured with whom the insurer has contact.

The extent of liability coverage provided to parties other than the named insured is determined by their relationship to the named insured as well as by the circumstances. For example, the liability coverage of a typical homeowners policy applies to:

- The named insured and the named insured's spouse, if the spouse is a resident in the household
- Relatives of the named insured or spouse, if the relatives reside in the household
- Children in the care of the named insured or spouse
- Any person or organization legally responsible for animals or watercraft owned by an insured (except in business situations)
- Employees using a covered vehicle, such as a lawn tractor, and other people using a covered vehicle on an insured location with the named insured's consent

Commercial liability policies also cover the named insured and certain others, depending on their relationship to the named insured. For example, a commercial general liability policy usually contains provisions that specify the relationships and circumstances that determine who is insured under the policy.

Reminder

The *named insured* is the policyholder whose name(s) appears on the declarations page of an insurance policy.

The *first named insured* is the person or organization whose name appears *first* as the named insured on a commercial insurance policy. Depending on the policy conditions, the first named insured might be the one responsible for paying premiums and the one who has the right to receive any return premiums, to cancel the policy, and to receive the notice of cancellation or nonrenewal.

One provision clarifies who is insured when the named insured is an individual, a partnership, or some other type of organization, such as a corporation. Another provision defines others who may be covered because of their business relationship to the named insured and the circumstances under which they are covered. The parties who are afforded liability coverage under this provision include:

- Employees of the named insured
- Real estate managers for the named insured
- Persons responsible for the property of a named insured who has died
- Any person who operates mobile equipment owned by the named insured while on a public highway
- Any organization that is newly acquired or formed by the named insured for up to a certain number of days after it is acquired or formed

As these examples illustrate, both personal and commercial liability insurance policies generally cover many individuals and organizations—including some that are not named in the policy declarations.

What Activities Are Covered?

A liability insurance policy must clearly express the insurer's intent to cover claims against the insured for which the insured is legally obligated to pay damages. It is not the insurer's intent to pay damages to every third party who suffers a loss and files a claim. The insurer will pay damages only to those who suffer injury or damage for which the insured is legally liable if the harm arose from a covered activity.

Just as property insurance policies use either a named perils or a special form coverage ("all-risks") approach to define covered causes of loss, liability insurance policies use two approaches to define covered activities. Certain policies state the specific activity or source of liability covered. For example, an auto insurance liability policy states that it applies to claims that result from covered auto accidents. In contrast, general liability insurance covers all activities or sources of liability that are not specifically excluded.

A commercial general liability policy (known as a "CGL" policy) is an example of general liability insurance. A general liability insurer agrees to pay damages "to which this insurance applies." However, the extent of coverage depends on the exclusions. That is, general liability policies essentially cover those claims that are not excluded and specifically exclude coverage for claims that are better handled by specific liability insurance policies, such as automobile liability insurance, workers compensation insurance, aircraft and watercraft liability insurance, and professional liability insurance.

In addition to excluding coverage for losses best handled elsewhere, general liability insurance policies contain exclusions dealing with uninsurable exposures, preventable losses, and exposures that would be too costly to insure. For example, like property insurance policies, nearly all liability policies exclude coverage for losses arising from war and nuclear reaction.

Educational Objective 8

Identify and describe the various types of injury or damage that are typically covered in liability insurance policies.

What Types of Injury or Damage Are Covered?

Liability policies typically cover claims for bodily injury and property damage for which the insured is legally liable. However, some liability policies, such as commercial general liability policies, also cover other types of injury, such as personal and advertising injury.

Bodily Injury

Since most liability policies provide coverage only for the insured's legal liability for bodily injury or property damage, the policy language must be precise. A typical commercial general liability policy defines **bodily injury** as follows:

> "Bodily injury" means bodily injury, sickness or disease sustained by a person, including death resulting from any of these at any time.

The term bodily injury is repeated in the definition for clarity. The definition indicates that, as used in the commercial general liability policy, the term bodily injury also includes some things that might not be included in the everyday use of that term. Sickness and disease are often considered forms of illness that do not result from physical accidents, that is, they do not involve injury. Death could be considered the severest form of injury, but unless it is specified in the policy, there might be reason to question whether coverage for claims for bodily injury liability includes coverage for death claims. Given the above definition, the commercial general liability policy clarifies that it covers claims for injury, sickness, disease, and death.

Bodily injury is any physical injury to a person, including sickness, disease, and death.

Property Damage

The definition of **property damage** in a typical commercial general liability policy reads in part as follows:

Property damage is physical injury to, destruction of, or loss of use of tangible property.

"Property damage" means:

a. Physical injury to tangible property, including all resulting loss of use of that property; or

b. Loss of use of tangible property that is not physically injured.

The definition of "property damage" as the term is used in a typical homeowners policy is considerably briefer and reads as follows:

"Property damage" means physical injury to, destruction of, or loss of use of tangible property.

Thus, according to both of these definitions, property damage includes both *direct losses* and *time element* (or *indirect*) *losses*. For example, the fire at AIC's plant caused *indirect* damage to the owners of surrounding businesses since they had to cease operations temporarily. Although there was no actual *direct* physical damage to these surrounding businesses, the business owners still lost the use of their property because of the explosion at AIC. As for the auto accident, if the owner of the other car temporarily lost the use of the car because of the accident, AIC might be liable not only for *direct* damage to the car but also for a *time element loss*, such as the cost of a rental car until the car was repaired or replaced.

Personal Injury

In addition to bodily injury, harm can be inflicted in other ways, such as damage to one's reputation. One might expect "bodily injury" and "personal injury" to mean the same thing. In fact, attorneys tend to use the term personal injury when referring to bodily injuries. However, when used in liability insurance policies, **personal injury** usually refers to a specific group of intentional torts, including defamation (which includes libel and slander), false arrest, and invasion of privacy. Any of these acts might cause harm to another person for which the tortfeasor may be held liable. For insurance purposes, intentional torts are usually considered personal injury offenses and are either excluded from coverage or are specifically covered as a separate coverage.

A few policies define personal injury in a way that includes not only the types of offenses listed above but also bodily injury. When that interpretation is used, personal injury coverage is broader than bodily injury coverage. However, the more common interpretation allows for separate coverage for bodily injury and personal injury, in which case personal injury coverage supplements bodily injury coverage. For example, the commercial general liability policy automatically includes personal injury coverage under a separate insuring agreement. Coverage for personal injury liability can be added by endorsement to a homeowners policy.

Reminder

Direct loss is a reduction in the value of property that results directly and often immediately from damage to that property.

Time element (or *indirect*) *loss* includes loss of income or extra expenses resulting from direct loss to property.

In insurance, the term **personal injury** is generally used to mean injury, other than bodily injury, arising from intentional torts such as libel, slander, or invasion of privacy.

Advertising Injury

Advertising injury, which is covered by most commercial general liability policies, typically includes the following types of offenses:

- Libel and slander
- Publication of material that constitutes an invasion of privacy
- Misappropriation of advertising ideas or business style
- Infringement of copyright, title, or slogan

The definitions of personal injury offenses and advertising injury offenses overlap somewhat. This overlap, however, does not result in duplicate coverage. Some versions of the commercial general liability policy, for example, include both personal and advertising injury in the same insuring agreement, so no coverage duplication results from repeating that a certain type of claim is covered. Furthermore, the policy clarifies that personal injury does not include offenses involving advertising activities and that advertising injury refers only to offenses committed in the course of advertising activities. Therefore, claims are covered as either personal injury or advertising injury, but not both. Newer versions of the commercial general liability policy include both personal injury and advertising injury coverages in a single coverage called "personal and advertising injury liability," which should eliminate any confusion that might have been present in the older policies about the difference in these two coverages.

Educational Objective 9

Describe the costs typically covered in liability insurance policies.

What Costs Are Covered?

Liability insurance policies typically cover two types of costs:

1. The damages that the insured is legally liable to pay
2. The cost of defending the insured against the claim

Some policies also cover other costs, such as supplementary payments and medical payments.

Damages

A person who has suffered bodily injury, property damage, or personal injury for which the insured is allegedly responsible might make a claim for damages. The claim is often settled out of court, and the insurer pays the claimant on behalf of the insured. If a case goes to court, the claimant might be awarded two types of damages, compensatory damages and punitive damages. These damages may or may not be covered by insurance.

Compensatory damages, intended to compensate the claimant for the injury or damage suffered, are covered by liability insurance if the insured is liable for a covered loss. As stated, compensatory damages include both special damages and general damages. A party who is held to be liable for another's injury might have to compensate the injured party for special damages, such as hospital bills, physicians' fees, lost income, and rehabilitation expenses. In addition to these actual expenses, the liable party might be required to pay general damages, such as pain and suffering, to compensate the victim for the physical and mental suffering experienced because of the bodily injury. AIC's liability insurer might have to pay both special damages and general damages if AIC is found liable for both types of compensatory damages because of the explosion and fire.

Most liability insurance policies do not specifically state whether punitive damages, intended to punish the insured for some outrageous conduct, are covered. Some states do not permit insurers to pay punitive damages for their insureds. The reason for this prohibition is that punishment is viewed as less effective if the responsible party does not personally pay the required damages. On the other hand, insurers may pay punitive damages if they are permitted to do so. Some people argue that punitive damages are as much a source of unexpected financial loss as compensatory damages, and that the insured should be entitled to insure against a judgment for punitive damages.

Out-of-Court Settlements

Very few liability claims are decided by the courts. Indeed, most liability claims are settled before the claimant even files a lawsuit. Most liability claims are settled privately between the claimant (or the claimant's lawyer) and the liability insurer (or the insurer's lawyer) on behalf of its insured.

Any party can decline to voluntarily settle a claim, in which case a lawsuit usually occurs, and a court eventually decides the claim. Parties agree to settle claims when they believe a proposed voluntary settlement is more attractive than a lawsuit and court verdict.

Generally, out-of-court settlements are attractive to both sides for two reasons:

1. *Out-of-court settlements resolve cases quickly.* Both sides to a lawsuit suffer significant financial and emotional costs. Out-of-court settlements spare the parties from these costs.

2. *Out-of-court settlements eliminate uncertainty about the outcome of a claim.* Court verdicts are very unpredictable, and either party might do worse than expected. A claimant or a defendant might bear all the costs of a lawsuit and receive a court verdict less favorable than an out-of-court settlement that

was available months or years earlier. Rather than face such an outcome, parties often prefer out-of-court settlements.

An out-of-court settlement is a voluntary agreement to close a claim in exchange for an agreed amount of money. Such settlements occur only after negotiation. Settlement negotiations consist of a series of communications between the parties in which one party suggests a settlement amount and the other party either accepts the amount, rejects it, or suggests another amount. Settlement negotiations can conclude quickly or go on for months, depending on the personalities and experience of the negotiators and on the underlying facts of the claim. Proposed settlement amounts should be based on each party's perception of what a likely court verdict would be. Thus, anything that would be relevant in court should be relevant in settlement negotiations, including the nature of the injuries or damage, the respective legal liability of the parties, and the quality of the witnesses or evidence for each side.

Once negotiations have concluded with a settlement, the parties sign a release, which is a binding contract. A release is a written agreement in which the claimant agrees to drop his or her claim and the insured, through the insurance company, agrees to pay the claimant the settlement amount. A release can be enforced as a legal obligation independent of the underlying claim, but it is not evidence of wrongdoing on the policyholder's part in the underlying claim.

Insurance companies depend on out-of-court settlements. They could not survive if they had to resolve all liability claims through the courts. An ordinary automobile accident claim can cost thousands of dollars in legal fees to prepare for trial and thousands more to put on trial. Legal fees and other defense costs are already a huge expense for insurers even when most claims are settled out of court.

The court system and society in general favor out-of-court settlements. The courts would be overwhelmed with cases and expenses if every legal issue had to go to court. Society benefits when injured parties receive prompt compensation and when all parties put their legal disputes behind them as quickly as possible.

Defense Costs and Expenses

It is sometimes said that an insurer's duty to defend insureds against liability claims is even more important than its duty to pay damages. If the defense is successful, the court delivers a judgment in favor of the defendant (that is, the insured), and no damages are awarded. In other cases, damages might be awarded, but an effective defense results in a lower award than the award sought by the plaintiff (the claimant).

Most liability insurance policies obligate the insurer to defend the insured against any claim or lawsuit in which a claimant seeks damages that would be covered by the policy; the insurer must pay the costs of such a defense. It is often possible to prove that the insured was not responsible for the alleged injury or damage. Even if the claim seems to have no legitimate basis, the insurer must defend the insured if no clear exclusion applies to the loss. Again, the insurer is obligated to defend an insured only when the claimant alleges that injury or damage was caused by a covered activity of the insured. If the claimant is ultimately awarded damages in a situation that originally seemed to be without merit, the insurer has to pay damages covered by the policy.

Litigation expenses are the expenses incurred for legal defense, such as attorneys' fees, expert witness fees, and the cost of legal research.

The expenses incurred for the defense, known as **litigation expenses**, are the insurer's responsibility. Some of these litigation expenses may be specifically described in the policy; others are implicit. The duty to defend, for example, implies that the insurer will retain the attorneys and pay their fees and expenses. Litigation expenses might also include investigation, legal research, expert witness fees, and similar costs incurred in preparing and presenting the case.

Supplementary Payments

In liability policies, **supplementary payments** are amounts the insurer agrees to pay (in addition to the liability limits) for items such as premiums on bail bonds and appeal bonds, loss of the insured's earnings because of attendance at trials, and other reasonable expenses incurred by the insured at the insurer's request.

Liability insurance policies typically include additional coverages stating the **supplementary payments** the insurer agrees to pay in addition to damages. These supplementary payments usually consist of the following:

- All expenses incurred by the insurer
- The cost (up to a specified limit) of bail bonds or other required bonds
- Expenses incurred by the insured at the insurer's request
- The insured's loss of earnings (up to a specified amount per day) because of attendance at hearings or trials at the insurer's request

Other costs that relate to the claim, such as *prejudgment* or *postjudgment interest*, might also be included in the list of supplementary payments.

Prejudgment Interest

Prejudgment interest is interest that might accrue on damages before a judgment has been rendered.

Liability claims that are not settled out of court often involve long delays between the time of the injury or damage and the time when a court awards a judgment to the claimant. The court award to the plaintiff might include damages as well as **prejudgment interest**. This additional sum of money represents the interest that could have been earned if the plaintiff had received compensation at the time of the injury or damage rather than at the time of the judgment.

Postjudgment Interest

When an award for damages is successfully appealed to a higher court, the plaintiff receives no payment. If, on the other hand, the higher court upholds the initial judgment, the plaintiff may also be entitled to receive **postjudgment interest** as compensation for the money that would have been earned if the insurer had paid the claim at the time of the first judgment. Postjudgment interest forces the insurer to bear the expense of the delay in payment caused by the appeal.

Postjudgment interest is interest that might accrue on damages after a judgment has been entered in a court and before the money is paid.

Medical Payments

Some liability policies also provide **medical payments coverage**, which is sometimes offered as an optional coverage the insured can purchase. Medical payments can help avoid larger liability claims. If a homeowners policy includes $1,000 of medical payments coverage, for example, a neighbor injured on the insured's property can receive emergency medical treatment up to that amount without having to sue the insured to recover the cost. Payment of this relatively modest amount reduces the prospect of a much more expensive claim for damages. In some cases, such as in homeowners policies, this coverage is called "medical payments to others" and *does not* cover injuries sustained by an insured or regular residents of his or her household. In other cases, such as in personal auto policies, medical payments coverage *does* cover an insured's injuries up to a specified limit.

Medical payments coverage pays necessary medical expenses incurred within a specified period by a claimant (and in certain policies, by an insured) for a covered injury, regardless of whether the insured was at fault.

What Time Period Is Covered?

Personal auto insurance is usually written for a six-month term. Other types of liability insurance are usually written for a one-year period, though other policy terms are also possible.

A liability insurance policy states what must happen during the policy period in order to "trigger" coverage. Depending on the type of policy, coverage is usually triggered by either:

- Events that occur during the policy period (in an *occurrence basis* policy)
- Claims made (submitted) during the policy period (in a *claims-made* policy)

Educational Objective 10

Demonstrate an understanding of the difference between occurrence basis and claims-made coverage.

Occurrence Basis Coverage

Bodily injury or property damage that occurs during the policy period triggers coverage under a liability policy that provides

Occurrence basis coverage covers liability claims that occur during the policy period, regardless of when the claim is submitted to the insurer.

occurrence basis coverage. In most situations, bodily injury or property damage is apparent at the time of the accident or shortly thereafter. Therefore, if a covered accident occurs during the policy period, the claim will be covered, regardless of when the claim is submitted. For example, if the claimant was injured in an automobile accident caused by the insured only a few hours before the policy period expired, the resulting claim would be covered, despite the fact that it might be submitted after the policy expired.

Occurrence policies do not limit the time period during which a claim can be submitted. As long as the injury or damage occurs during the policy period, coverage applies even to claims made years later. From the insured's standpoint, this coverage offers valuable protection for unknown and unforeseen claims. For the insurer, however, occurrence coverage means that liability claims might surface long after a policy has expired. This particular problem contributed to the development of claims-made coverage.

Claims-Made Coverage

Claims-made coverage covers liability claims that are made (submitted) during the policy period for covered events that occur on or after the *retroactive date* and before the end of the policy period.

A **retroactive date** in a claims-made policy is the date on or after which injury or damage must occur in order to be covered.

Although personal liability insurance policies and most commercial general liability insurance policies are written on an occurrence basis, claims-made coverage is sometimes used to insure business organizations that face certain types of liability loss exposures. Under a liability policy that provides **claims-made coverage**, the insurer agrees to pay all claims that are made (submitted) during the policy period (or before the end of some extended period specified in the policy) if the covered event occurs on or after a specified date (called a **retroactive date**) and before the end of the policy period.

In theory, the claims-made approach is ideal. An insured buys a series of claims-made policies, and each succeeding policy becomes effective when the preceding one expires. Unless coverage lapses, the insured will never be without coverage, since there is always a current policy to provide coverage when a claim is presented.

The situation becomes more complicated in practice, however. Most claims-made policies contain a retroactive date. Claims due to injuries that occur before that retroactive date are not covered even if the claim is made during the policy period. Occurrence policies also do not cover claims arising from occurrences before the policy's inception date. Therefore, an insured who replaces a claims-made policy either with an occurrence policy or with a claims-made policy with a new retroactive date might face a gap in coverage.

Because of periodic renewals and the possibility that the insured will shift coverage from one insurer to another, maintaining continuous coverage without gaps is perhaps the greatest difficulty with claims-made coverage. Thus, insurers, producers, and insureds must pay careful attention to the details of claims-made and occurrence basis policies.

Educational Objective 11

Explain how claim payments are affected by various limits and provisions in liability insurance policies.

What Factors Affect the Amount of Claim Payments?

Even when a liability claim is covered, an insurer does not necessarily pay the full amount of the judgment awarded to a claimant. The extent of the insurer's payment depends on the following types of policy provisions:

- Policy limits
- Defense cost provisions
- "Other insurance" provisions

Policy Limits

It is difficult to predict the dollar amount of liability insurance needed to cover an insured's future claims. Legal obligations depend on uncertain future events in a changing legal environment. Still, it is necessary for the insured and the insurer to agree on some dollar amount of coverage. As with property insurance, policy limits help an insurer measure the extent of its obligation. Limits also give options to the insured, who must decide not only how much coverage is desirable but also how much is affordable. Liability insurance limits are generally round numbers such as $100,000, $500,000, or $1,000,000.

Types of Limits

Limits are expressed in different ways, as follows:

- An **each person limit** is a specific upper limit on the amount an insurer will pay for injury to any one person. If several persons are injured in a given occurrence, this limit applies separately to each one.

- An **each occurrence limit** is a specific upper limit on the amount an insurer will pay for all covered losses from a single occurrence, regardless of the number of persons injured or the number of parties claiming property damage. There might be several different covered occurrences during one policy period.

- An **aggregate limit** is a specific upper limit on the amount an insurer will pay for *all* covered losses during the covered period, which is usually the same as the policy period.

An **each person limit** is the maximum amount an insurer will pay for injury to any one person for a covered loss.

An **each occurrence limit** is the maximum amount an insurer will pay for all covered losses from a single occurrence, regardless of the number of persons injured or the number of parties claiming property damage.

An **aggregate limit** is the maximum amount an insurer will pay for *all* covered losses during the covered policy period.

Split limits are separate limits that an insurer will pay for bodily injury and for property damage.

A **single limit** of liability is the maximum amount an insurer will pay for the insured's liability for both bodily injury and property damage that arise from a single occurrence.

Split Limits and Single Limits

Separate limits for bodily injury and property damage liability coverage are known as **split limits**. For example, a personal auto policy might provide bodily injury liability coverage with a $100,000 limit for each person and a $300,000 limit for each occurrence with a separate limit of $50,000 for each occurrence for property damage liability coverage. A **single limit** applies to any combination of bodily injury and property damage liability claims arising from the same occurrence. For example, a $300,000 single limit covers a bodily injury loss up to $300,000, a property damage liability loss up to $300,000, or any combination of bodily injury and property damage arising from a single occurrence up to $300,000.

Examples of Split Limits and Single Limits

Split Limits

Jessica has a personal auto policy with the following split limits:

Bodily Injury

$100,000 each person
$300,000 each occurrence

Property Damage

$50,000 each occurrence

Jessica is liable for a covered auto accident resulting in injuries to Richard, the driver of the other car, and Marcy, his passenger. When the case went to trial, the court awarded $200,000 in bodily injury damages to Richard and $150,000 to Marcy. In addition, the damage to Richard's car amounted to $10,000, which Jessica was also ordered to pay. Jessica's insurer would pay $110,000 to Richard ($100,000 each person limit for bodily injury plus $10,000 for property damage) and $100,000 to Marcy (the each person limit). Thus, the insurer would pay a total of $210,000 for this accident (plus Jessica's defense costs, which are paid in addition to the policy limits in a personal auto policy). Jessica would have to pay the remaining bodily injury damages of $150,000 from her own pocket.

Single Limit

If Jessica's personal auto policy had a single limit of $300,000 in lieu of the split limits shown above, her insurer would pay a total of $300,000 to Richard and Marcy for both bodily injury and property damage (plus defense costs) in the above accident. (A determination of exactly how much each party receives would depend on the circumstances of this particular claim.)

In this situation, Jessica's insurer would pay more under the single limit policy than the split limits policy, but such is not always the case. For example, if three people had had bodily injury of $150,000 each plus the $10,000 property damage, the

> insurer would have paid a total of $310,000 under the split
> limits policy ($100,000 bodily injury for each person plus
> $10,000 property damage); under the single limits policy, the
> insurer would pay only $300,000, the maximum payable for any
> one occurrence.

Defense Cost Provisions

Most liability policies place no dollar limit on the defense costs
payable by the insurer. The only limitation is that the insurer is
not obligated to provide further defense once the entire policy
limit has been paid in settlement or judgment for damages.

Stated differently, defense costs are usually payable *in addition to*
the policy limits, and policy limits include only payment for
damages. Practical limitations, however, tend to restrict defense
costs. For example, an insurer is not likely to spend $100,000
defending a claim for $10,000 in damages.

Certain policies exist, however, that place defense costs within
the overall policy limit. In such policies, for example, if the
policy limit is $100,000 and the insured has a covered claim
involving damages of $90,000 and defense costs of $30,000, the
insurer would pay a total of $100,000 for both the damages and
the defense. The insured would be responsible for paying the
additional $20,000.

"Other Insurance" Provisions

In some cases, more than one policy or coverage might cover
the same claim. As with property insurance, liability insurance
policies contain "other insurance" provisions to resolve this
problem and preserve the principle of indemnity. Several
approaches are used, and the applicable approach depends on
the wording of the particular policy and on the situation.

Educational Objective 12

Define or describe each of the Key Words and Phrases for this
assignment. (All Key Words and Phrases appear in bold print in
the text and in the margins throughout this chapter.)

Summary

This chapter discusses liability loss exposures and the liability
policy provisions that deal with those exposures. Liability loss
exposures are based on the concept of legal liability. By holding
individuals and business organizations responsible for their
conduct, the legal system protects the rights of individuals and
businesses. The legal system in the United States derives
essentially from the following:

- The Constitution, which is the source of *constitutional law*
- Legislative bodies, which is the source of *statutory law*
- Court decisions, which is the source of *common law*

An important distinction exists in the U.S. legal system between criminal law and civil law. Criminal law imposes penalties on those who commit wrongs against society. Civil law provides a means to settle disputes among individuals and to determine responsibility for injuries or damage.

Liability loss exposures involve the following elements:

- The legal basis of a claim by one party against another for damages
- The financial consequences that might occur from a liability loss

Many legal principles can serve as a basis for holding one party responsible for another's injury. Most liability cases rely on tort law, which allows an injured party to sue for damages if the other party's negligence, intentional tort, or absolute liability (from an inherently dangerous activity) caused the injury or damage. Liability can also arise from a breach of contract, which allows one party to seek relief in court from the other party to a contract. Statutes, such as workers compensation laws, also impose liability on certain parties when a legislative body has determined that it is in the interest of society to hold those persons liable.

A liability loss occurs only if an insured causes another person to suffer some definite harm. A liability claim can lead to compensatory damages, consisting of special damages (for medical expenses, lost income, and rehabilitation expenses) as well as general damages (for pain and suffering). Many liability claims also lead to defense costs, including legal fees, investigation expenses, and other expenses to defend the claim.

Innumerable activities and situations can create liability to someone else. These include owning or operating an automobile, owning or occupying property, conducting business operations, manufacturing or selling products, advertising, polluting the environment, selling or otherwise providing alcoholic beverages, and practicing a profession.

Liability insurance policies cover damages for which the insured becomes legally obligated to pay and that arise out of the activities covered by the policy. The following questions must be answered in the provisions of liability insurance policies:

- What parties are insured?
- What activities are covered?
- What types of injury or damage are covered?
- What costs are covered?
- What time period is covered?
- What factors affect the amount of claim payments?

Chapter 10

Managing Loss Exposures: Risk Management

Educational Objectives

After studying this chapter, you should be able to:

1. Identify and describe the steps in the risk management process. (pp. 10-4 to 10-20)

2. Identify and describe various methods of identifying loss exposures. (pp. 10-5 to 10-8)

3. Explain why measuring loss frequency and loss severity is important in analyzing loss exposures. (pp. 10-8 to 10-10)

4. Identify and describe various risk management techniques. (pp. 10-10 to 10-14)

5. Describe the financial criteria and the guidelines for selecting the risk management techniques that are most appropriate in a given situation. (pp. 10-14 to 10-17)

6. Describe procedures for implementing risk management techniques. (pp. 10-18 to 10-19)

7. Describe procedures for monitoring and modifying a risk management program. (pp. 10-19 to 10-20)

8. Explain how each of the following can benefit from sound risk management: (pp. 10-20 to 10-22)

   a. Businesses

   b. Individuals and families

   c. Society

   d. Insurers

9. In a given case, recommend and justify risk management techniques appropriate for an individual, a family, or a business. (pp. 10-22 to 10-25)

10. Define or describe each of the Key Words and Phrases for this assignment. (All Key Words and Phrases appear in bold print in the text and in the margins throughout this chapter.)

Chapter 10

Managing Loss Exposures: Risk Management

In the previous two chapters, you learned about property and liability loss exposures and the insurance policy provisions that deal with those exposures. This final chapter will help you understand that insurance is just one way of managing loss exposures.

As described in the beginning of this book, insurance is three things: a transfer system, a business, and a contract. As a transfer system, insurance is a risk management technique, but it is not the only one. Whether you know it or not, you practice risk management informally throughout your life. For instance, if you decide not to take up skiing because you are afraid of being injured, you are practicing the risk management technique of *avoidance*. If you do decide to ski, but choose to wear a helmet while skiing, you are practicing the risk management technique of *loss control*. When you accept the lift ticket from the ski resort, you can read on the back that you have accepted a form of *noninsurance transfer* in which you agree to not hold the resort responsible for any injury that you might incur. If you ski and do not have insurance against accidental injury, you are practicing the risk management technique of *retention*. Finally, if you purchase an insurance policy to cover accidental injuries, including skiing injuries, you are handling your loss exposure by purchasing *insurance*. You will learn about all of these techniques for handling loss exposures in this chapter, which introduces risk management as a formal process. Keep in mind, however, that informal risk management occurs every day in everyone's life and in every business.

Everything people or organizations do exposes them to possible accidental losses. Whenever accidental losses occur, they can create serious financial consequences for the individuals, households, or organizations that suffer the loss. Such losses can also prevent persons or organizations from achieving their goals. Identifying and finding ways to deal with these potential losses is what risk management is all about. Insurance, which cannot prevent accidental losses, works best when it is part of a well-designed risk management program tailored to the loss exposures of each insured.

Educational Objective 1

Identify and describe the steps in the risk management process.

The Risk Management Process

Risk management is the process of making and implementing decisions to deal with loss exposures. It involves identifying loss exposures and then applying various techniques to eliminate, control, finance, or transfer those exposures.

Although it is defined in various ways, **risk management** is essentially the process of managing exposures to accidental losses. Whether those practicing risk management are company executives, individuals planning for themselves or their families, or professionals working with clients, the goal of risk management is the same: to minimize the adverse effects of loss exposures. For every risk management professional relying on computers and sophisticated systems to assist with decision making, there are hundreds who jot their solutions on scratch pads or simply note them mentally. Risk management is not just a process used by large corporations. Risk management concepts are also used, consciously or not, by small and medium-sized companies, communities, families, and individuals.

The risk management process needs specific attention in every well-managed household or organization, regardless of its nature or its size. The person who performs the risk management function differs, depending on the household or organization. The responsible person in an organization might be an employee known as the risk manager, as the director of risk management, or by some other title. In other organizations, risk management is performed in part by someone outside the firm—for example, a risk management consultant. An insurance agent or broker can assist organizations with their risk management process by helping them determine what loss exposures they have and by suggesting the types and amounts of insurance they need; however, decisions should be made by the client, not by the agent or broker. In a household, the person who performs risk management might be the primary wage earner or the person who handles the household finances. In this chapter, the term "risk manager" refers in a broad sense to anyone who is primarily responsible for risk management, regardless of title or status within the organization or household. The term "household" refers to any household unit, whether an individual, a traditional family, or individuals living together in a single household. The term "organization" refers to any business, organization, or community, whether operating as a for-profit or nonprofit organization. Risk management concepts are valid for all of these types of households and organizations.

Risk managers in households or organizations should be responsible for seeing that all the steps of the risk management process are properly performed:

1. Identifying and analyzing loss exposures
2. Examining possible risk management techniques for handling those loss exposures
3. Selecting the most appropriate risk management techniques
4. Implementing the chosen techniques in a risk management program
5. Monitoring and modifying the risk management program

Exhibit 10-1 shows the main components of each of these steps in the risk management process.

Step 1: Identifying and Analyzing Loss Exposures

Identifying exposures to accidental losses involves developing a complete list of loss exposures and possible accidental losses that can affect a particular household or organization. *Analyzing* these loss exposures requires estimating how large the losses might be and how often they might occur to determine how these losses might interfere with the activities and objectives of the household or organization.

Educational Objective 2

Identify and describe various methods of identifying loss exposures.

Identifying Loss Exposures

To handle *loss exposures*, a risk manager must first identify them. The key to identifying loss exposures is a thorough knowledge of how the household or organization operates. The risk manager can start with a physical inspection of the premises and then use other tools that aid in the identification process, such as loss exposure surveys and flowcharts.

Reminder

A *loss exposure* (or simply an *exposure*) is any condition or situation that presents the possibility of a loss.

Major Types of Loss Exposures

- *Property loss exposures* can lead to losses from damage to or loss of tangible or intangible assets. Property loss exposures include exposure to *net income* losses, which are decreases in revenues or increases in expenses that result from property losses.

- *Liability loss exposures* present the possibility of a claim for damages against a person or business for negligence or for other alleged wrongdoing.

- *Human and personnel loss exposures* present the possibility of a direct financial loss by causes such as death, illness, injury, or disability. When such exposures affect individuals or families, they are called *human* (or *personal*) *loss exposures*. When similar exposures affect businesses, they are called *personnel loss exposures*.

Exhibit 10-1

Steps in the Risk Management Process

1. Identifying and analyzing loss exposures

Identifying	Analyzing
Physical inspection Loss exposure survey Flowchart	Loss frequency Loss severity

2. Examining risk management techniques

Avoidance
Loss control:
   Loss prevention
   Loss reduction
Retention
Noninsurance transfer
Insurance

Decisions based on financial criteria
Decisions based on informal guidelines:
   Do not retain more than you can afford to lose.
   Do not retain large exposures to save a little premium.
   Do not spend a lot of money for a little protection.
   Do not consider insurance a substitute for loss control.

4. Implementing the chosen techniques

Decide what should be done.
Decide who should be responsible.
Communicate risk management information.
Allocate costs of the risk management program.

5. Monitoring and modifying the risk management program

Continuously monitor the risk management program.
Periodically review the insurance program.
Revise the risk management program as needed.

Physical Inspection

A risk manager cannot gain a clear picture of operations by sitting in an easy chair or behind a desk. The most straightforward method of identifying loss exposures is a physical inspection of all locations, operations, maintenance routines, safety practices, work processes, and other activities. Physical inspection by itself usually does not suffice, however, because the risk manager might not have sufficient knowledge of the operations to identify all exposures or to ask others the right questions to uncover all loss exposures.

Loss Exposure Survey

A **loss exposure survey**, or checklist, is a document listing potential loss exposures that a household or an organization might face. Independent risk management consultants as well as insurance companies, agents, and brokers often design such surveys to be comprehensive enough to apply to almost any household or organization. However, a given household or organization is unlikely to face all of the loss exposures detailed in such surveys.

The risk manager uses the survey to indicate areas in which the organization faces the particular loss exposures listed on the survey. In an organization, the risk manager usually discusses the items on the survey with managers, supervisors, and other employees working in various areas who can explain the details involved in the exposures the organization faces.

A loss exposure survey can be a valuable tool to help the risk manager identify the organization's loss exposures. If used appropriately, the survey also familiarizes the risk manager with all the organization's operations. The survey's major weakness is that it might omit an important exposure, especially if the organization has unique operations not included on a standard survey form. Risk managers cannot depend solely on surveys because they might miss important loss exposures. Instead, risk managers should use the survey as a guide to develop a comprehensive picture of the organization's operations and loss exposures.

Exhibit 10-2 presents a sample of questions frequently asked on loss exposure surveys for organizations. Such surveys usually group similar exposures together, such as exposures from manufacturing operations, from the sale of products, from the use of vehicles, and so forth. Similar but less extensive surveys are available (often from insurance agents, brokers, or companies) to help households identify the loss exposures they face.

Flowchart

Risk managers can use a **flowchart** to identify specific types of loss exposures. A flowchart complements the loss exposure survey by providing a diagram of loss exposures from certain operations. As with a loss exposure survey, a flowchart is beneficial because it forces the risk manager to examine each aspect of the operation in detail.

Flowcharts can be complex or relatively simple. Exhibit 10-3 is a simplified flowchart for a winery in California that grows its own grapes. In the case of the winery, the flowchart reveals potential bottlenecks in production. For example, the grape crusher is vitally important because production cannot continue

A **loss exposure survey** is a risk management tool in the form of a checklist or questionnaire listing potential loss exposures that a household or an organization might face.

A **flowchart** is a diagram that depicts the flow of a particular operation or set of related operations within an organization.

Exhibit 10-2

Sample of Questions Frequently Asked on Loss Exposure Surveys

Yes	No	
❏	❏	1. Do you have a brochure or other written material that describes your business operations or products?
❏	❏	2. Is your business confined to one industry?
❏	❏	3. Is your business confined to one product?
❏	❏	4. Do you own buildings?
❏	❏	5. Do you lease buildings *from* others?
❏	❏	6. Do you lease buildings *to* others?
❏	❏	7. Do you plan any new construction?
❏	❏	8. Are your fixed asset values established by certified property appraisers?
❏	❏	9. Do you own any vacant land?
❏	❏	10. Are any properties located in potential riot or civil disturbance areas?
❏	❏	11. Are any properties located in potential flood or earthquake areas?
❏	❏	12. Do your properties have security alarm systems? (Fire-sprinkler discharge, burglary, smoke detection, etc.)
❏	❏	13. Are there any unusual fire or explosion hazards in your business operation? (Welding, painting, woodworking, boilers or pressure vessels, etc.)
❏	❏	14. Do you take a physical count of inventory at least once a year?
❏	❏	15. Do you lease machinery or equipment other than automotive?
❏	❏	16. Do you stockpile inventory, either raw or finished?
❏	❏	17. Could you conveniently report inventory values on a monthly basis?
❏	❏	18. Do you buy, sell, or have custody of goods or equipment of extremely high value? (Radium, gold, etc.)
❏	❏	19. Do you use any raw stock, inventory, or equipment that requires substantial lead time to reproduce?
❏	❏	20. Do you export or import?

Condensed and adapted with permission from George L. Head and Stephen Horn II, *Essentials of Risk Management,* vol. 1, 3rd ed. (Malvern, PA: Insurance Institute of America, 1997), pp. 155-156. For the complete survey, refer to that text.

if that single piece of machinery breaks down. The bottling process is another potential source of trouble because the bottling equipment could be difficult to replace quickly if damaged or destroyed. The flowchart also illustrates certain exposures beyond the winery's control. For example, suppose the bottle or box manufacturer sustains a loss and is unable to supply the winery. Are alternative suppliers available? The flowchart by itself is useful, but to gain maximum benefit from a flowchart, a risk manager must use it in conjunction with other methods of exposure identification.

Educational Objective 3

Explain why measuring loss frequency and loss severity is important in analyzing loss exposures.

Exhibit 10-3

Flowchart for a Winery

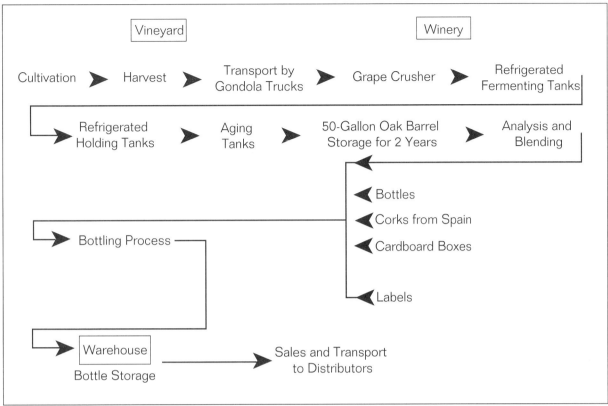

This flowchart was prepared by and is reproduced with the permission of Stephen J. Horn II, CPCU, ARM, AAI.

Analyzing Loss Exposures

Analyzing loss exposures involves determining the financial effect of a potential loss on the household or organization. To determine the financial effect of losses, a risk manager needs to measure both the likely frequency and likely severity of those losses. This analysis enables the risk manager to give priority to the most significant exposures.

Loss Frequency

Loss frequency indicates how often a loss occurs or is expected to occur. Frequent losses include abrasions and minor lacerations of employees at a manufacturing plant, minor auto accidents with a large fleet of autos, and spoilage of produce at a supermarket. Other losses, such as those caused by earthquakes, tornadoes, and hurricanes, occur much less frequently.

Accurate measurement of loss frequency is important because the proper treatment of the loss exposure often depends on how frequently the loss is expected to occur. If a particular type of loss occurs frequently, or if its frequency has been increasing in recent years, the risk manager might decide that procedures for controlling losses are necessary to decrease the frequency of losses.

Loss frequency is a term used to indicate how often losses occur or are expected to occur. Loss frequency is used to predict the likelihood of similar losses in the future.

Loss severity is a term that refers to the dollar amount of damage that results or might result from loss exposures. Loss severity is used to predict how costly future losses are likely to be.

Loss Severity

Loss severity refers to the dollar amount of damage that results or might result from a loss exposure. It is much easier to gauge the potential severity of property losses than of liability losses. Most property losses have a finite value, and whether the property is partially or completely destroyed, the severity of the loss is usually calculable. The severity of liability exposures is much harder to calculate. If a paint manufacturer sells paint that produces toxic fumes when used, the severity of the potential liability loss is almost unlimited.

Likewise, the severity of the property loss from an airplane crash might equal several million dollars, a calculable amount. However, if an aircraft loaded with passengers crashes in a densely populated metropolitan area, the potential severity of the liability loss is difficult, if not impossible, to estimate accurately.

Properly estimating loss severity is also essential in order to treat the exposure to loss. The potential severity of losses is a major consideration in determining whether the household or organization should insure a particular exposure or retain all or part of the financial consequences of the loss.

Educational Objective 4

Identify and describe various risk management techniques.

Step 2: Examining Risk Management Techniques

Once the identification and analysis of loss exposures is complete, the risk manager should examine all possible techniques for treating the exposures. These techniques include the following:

- Avoidance
- Loss control
- Retention
- Noninsurance transfer
- Insurance

Avoidance

Avoidance is a risk management technique that eliminates a loss exposure and reduces the chance of loss to zero.

Avoidance is a risk management technique that eliminates the chance of a particular type of loss by either disposing of an existing loss exposure or by not assuming a new exposure. For example, a manufacturer of sports equipment might decide not to add football helmets to its line of products to avoid the possibility of large lawsuits from head injuries. A family might decide not to purchase a motor boat in order to avoid the potential property and liability exposures that accompany boat ownership.

The advantage of avoidance as a risk management technique is that the probability of loss equals zero—no doubt or uncertainty about the loss exposure exists because a loss is not possible. If this objective is not accomplished, the exposure has not been avoided. Often, discontinuing an existing activity avoids losses from *future activities*, but it does not eliminate outstanding exposures that might still arise from *past activities*. In the case of the sports equipment manufacturer, if it were already making football helmets and quit making them because of claims for injuries connected with their use, it has avoided liability loss exposures arising out of *future* helmet sales, but claims could still arise from the helmets sold in the *past*. Thus, the manufacturer has not really achieved complete avoidance of these exposures.

Avoidance has the disadvantage of sometimes being impractical and is often difficult, if not impossible, to accomplish. Suppose Suzanne is contemplating the purchase of her first automobile, but she is worried about the exposures inherent in automobile ownership. She might believe the chance of damage to the car is too great. Further, Suzanne might be unwilling to assume the chance of liability imposed by law, or perhaps she cannot afford automobile insurance. However, avoidance of these exposures might pose additional problems for Suzanne. Does she need a car for commuting to work or for other activities? If so, she will have to exchange the exposures of automobile ownership for the exposures inherent in some other type of transportation. Renting or leasing a car might be more expensive than auto ownership, and Suzanne would still be liable for any accidents she might cause. Doing totally without a car would mean traveling by public transportation, by hitchhiking, by bicycle, by motorcycle, or on foot; any of these alternatives could prove more hazardous to Suzanne than riding in her own car. Thus, Suzanne might decide that avoidance is not a feasible technique and choose to purchase a car and buy automobile insurance to cover her automobile loss exposures.

Loss Control

Loss control is an effective risk management technique that involves taking steps to lower the frequency or severity of losses. Controlling loss frequency is called **loss prevention**; controlling loss severity is referred to as **loss reduction**. The loss control technique is rarely used by itself and is often most effective when used in conjunction with other risk management techniques, such as insurance.

Loss Prevention

Risk managers often attempt to control losses by practicing loss prevention: trying to keep losses from occurring in the first place. Examples of loss prevention are commonplace:

- Keeping doors and windows locked to prevent burglaries

Loss control is a risk management technique that attempts to decrease the frequency or severity of losses. Loss control includes *loss prevention* and *loss reduction*.

Loss prevention seeks to lower the *frequency* of losses, in other words, to decrease the *number* of losses.

Loss reduction seeks to lower the *severity* of losses that do occur, in other words, to decrease the *dollar amount* of losses.

- Instituting a regular program of vehicle maintenance to prevent accidents due to faulty equipment

Loss Reduction

In addition to trying to prevent losses from occurring, a risk manager might attempt to reduce the severity of losses if they do occur. Common loss reduction devices include:

- Installing a sprinkler system, which does not usually prevent fires, but which limits damage once a fire occurs.

- Posting signs in a convenience store stating that the "cashier cannot open the safe"; while the sign might not prevent a robbery from occurring, the fact that most of the money is locked in the safe can limit the severity of a potential robbery loss to the amount of money in the cash register.

Use of Inspection Reports in Loss Control

Insureds often use loss control measures because the insurer has recommended them. Insurers focus considerable loss control efforts on commercial insurance accounts. The loss control programs recommended by insurers are generally based on *inspection reports* prepared by the insurers' loss control representatives. An inspection report is one of the best sources of underwriting information and supplements the application.

When an underwriter receives an application for a commercial account, one of the underwriter's first tasks is often to request an inspection report from the insurance company's loss control department. A loss control engineer or representative visits the applicant's location or locations to inspect the premises and operations and submits an inspection report.

An inspection report usually has two main objectives:

- To provide a thorough description of the applicant's operation so that the underwriter can make an accurate assessment when deciding whether to accept the application for insurance.

- To provide an evaluation of the applicant's current loss control measures and recommend improvements in loss control efforts. The underwriter may require that the applicant implement the loss control recommendations in order for the application to be accepted.

Retention is a risk management technique that involves retaining all or part of a particular loss exposure. When the household or organization retains the exposure, it must pay for any losses resulting from the exposure with its own funds or from its own assets.

Retention

As a risk management technique, **retention** simply means that the household or organization retains the financial consequences of a loss exposure. The entity must draw on its own financial resources to pay for part or all of the consequences of a particular loss exposure. The financial consequences of any exposure that has not been avoided or transferred are invariably retained.

Retention can be intentional, but it is often unintentional. After thoroughly analyzing the alternatives, a risk manager might decide that retention is the best means of handling a given exposure, perhaps because insurance is not available or is too expensive. As an example of such intentional retention, a risk manager might decide that purchasing collision coverage on a fleet of older vehicles is not worth the premium; he or she might therefore decide to retain the organization's exposure to collision losses and to pay for any collision losses from the company's operating funds. Unintentional retention might result from inadequate exposure identification and analysis or from incomplete evaluation of risk management techniques. For example, a restaurant might not identify its liability exposure for serving too much alcohol to a customer and therefore fail to purchase liquor liability insurance to cover this exposure.

Retention can be partial or total. An example of partial retention would be a $500 deductible on a personal auto policy or a $10,000 per building deductible on a commercial property insurance policy. An example of total retention would be a husband and wife choosing not to purchase flood insurance on their home by the lake because they think it is too expensive. They are thus totally retaining their exposure to flood losses.

Retention is usually used in combination with other risk management techniques, particularly loss control and insurance. A deductible in a business auto policy is an example of the combination of retention and insurance. If the risk manager also implements a driver safety program to lower the frequency of corporate auto accidents, loss control, retention, and insurance combine to treat the exposure economically.

Noninsurance Transfer

Business organizations often treat loss exposures by transferring the potential financial consequences of loss to another party. When the other party is *not* an insurance company, this method of treating loss exposures is called **noninsurance transfer**. For example, the landlord of a commercial building might wish to transfer the liability exposure arising out of activities of a tenant. The landlord accomplishes this transfer by having the tenant sign a *hold harmless agreement*. The agreement can be either a separate contract or a provision included in the lease. A hold harmless agreement states that one party (in this case, the tenant) agrees to hold the other party (the landlord) harmless, or not legally responsible, for any liability arising from the tenant's use of the premises. Since there is a possibility of members of the public sustaining an injury on the rented property, the landlord has transferred this liability exposure to the tenant, who will be responsible for any such loss.

A **noninsurance transfer** is a risk management technique in which one party transfers the potential financial consequences of a particular loss exposure to another party that is not an insurance company.

Reminder

A *hold harmless agreement* is a contractual provision that obligates one party to assume the legal liability of another party.

Insurance

In addition to other techniques for handling loss exposures, households and small businesses depend heavily on insurance. Most medium-sized and large corporations also rely on insurance as a major component of their risk management programs, but they might be less dependent on insurance and employ other risk management techniques more systematically than households and small businesses.

Even the largest corporations face exposures to loss that they simply cannot handle in any other way as economically as through the purchase of insurance. No viable alternative exists for highly unpredictable loss exposures that could result in catastrophic financial consequences. Major corporations might use large retention amounts (deductibles or self-insurance) and purchase insurance policies to provide coverage above these amounts to protect them against large losses.

By working closely with the organization's insurance agent or broker, a risk manager can develop an insurance program tailored to the company's needs and coordinate the insurance program with the techniques of avoidance, loss control, retention, and noninsurance transfer to form a complete risk management program.

Exhibit 10-4 lists the various risk management techniques, explains what each technique does, and gives an example of each.

Educational Objective 5

Describe the financial criteria and the guidelines for selecting the risk management techniques that are most appropriate in a given situation.

Step 3: Selecting the Most Appropriate Risk Management Techniques

If it were possible to predict accidental losses accurately, selecting risk management techniques would be easy: prevent or avoid the losses that are most likely to happen and buy insurance against the losses that cannot be prevented or avoided. However, because no one can predict accidental losses with such accuracy, choices of risk management techniques must be based on forecasts of expected losses—where they are most likely to happen, how often they are likely to occur, and how large they will probably be. No one can know in advance which risk management techniques will be the best—risk managers can only make decisions about the techniques that appear to be the most appropriate.

Business organizations that are accustomed to reaching decisions based on expected profits or other financial criteria will probably use these same financial standards to select the most promising risk management techniques. Organizations that are less financially oriented are more likely to apply less formal guidelines to choose risk management techniques.

Exhibit 10-4

Risk Management Techniques

Technique	What the Technique Does	Example
Avoidance	Eliminates the chance of a particular type of loss by either disposing of an existing loss exposure or by not assuming a new exposure	A family decides not to purchase a boat and therefore avoids the property and liability loss exposures associated with boat ownership.
Loss Control	Lowers frequency and/or severity of losses	
1. Loss prevention	Lowers loss *frequency* (number of losses)	A business installs a burglar alarm system in an attempt to prevent burglaries.
2. Loss reduction	Lowers loss *severity* (dollar amount of losses)	A business installs a sprinkler system to reduce the amount of fire damage from potential fires.
Retention	Retains all or part of a loss exposure (intentionally or unintentionally), which means that losses must be paid for with available funds or other assets	A business decides not to purchase collision coverage for its fleet of vehicles and sets aside its own funds to pay for possible collision losses.
Noninsurance transfer	Transfers potential financial consequences of a loss exposure from one party to another party that is not an insurance company	In a lease, a landlord transfers the liability exposures of a rented building to the tenant.
Insurance	Transfers financial consequences of specified losses from one party (the insured) to an insurance company in exchange for a specified fee (premium)	A family purchases homeowners and personal auto policies from an insurance company.

Decisions Based on Financial Criteria

Financial management standards typically call for making those choices that promise to increase profits and/or operating efficiency. Risk management decisions can be based on the same criteria. When an organization undertakes an activity to achieve profit goals or other objectives, it also assumes the exposures to accidental loss that are inherent in that activity. How the organization deals with those loss exposures affects the profits or output from the activity. By forecasting how a particular risk management decision will affect profits or output, an organization can project which risk management choice is likely to be the most financially beneficial. For example, a corporation might analyze its financial position and decide that it does not want any retained loss exposures to affect annual corporate earnings by more than five cents per share of stock. If the corporation has one hundred million shares outstanding, the risk management department can retain up to $5 million for all exposures in a fiscal year. The risk management department makes its retention decisions for the coming year based on this strategy of protecting corporate earnings.

Decisions Based on Informal Guidelines

Most households and small organizations follow less formal guidelines in selecting risk management techniques.

Do Not Retain More Than You Can Afford To Lose

This rule sets the upper limit on the proper retention level; the amount that a household or organization can afford to lose depends on its financial situation. For example, if a family has only $500 in its savings account and lives from paycheck to paycheck, it probably cannot afford to carry a $1,000 deductible on either its homeowners or personal automobile policies. The family will probably choose to carry whatever minimum deductibles the insurer offers, despite the fact that the family could save premium dollars by choosing a higher deductible. The family simply cannot afford to lose more than a few hundred dollars for any loss.

Do Not Retain Large Exposures To Save a Little Premium

A risk manager should not retain a large exposure to loss, such as auto liability, in order to save a small amount of insurance premium. Depending on market conditions, certain types of liability insurance coverage, such as some umbrella policies (designed to cover large liability losses), can cost relatively little because the potential frequency of large liability losses is low.

Exposures with the potential of low frequency but high severity should generally be insured because they are highly unpredictable. For example, the probability of a building suffering a total fire loss is low because total fire losses happen infrequently; however, if a multi-million-dollar commercial building does burn to the ground, the severity of the loss would be great. One such loss would cost the organization many times a year's insurance premium, so the organization should fully insure the building.

Do Not Spend a Lot of Money for a Little Protection

Risk managers should spend insurance dollars where they will do the most good. Spending a relatively high premium to buy a little protection usually amounts to "trading dollars" with the insurance company. If the exposure is almost certain to lead to a loss, the insurer must charge a premium close to the expected cost of the loss plus expenses. It is better to retain exposures of this type because the household or organization could absorb the cost of a loss almost as easily as the cost of the insurance. For loss exposures with high frequency and low severity, retention and loss control are usually the best alternatives. For example, the owner of a candy shop might decide not to purchase crime insurance on its stock of candy because it knows that customers and employees often steal small amounts of candy. The severity of these small thefts is low even though the frequency is high. The probability of a burglar stealing large amounts of candy is also low (the burglar would probably go instead for the money in the safe or cash register). The cost of insurance against theft of the candy would probably be higher than the frequent small losses the shop incurs, so the shop owner's decision not to purchase theft insurance for the candy is probably a good one.

Do Not Consider Insurance a Substitute for Loss Control

A risk manager might evaluate a particular exposure, such as automobile collisions, and discover that the frequency of accidents has been increasing in recent years. If the company has a $1,000 collision deductible for each accident, the risk manager might decide that something must be done to reduce the organization's total annual retention for auto accidents.

One approach might be to lower the deductible to $500 so that the company retains less on each accident. This step would not solve the real problem, however, which is the increase in loss frequency. The insurance cost increases with the lower deductible, and the increase in loss frequency is likely to continue. In this case, the risk manager would be using the purchase of insurance in lieu of loss control.

Instead, the company could implement a loss control program to prevent accidents from occurring. This program could include more careful screening of company drivers, periodically reviewing drivers' motor vehicle records, training employees in safe driving practices, ensuring vehicle safety through regular vehicle maintenance, and implementing other loss control activities to reduce the frequency of collisions. If the program works and fewer accidents occur, the organization's overall retention from absorbing deductibles decreases, although the cost of the loss control program must be considered. Future insurance premiums might be lower as well, because the insurer might give a premium credit for the improved accident record.

When insurance takes the place of loss control, the insured simply passes the cost of absorbing additional losses to the insurance company and is once again trading dollars with the insurer. It might be more economical to spend dollars on a loss control program that will prevent and reduce losses and lower the long-term cost of insurance and the risk management program.

> **Educational Objective 6**
>
> Describe procedures for implementing risk management techniques.

Step 4: Implementing the Chosen Risk Management Techniques

Implementing the risk management techniques that an organization has chosen requires that the risk manager make decisions concerning:

- What should be done
- Who should be responsible
- How to communicate risk management information
- How to allocate the costs of the program

Deciding What Should Be Done

Once the risk manager has decided what risk management techniques to use, he or she must work out the details of how to implement them. For example, Helen, the risk manager of Goodfood Supermarket, has decided that the store needs a sprinkler system, but she must now decide how much Goodfood can afford to spend on the system, what kind of system should be installed, and which contractor should install it. She might also need to check on local water supply and building permits and decide what is necessary to be in compliance with local ordinances. Since the top management of Goodfood will certainly want to see that customer disruption at the store is kept to a minimum, Helen must decide how to accomplish this objective. She must also consult with Goodfood's insurance agent to make sure that proper property and liability coverages are in place during and after the installation of the system and that an insurance credit is given for the sprinkler system. Helen must take these considerations and many others into account before deciding exactly how to implement the loss control technique she has chosen. She must also consult with the necessary people both inside and outside the business to help make these decisions.

Deciding Who Should Be Responsible

The risk manager does not usually have complete authority to implement risk management techniques and must depend on others to implement the program based on the risk manager's advice. The risk manager must seek authority for the risk management program from senior management. Larger organizations might have a written risk management statement and a risk management manual outlining guidelines, procedures, and authority for implementing risk management techniques. In smaller organizations and in households, the person making risk management decisions is often the person implementing the program because that person is the organization's owner or the household's primary wage earner.

Communicating Risk Management Information

Any risk management program must include a communications network. Risk management departments of large organizations generally rely on a risk management manual to inform others of how to identify new exposures, what risk management techniques are currently in place, how to report insurance claims, and other important information. The communication process must be two-way. Management and other employees must funnel information to the risk manager so that he or she can adjust the program for new exposures and evaluate the effectiveness of the techniques used.

Allocating Costs of the Risk Management Program

Also important is the allocation of risk management costs. When numerous operations or locations exist, the costs of loss control, retention, noninsurance transfers, and insurance, as well as the expenses of the risk management department, must be spread appropriately across all departments and locations.

In small organizations or within households, allocating costs is also feasible. For example, an employee of a small business might be required to pay the deductible arising from damage she caused to a company car, or a teenager might have to pay to fix a neighbor's window that he accidentally broke.

Educational Objective 7

Describe procedures for monitoring and modifying a risk management program.

Step 5: Monitoring and Modifying the Risk Management Program

Monitoring the risk management program is an ongoing activity that a risk manager must carefully perform. Because the needs of all households and organizations change over time, a risk management program should not become outdated. Monitoring the program ranges from handling routine matters, such as updating fleets of vehicles, to making complex decisions concerning new activities to initiate or avoid.

Each year the household or organization should thoroughly review its insurance program with its agent or broker. Because decisions regarding insurance are usually interrelated with other risk management techniques, any change in this area of the risk management program necessarily affects the other areas.

In effect, the last step in the risk management program is really a return to the first. In order to monitor and modify the risk management program, the risk manager must periodically identify and analyze new and existing loss exposures and then reexamine, select, and implement appropriate risk management techniques. Thus, the process of monitoring and modifying the risk management program begins the risk management process once again.

Educational Objective 8

Explain how each of the following can benefit from sound risk management:

a. Businesses

b. Individuals and families

c. Society

d. Insurers

Benefits of Risk Management

Few businesses, individuals, or families are financially able to retain all their loss exposures and must transfer much of the financial burden of their potential losses. Therefore, insurance is an essential part of almost all sound risk management programs. However, insurance must be considered in its proper place in a well-balanced program of risk management that also includes other risk management techniques. Risk management has many advantages over merely buying insurance. These advantages benefit businesses, individuals, families, and society, as well as insurers.

Benefits of Risk Management to Businesses

Making insurance part of an overall risk management program instead of relying solely on insurance provides many benefits to an organization, including:

- Improved access to affordable insurance
- Increased opportunities
- Achievement of business goals

Improved Access to Affordable Insurance

Insurers often prefer to insure an organization that practices good risk management rather than one that relies only on insurance to protect it against the financial consequences of accidental losses. An insured who combines a sound insurance program along with the risk management techniques of avoidance, loss control, retention, and noninsurance transfer usually has fewer and smaller losses than do other insureds. Therefore, insurers are likely to generate better loss ratios and underwriting results by insuring policyholders that have sound risk management programs. Consequently, such insureds are often able to obtain broader coverage at lower premiums than are insureds that do not practice risk management.

Increased Opportunities

The fear of uncertain future losses tends to make many business owners and executives reluctant to undertake activities they consider too risky. This reluctance deprives an organization of the benefits that could be derived from undertaking certain activities. A business that can worry less about its loss exposures because of effective risk management is financially and psychologically better prepared to seek other opportunities that might increase its profits. For example, if a business feels secure in the way it has managed its present property and liability loss exposures, it might consider more favorably a proposal to manufacture a new product or to expand its present sales territory.

Achievement of Business Goals

Risk management makes it possible for a business to achieve its business and financial goals, such as stability, growth, and continuity, in a cost-effective manner and can thus help improve profitability. Profits can be increased directly by reducing expenses. For example, a firm might reduce its insurance costs because the risk manager chooses to retain a loss exposure instead of insuring it.

Benefits of Risk Management to Individuals and Families

Like businesses, individuals and families benefit in several ways from effective risk management:

- *Coping more effectively with financial disasters* that might otherwise cause a greatly reduced standard of living, personal bankruptcy, family discord, or even family breakups.

- *Enjoying greater peace of mind* from knowing that their loss exposures are under control. They have less physical and mental strain and can become more involved in other activities.

- *Reducing expenses* by handling loss exposures in the most economical fashion.

- *Taking more chances and making more aggressive decisions* on ventures with high profit potential such as investing in the stock market, changing careers, or starting a part-time business.

- *Continuing activities following an accident or other loss*, and thus reducing inconvenience.

- *Improving image in the community* by successfully preparing for and handing adversity and satisfying to some degree a sense of social responsibility.

Benefits of Risk Management to Society

By benefiting themselves through effective risk management, businesses, individuals, and families also benefit society in various ways:

- *Stimulating economic growth* because fewer and less costly losses mean that more funds are available for other uses, such as investment, which can spur economic growth

- *Reducing the number of persons dependent on society for support* (and thus increasing the number of taxpayers) because businesses and families plan for financial crises through risk management

- *Causing fewer disruptions in the economic and social environment* because companies and families practice risk management

Benefits of Risk Management to Insurers

From an insurer's point of view, risk management is beneficial in many ways:

- *Creating a positive effect on an insurer's underwriting results, loss ratio, and overall profitability* because insureds who practice sound risk management tend to experience fewer or less severe insured losses than those who do not.

- *Providing more thoughtful consumers of insurance* because those who practice risk management are likely to combine insurance with other techniques for handling loss exposures.

- *Creating innovative products and competitive prices and services* because professional risk managers seek to get the most for their insurance dollars and are often willing to pay higher premiums in exchange for greater insurance value. As a result, these risk managers may encourage insurers to be more innovative and competitive in the insurance products, prices, and services they provide.

- *Obtaining the respect and business of risk managers and companies* that have a risk management program if the insurers and their producers are knowledgeable about risk management.

Educational Objective 9

In a given case, recommend and justify risk management techniques appropriate for an individual, a family, or a business.

An Example of a Risk Management Program

An example of a simple risk management program might help to clarify the risk management process. To show that a risk management program need not be complicated, this example applies the risk management process to a family situation. Keep in mind, however, that risk management programs for organizations can be either simple or sophisticated. These programs become more complex as organizations increase in size and their loss exposures become more extensive and complicated.

A typical household faces many loss exposures, such as various property and liability exposures from home and automobile ownership. For example, Tony and Maria Garcia both work outside their home, and they have three school-aged children. The Garcias own two automobiles and a home with a pool, have a modest savings account, and have made some investments in the stock market. After attending a seminar at his company on risk management, Tony has decided that the family should initiate a risk management program of its own. Remembering the steps in the risk management program, Tony knows that the family must:

1. Identify and analyze its loss exposures
2. Examine various risk management techniques
3. Select techniques appropriate for the family
4. Implement the chosen techniques
5. Monitor and modify its risk management program

Tony and Maria started the process of identifying loss exposures by listing the exposures they could think of and then inspecting their home, looking for other exposures they had not yet considered. For example, when Tony spotted his daughter's field hockey stick, he realized that they have a liability exposure arising from the children's various athletic activities. His son's saxophone in his bedroom reminded Tony that the saxophone was not specifically insured and that they did not have the funds readily available to replace it if it were stolen or damaged. Tony gulped when he viewed their swimming pool full of neighborhood children, and realized that they needed higher liability limits than their current homeowners policy provided. After a physical inspection of their home and property, Maria called their insurance agent and obtained a household inventory form that they used to inventory their household contents and other possessions to determine their property loss exposures. The agent also sent them a survey form to complete, which they used to list potential liability exposures for the family. Maria and Tony then analyzed all the loss exposures they had identified and attempted to determine which ones could cause the most frequent or most severe losses.

After identifying and analyzing their property and liability exposures, the Garcias next step was to examine risk management techniques. Tony knew from the seminar that possible techniques included avoidance, loss control, noninsurance transfer, and retention, as well as insurance. The Garcias had been thinking of buying a new home near the local river, but Tony and Maria were afraid the exposure to flooding was too great; therefore, they decided not to buy the house and thus used avoidance to eliminate this exposure. In an attempt to practice sound loss control, they decided to install deadbolt locks on all their doors and locks on all their windows; they also installed smoke detectors in several places in their home, and they are contemplating installing a burglar alarm system if they can find one that is both effective and within the family budget. Tony and Maria explored noninsurance transfer by checking into leasing a car, but they found that they would still be responsible for all liability connected with the use of the vehicle and would still have to purchase insurance, so they decided this was not a good risk management technique for them.

Since the Garcias do not have much disposable income after they pay their mortgage, car payments, and other household bills each month, they know that they must rely heavily on insurance to cover their loss exposures. Although they cannot afford to retain much of their exposure, they did raise the deductibles on both their homeowners and personal auto policies from $250 to $500, thereby saving them some money on their premiums. They decided not to specifically insure their son's saxophone because their homeowners policy already covered it for fire, theft, lightning, and other causes of loss. They decided to apply the retention technique if their son simply lost or damaged the saxophone; in other words, they would just replace the saxophone from their personal funds, make their son earn money to replace it, or not buy a new one. They decided to purchase an umbrella policy to cover large liability losses such as those that might arise from the children's sporting activities or the pool exposure. The increased deductibles and retaining the property loss exposures for the saxophone were about all the retention Tony and Maria thought they could handle. Thus, as in most households, insurance will play a dominant role in treating loss exposures for the Garcia family.

By deciding not to purchase the house near the river, installing locks and smoke detectors, purchasing umbrella insurance, and deciding to retain some exposures, the Garcias effectively completed the third and fourth steps in the risk management process: selecting and implementing their risk management techniques.

The last step in the Garcias' risk management program is periodically monitoring and modifying the program. For a family, an annual review of their situation is probably sufficient unless their circumstances change significantly. An ideal time for the Garcias to do another physical inspection and inventory would be at the renewal of their homeowners policy or if either Tony or Maria changes jobs, receives a large bonus, has a salary increase, or purchases any type of high-valued property. When

Tony first began to monitor their risk management program, he realized that they had neglected to consider their human loss exposures, such as death, illness, injury, or unemployment. Tony and Maria immediately took steps to modify their risk management program to include their human loss exposures and began the process of exposure identification and analysis all over again to include those important exposures.

Educational Objective 10

Define or describe each of the Key Words and Phrases for this assignment. (All Key Words and Phrases appear in bold print in the text and in the margins throughout this chapter.)

Summary

Insurance is one of the fundamental techniques of risk management, but it is not the only one. Risk management can enable a person, family, or business to handle exposures to accidental losses effectively. Risk management is the process of making and carrying out decisions to minimize the adverse effects of accidental losses and involves the following steps:

1. Identifying and analyzing loss exposures
2. Examining possible risk management techniques for handling those loss exposures
3. Selecting the most appropriate techniques
4. Implementing the chosen techniques in a risk management program
5. Monitoring and modifying the risk management program

A risk manager, who is the person responsible for the risk management process, can conduct a physical inspection to identify loss exposures and can also use tools such as loss exposure surveys and flowcharts. Analyzing loss exposures includes measuring loss frequency (how often losses occur) and loss severity (the dollar amount of losses).

After identifying and analyzing all loss exposures, the risk manager must examine possible risk management techniques, which are methods of handling the loss exposures. These techniques include:

- Avoidance
- Loss control (which includes both loss prevention and loss reduction)
- Retention
- Noninsurance transfer
- Insurance

Selecting the most appropriate techniques involves making decisions based on financial criteria as well as informal guidelines. Implementing the chosen techniques calls for making decisions on what should be done, who should be responsible, how to communicate risk management information, and how to allocate costs of the risk management program.

The final step in the process of risk management is actually a return to the first. To properly monitor and modify the program, the risk manager must go back to step one and once again begin to identify and analyze new and existing loss exposures. Thus, the process begins anew.

Risk management has many advantages over merely buying insurance. These advantages benefit businesses, individuals, families, society, and insurers in various ways. Although formal risk management programs are used primarily by business organizations, individuals and families can also benefit from applying risk management to their exposures to accidental losses. While a risk management program for a large business can be complex and sophisticated, a risk management program for a family can be simple and informal and is well worth the time and effort to implement.

Glossary

This glossary includes all Key Words and Phrases found in bold print in the text and in boxes in the margins.

ACV. See **Actual cash value.**

Absolute liability (strict liability) Legal liability that arises from inherently dangerous activities or dangerously defective products that result in injury or harm to another, regardless of how much care was used in the activity. Absolute liability does not require proof of negligence.

Actual cash value (ACV) The replacement cost of property minus depreciation. (Actual cash value can also be determined by market value, if any.)

Actuarial equity A ratemaking concept through which actuaries base rates on actuarially calculated loss experience and place insureds with similar characteristics in the same rating class.

Actuary A person who uses complex mathematical methods and technology to analyze loss data and other statistics and develop systems for determining insurance rates.

Additional living expense A coverage in homeowners policies that indemnifies the insured for the additional expenses that are incurred following a covered property loss so that the household can maintain its normal standard of living while the dwelling is uninhabitable.

Adjuster. See **Claim representative.**

Admitted assets Types of property, such as cash and stocks, that regulators allow insurers to show as assets on their financial statements. Such assets are easily convertible to cash at or near the property's market value.

1

Admitted insurer. See **Licensed insurer**.

Adverse selection A situation that occurs because people with the greatest probability of loss are the ones most likely to purchase insurance. Adverse selection normally occurs if the premium is low relative to the loss exposure for such people.

Agency A legal relationship created when one party, the principal, authorizes another party, the agent, to act as a legal representative of the principal.

Agency agreement. See **Agency contract**.

Agency contract (agency agreement) A written agreement between an insurance company and an agent that specifies, among other things, the scope of the agent's authority to conduct business for the insurer.

Agency expiration list The record of an insurance agency's present clients and the dates their policies expire.

Agent In any agency relationship, the party that is authorized by the principal to act on the principal's behalf.

Aggregate limit The maximum amount an insurer will pay for all covered losses during the covered policy period.

Agreed value A method of valuing property in which the insurer and the insured agree on the value of the property at the time the policy is written. That amount is stated in the policy declarations and is the amount the insurer will pay in the event of a total loss to the property.

Alien insurer An insurer incorporated in another country.

Apparent authority Authority based on a third party's reasonable belief that an agent has authority to act on behalf of the principal.

Assault The intentional threat of bodily harm.

Assets Property (both tangible and intangible) owned by an entity.

Assignment The transfer of rights or interest in a policy to another party by the insured; assignment usually requires the insurer's written permission.

Attitudinal hazards. See **Morale hazards**.

Attorney-in-fact The contractually authorized manager of a reciprocal insurance exchange who administers its affairs and carries out its insurance transactions.

Auto In insurance policies: cars, trucks, buses, and other motorized vehicles designed for use on public roads.

Auto liability insurance A type of insurance that covers an insured's liability for bodily injury to others and damage to the property of others resulting from automobile accidents.

Auto physical damage insurance   A type of property insurance that covers loss of or damage to specified vehicles owned by the insured and sometimes covers vehicles borrowed or rented by the insured.

Avoidance   A risk management technique that eliminates a loss exposure and reduces the chance of loss to zero.

Balance sheet   A type of financial statement that shows an insurance company's financial position at a particular point in time and includes the company's admitted assets, liabilities, and policyholders' surplus.

Bailee   A person or business that holds the property of others for some specific purpose.

Battery   Unlawful physical contact with another person.

Binder   A temporary contract of insurance that is either written or oral.

Binding authority   The authority of an insurance agent, usually granted in the agency contract, to effect coverage on behalf of a particular insurer.

Bodily injury   Any physical injury to a person, including sickness, disease, and death.

Book of business (portfolio)   A group of policies with a common characteristic, such as territory or type of coverage, or all policies written by a particular insurer, producer, or agency.

Broker   An independent business owner or firm that sells insurance by representing customers rather than insurers.

Burglary   In insurance, the taking of property from inside a building by someone who unlawfully enters or exits the building.

Business income insurance   A type of property insurance that covers the loss of net income or additional expenses incurred by a business as the result of a covered loss to its property.

Cancellation   The termination of a policy, by either the insurer or the insured, during the policy period.

Capacity   The amount of business an insurer is able to write, usually based on a comparison of the insurer's written premiums to the size of its policyholders' surplus.

Capacity ratio (premium-to-surplus ratio)   An insurer's written premiums divided by its policyholders' surplus.

Captive insurance company (captive)   An insurer that is formed as a subsidiary of its parent company, organization, or group, for the purpose of writing all or part of the insurance on the parent company or companies.

Case law. See **Common law**.

Cash value A savings fund that accumulates in a whole life insurance policy and that the policyholder can access in several ways, including borrowing, purchasing paid-up life insurance, and surrendering the policy in exchange for the cash value.

Cause of loss (peril) The actual means by which property is damaged or destroyed. Examples include fire, lightning, and theft.

Centralized When all activities are conducted in a central location, such as the home office.

Civil law A category of law that deals with the rights and responsibilities of citizens with respect to one another. Civil law applies to legal matters not governed by criminal law.

Claim A demand by a person or business seeking to recover from an insurance company for a loss that might be covered by an insurance policy.

Claim representative (adjuster) A person responsible for investigating, evaluating, and settling insurance claims.

Claimant Anyone who submits a claim to an insurance company. Insurance professionals usually use the term claimant to refer to a third party that has suffered a loss and seeks to collect for that loss from an insured.

Claims-made coverage A type of liability coverage that covers claims that are made (submitted) during the policy period for covered events that occur on or after the retroactive date and before the end of the policy period.

Class rates (manual rates) Rates that apply to insureds with similar loss exposures who are grouped into the same rating category, or rating class.

Coinsurance An insurance-to-value provision in many property insurance policies. If the property is underinsured, the coinsurance provision reduces the amount that an insurer will pay for a covered loss.

Collision Coverage for damage to an insured motor vehicle caused by its impact with another vehicle or object or by its upset or overturn.

Combined ratio The sum of the loss ratio and the expense ratio.

Commensurate with the exposure An appropriate relationship existing between the size of the premium and the exposure assumed by the insurer.

Commercial general liability insurance A type of insurance that covers businesses for their liability for bodily injury and property damage. It can also include liability coverage for various other offenses that might give rise to claims, such as libel, slander, false arrest, and advertising injury.

Commission. See **Sales commission.**

Common law (case law) Law that consists of a body of principles and rules established over time by courts on a case-by-case basis.

Compensatory damages Damages, which include both special and general damages, that are intended to compensate a victim for harm actually suffered.

Competitive state fund A state workers compensation insurance plan that competes with private insurers to provide workers compensation insurance.

Comprehensive. See **Other than collision.**

Concealment An intentional failure to disclose a material fact.

Conditional contract A contract in which one or more parties must perform only under certain conditions.

Consideration Something of value given by each party to a contract.

Constitutional law Law that is based on the Constitution of the United States and all the decisions of the U.S. Supreme Court that involve the Constitution.

Constructive total loss A loss in which the property cannot be repaired for less than its actual cash value minus the anticipated salvage value.

Contingent commission A commission that an insurer pays, usually annually, to an independent agency and that is based on the premium volume and profitability level of the agency's business with that insurer.

Contract A legally enforceable agreement between two or more parties.

Contract of adhesion A contract in which one party (the insured, in insurance) must adhere to the agreement as written by the other party (the insurer).

Contract of indemnity A contract (policy) in which the insurer agrees, in the event of a covered loss, to pay an amount directly related to the amount of the loss.

Contract law The branch of civil law that deals with contracts and the settlement of contract disputes.

Covered losses The events for which insurance pays.

Crime insurance A type of insurance that protects the insured against loss to covered property from various causes of loss such as burglary, robbery, theft, and employee dishonesty.

Criminal law A category of law that applies to wrongful acts that society deems so harmful to the public welfare that government takes the responsibility for prosecuting and punishing the wrongdoers.

Damages A monetary award that one party is required to pay to another who has suffered loss or injury for which the first party is legally responsible.

Dec. See **Declarations page**.

Decentralized The process of moving activities away from a central location.

Declarations page (declarations or dec) An information page in an insurance policy that provides specific details about the insured and the subject of insurance.

Deductible A portion of a covered loss that is not paid by the insurer. The deductible is subtracted from the amount the insurer would otherwise be obligated to pay the insured.

Demutualization The process by which a mutual insurer, which is owned by its policyholders, becomes a stock company, which is then owned by its stockholders.

Depreciation Physical wear and tear or technological or economic obsolescence.

Direct loss A reduction in the value of property that results directly and often immediately from damage to that property.

Direct response system An insurance marketing system that includes any system that does not depend primarily on individual producers to locate customers and sell insurance but relies primarily on mail, phone, and/or Internet sales.

Direct writer An insurer that uses the direct writing system to market insurance.

Direct writing system An insurance marketing system that uses sales representatives who are employees of an insurance company.

Disability income insurance A type of health insurance that pays periodic income payments to an insured who is unable to work because of sickness or injury.

Domestic insurer An insurer incorporated in the same state in which it is transacting business.

Draft authority Authority expressly given to an agent by an insurer to settle and pay certain types of claims by writing a claim draft up to a specified limit.

E&O. See **Errors and omissions**.

E&S insurance. See **Excess and surplus lines insurance**.

Each occurrence limit The maximum amount an insurer will pay for all covered losses from a single occurrence, regardless of the number of persons injured or the number of parties claiming property damage.

Each person limit   The maximum amount an insurer will pay for injury to any one person for a covered loss.

Earned premium   The portion of the written premium for a particular policy that applies to the part of the policy period that has already occurred.

Endorsement   A document that amends an insurance policy by adding or deleting coverage or otherwise modifying the coverage.

Errors and omissions (E&O)   Negligent acts (errors) or failures to act (omissions) committed by a professional (such as an insurance agent) in the conduct of business that give rise to legal liability for damages.

Excess and surplus lines (E&S) insurance   Insurance coverages, usually unavailable in the standard market, that are written by nonadmitted (unlicensed) insurers.

Exclusions   Policy provisions that eliminate coverage for specified exposures.

Exclusive agent   An agent that has a contract to sell insurance exclusively for one insurance company or a group of related companies.

Expense ratio   An insurer's incurred underwriting expenses for a given period divided by its written premiums for the same period.

Expert systems (knowledge-based systems)   Computer software programs that supplement underwriting decision-making.

Exposure.   See **Loss exposure**.

Exposure unit   A measure of loss potential, used in rating insurance. For example, in homeowners insurance, each home insured is an exposure unit.

Express authority   Authority that the principal expressly grants to the agent.

Extra expenses   Expenses incurred to continue the operation of a business or expenses that reduce the length of a business interruption when the property has been damaged by a cause of loss covered by insurance.

Facultative reinsurance   An arrangement in which a reinsurer evaluates individually each policy that the primary insurer asks the reinsurer to cover.

False arrest   An unlawful physical restraint of another's freedom.

Field claim representative.   See **Outside claim representative**.

File-and-use laws State rating laws in which insurance rates must be filed with the state insurance department but do not have to be approved before use.

Fire and allied lines A type of property insurance that covers direct damage to or loss of insured property.

First named insured The person or organization whose name appears first as the "named insured" on a commercial insurance policy. Depending on the policy conditions, the first named insured might be the one responsible for paying premiums and the one who has the right to receive any return premiums, to cancel the policy, and to receive the notice of cancellation or nonrenewal.

Flex rating laws State rating laws in which prior approval by the state insurance department is required only if the new insurance rates are a specified percentage above or below previously filed rates.

Floater Policies that are designed to cover property that "floats," or moves from location to location.

Flowchart A diagram that depicts the flow of a particular operation or set of related operations within an organization.

Foreign insurer An insurer licensed to operate in a state but incorporated in another state.

Friendly fire A fire that stays in its intended place.

General damages Compensatory damages awarded for losses, such as pain and suffering, that do not have a specific economic value.

Guaranty fund A state fund that provides a system to pay the claims of insolvent insurers; the money in the guaranty fund comes from assessments collected from all insurers licensed in the state.

Hazards Conditions that increase the chance of loss.

Hold harmless agreement A contractual provision that obligates one party to assume the legal liability of another party.

Hostile fire A fire that leaves its intended place.

Human loss exposure (personal loss exposure) Any condition or situation that presents the possibility of a financial loss to an individual or family by causes such as death, sickness, injury, or unemployment. (In a broader sense, the term personal loss exposure can also be used to include all loss exposures faced by individuals and families, including property and liability loss exposures.)

Implied authority Authority that is considered to be within the scope of authority granted by a principal to an agent, even though such authority is not expressly granted orally or in an agency contract. Implied authority arises from actions of the agent that are in accord with accepted custom.

Income statement   A type of financial statement that shows a company's revenues, expenses, and net income for a particular period, usually one year.

Incurred losses   The sum of paid losses and changes in loss reserves (loss reserves at the end of the period minus loss reserves at the beginning of the period) for all claims during a particular period.

Indemnify   To restore a party who has had a covered loss to the same financial position that party held before the loss occurred.

Independent adjusters   Independent claim representatives who offer claim handling services to insurance companies for a fee. Independent adjusters are either self-employed or work for an independent adjusting firm.

Independent agency   An independent firm that sells insurance, usually as a representative of several unrelated insurance companies.

Independent agent   A producer who works for an independent agency and who can be either the owner or an employee of the agency.

Indirect loss.   See **Time element loss.**

Individual rates (specific rates)   A specific insurance rate that reflects the unique characteristics of an insured or the insured's property.

Inland marine insurance   A type of insurance that covers miscellaneous types of property, such as movable property, goods in domestic transit, and property used in transportation and communication.

Inside claim representative   An insurance company employee who handles claims that can be settled, usually by telephone or letter, from inside the insurer's office.

Insurable interest   The right of a person or entity to property such that a loss to that property would cause a direct monetary loss to that person or entity.

Insurance agents   Legal representatives of an insurance company (or insurance companies) for which they have contractual agreements to sell insurance.

Insurance Regulatory Information System (IRIS)   An analytical system designed by the NAIC to monitor an insurer's overall financial condition.

Insurance-to-value provisions Provisions in property insurance policies that encourage insureds to purchase an amount of insurance that is equal to, or close to, the value of the covered property.

Insured A person, a business, or an organization whose property, life, or legal liability is covered by an insurance policy.

Insurer An insurance company.

Insuring agreement A statement in an insurance policy that the insurer will, under certain circumstances, make a payment or provide a service.

Intentional tort A deliberate act (other than a breach of contract) that causes harm to another person.

Interinsurance exchange. See **Reciprocal insurance exchange**.

Invasion of privacy An encroachment on another person's right to be left alone.

Investment income ratio Net investment income divided by earned premiums for a particular period.

IRIS. See **Insurance Regulatory Information System**.

Judgment rate A type of individual rate, usually based on the underwriter's experience, used to develop a premium for a unique exposure for which there is no established rate.

Knowledge-based systems. See **Expert systems**.

Law of large numbers A mathematical principle stating that as the number of similar but independent exposure units increases, the relative accuracy of predictions about future outcomes (losses) based on these exposures also increases.

Legal hazards Characteristics of the legal or regulatory environment that affect an insurer's ability to collect a premium commensurate with the exposure to loss.

Legal liability The legal responsibility of a person or organization for injury or damage suffered by another person or organization.

Liabilities Financial obligations, or debts, owed by a company to another entity, usually the policyholder in the case of an insurance company.

Liability insurance A type of insurance that covers losses resulting from bodily injury to others or damage to the property of others for which the insured is legally liable and to which the coverage applies.

Liability loss A claim for monetary damages because of injury to another party or damage to another party's property.

Liability loss exposure Any condition or situation that presents the possibility that a liability loss will happen.

Libel   A written or printed untrue statement that damages a person's reputation.

Liberalization clause   A policy condition stating that if a policy form is broadened at no additional premium, the broadened coverage automatically applies to all existing policies of the same type.

Licensed insurer (admitted insurer)   An insurer authorized by the state insurance department to transact business within that state.

Litigation expenses   Expenses incurred for legal defense, such as attorneys' fees, expert witness fees, and the cost of legal research.

Loss control   A risk management technique that attempts to reduce loss frequency (how often losses occur) or loss severity (the amount of damage caused by losses).

Loss exposure (exposure)   Any condition or situation that presents the possibility of a loss occurring.

Loss exposure survey   A risk management tool in the form of a checklist or questionnaire listing potential loss exposures that a household or an organization might face.

Loss frequency   A term used to indicate how often losses occur or are expected to occur. It is used to project the likelihood of similar losses in the future.

Loss payable clause   A provision in some property insurance policies that states that a loss will be paid to both the insured and the loss payee as their interests appear and gives the loss payee certain rights.

Loss payee   A party, usually a lender or creditor, who is named on a policy and is entitled to be included as a payee on any loss payments made by an insurer.

Loss prevention   A type of loss control that seeks to lower the frequency of losses (to decrease the number of losses).

Loss ratio   The insurer's incurred losses (including loss settlement expenses) for a given period divided by its earned premiums for the same period.

Loss reduction   A type of loss control that seeks to lower the severity of losses that occur (to decrease the dollar amount of losses).

Loss reserves   Amounts designated by insurance companies to pay claims for losses that have already occurred but are not yet settled.

Loss severity   A term that refers to the dollar amount of damage that results or might result from loss exposures. It is used to project how costly future losses are likely to be.

Losses. See **Covered losses.**

Managing general agency (MGA) An independent business organization that functions almost as a branch office for one or more insurance companies. The MGA appoints and supervises independent agents for insurance companies that use the independent agency system.

Manual rates. See **Class rates.**

Manuscript policy An insurance policy that is specifically drafted according to terms negotiated between a specific insured (or group of insureds) and an insurer.

Market conduct regulation State laws that regulate the practices of insurers in regard to four areas of operation: sales and advertising, underwriting, ratemaking, and claim settlement.

Marketing The process of identifying customers and their needs and then creating, pricing, promoting, selling, and distributing products or services to meet those needs.

Marketing representatives Insurance company employees whose role is to visit agents representing the insurer, to develop and maintain sound working relationships with those agents, and to motivate the agents to produce a satisfactory volume of profitable business for the insurer.

Material fact Information that would affect the insurer's underwriting decision to provide or maintain insurance or that would affect a claim settlement.

Medical insurance Health insurance that covers the cost of medical care, including doctors' bills, hospital charges (including room and board), laboratory charges, and related expenses.

Medical payments coverage Coverage for necessary medical expenses incurred within a specified period by a claimant (and in certain policies, by an insured) for a covered injury, regardless of whether the insured was at fault.

Merit rating plans Rating plans that modify class rates to reflect the loss characteristics of a particular insured.

Mine subsidence A cause of loss involving the sinking of ground surface when underground open spaces, resulting from the extraction of coal or other minerals, are gradually filled in by rock and earth from above.

Misrepresentation A false statement of a material fact.

Mixed marketing system The use of more than one marketing system by an insurer.

Mobile equipment As defined in commercial insurance policies: various types of land vehicles, usually designed for use principally off public roads, including equipment attached to them.

Model law   A document drafted by the NAIC, in a style similar to a state statute, that reflects the NAIC's proposed solution to a given problem and provides a common basis to the states for drafting laws that affect the insurance industry.

Modular policy   A policy that consists of several documents, none of which by itself forms a complete policy.

Money   As defined in insurance policies: currency, coins, and bank notes; also traveler's checks, credit card slips, and money orders held for sale to the public.

Monopolistic state fund   A state-operated workers compensation insurance plan that is the only source of workers compensation insurance allowed in that state.

Moral hazards   Dishonest tendencies in the character of the insured (or applicant) that increase the probability of a loss occurring.

Morale hazards (attitudinal hazards)   Carelessness or indifference to potential loss on the part of an insured (or applicant).

Mortgage clause (mortgage holders clause)   A provision in some property insurance policies that protects the insurable interest of the mortgagee by giving it certain rights, such as the right to be named on claim drafts for losses to insured property and the right to be notified of policy cancellation.

Mortgage holder.   See **Mortgagee**.

Mortgagee (mortgage holder)   A lender that loans money on a home, building, or other real property.

Mortgagor   The person or organization that borrows money from a mortgagee to finance the purchase of real property.

Mutual insurance company   An insurer that is owned by its policyholders and formed as a corporation for the purpose of providing insurance to its policyholder-owners.

NAIC.   See **National Association of Insurance Commissioners**.

Named insured   The policyholder whose name(s) appears on the declarations page of an insurance policy.

Named perils   The perils listed and described in a policy. In a named perils policy, only losses caused by those listed perils are covered.

National Association of Insurance Commissioners (NAIC)
An association consisting of the heads (usually called commissioners) of the insurance departments of each state plus the District of Columbia and U.S. territories and possessions. The NAIC coordinates insurance regulation activities among the various insurance departments.

Negligence   Failure to act in a manner that is reasonably prudent; failure to exercise the appropriate degree of care under given circumstances.

Net income   Revenue minus expenses during a given period.

Net underwriting gain or loss   An insurer's earned premiums minus its losses and underwriting expenses for a specific period.

No-file laws.   See **Open competition**.

Nonadmitted assets   Types of property, such as office furniture and equipment, that insurance regulators do not allow to be shown as assets on an insurer's financial statements because they cannot be readily converted to cash at or near their market value.

Nonadmitted (unlicensed) insurers   Insurers that are not licensed in many of the states in which they operate and that write excess and surplus lines insurance coverages.

Noninsurance transfer   A risk management technique in which one party transfers the potential financial consequences of a particular loss exposure to another party that is not an insurance company.

Occurrence basis coverage   A type of liability coverage that covers claims that occur during the policy period, regardless of when the claim is submitted to the insurer.

Ocean marine insurance   A type of insurance that includes hull insurance (which covers ships) and cargo insurance (which covers the goods transported by ships). Ocean marine insurance can also include liability insurance for the operation of ships.

Open competition (no-file laws)   A state rating system in which insurance rates do not have to be filed with the state.

Open perils.   See **Special form coverage**.

Other than collision (comprehensive)   A coverage for losses to a covered auto by fire, theft, vandalism, falling objects, flood, and various other perils.

Outside claim representative (field claim representative)   An insurance company employee who handles claims that cannot be handled easily by phone or mail. Outside claim representatives visit the scene of a loss, conducting interviews, investigations, and meetings with all parties involved.

Overall gain or loss from operations   An insurer's net investment gain or loss plus its net underwriting gain or loss.

Overall operating ratio   An insurer's investment income ratio subtracted from its combined ratio.

Paid losses   Claim payments that an insurer has made.

Peril.   See **Cause of loss**.

Personal injury   In most insurance policies, injury (other than bodily injury) arising from intentional torts such as libel, slander, or invasion of privacy.

Personal liability insurance   A type of insurance that provides liability coverage to individuals and families for bodily injury and property damage arising from the insured's personal premises or activities.

Personal loss exposure.   See **Human loss exposure**.

Personal property   All tangible or intangible property that is not real property.

Personnel loss exposure   The possibility of a financial loss to a business because of the death, disability, retirement, or resignation of key employees.

Physical hazards   Tangible characteristics of property, persons, or operations that tend to increase the probable frequency or severity of loss.

Policy   A complete written contract of insurance.

Policyholders' surplus   An insurance company's total admitted assets minus its total liabilities.

Portfolio.   See **Book of business**.

Postjudgment interest   Interest that might accrue on damages after a judgment has been entered in a court and before the money is paid.

Prejudgment interest   Interest that might accrue on damages before a judgment has been entered in a court.

Premium   A periodic payment by an insured to an insurance company in exchange for insurance coverage.

Premium-to-surplus-ratio.   See **Capacity ratio**.

Primary insurer   An insurer that transfers its loss exposures to a reinsurer.

Principal   The party that authorizes an agent to act on its behalf in an agency relationship.

Principle of indemnity   An insurance principle that states that the insured should not be better off financially after a loss than before; thus, the insured should not profit from any insured loss.

Prior-approval laws   State rating laws in which insurance rates must be approved by the state insurance department before they can be used.

Pro rata refund   The unused premium (based on the pro rata portion of the premium for the number of days remaining in the policy) returned to the insured when a policy is canceled.

Producer   A person who sells insurance products for an insurance company or companies.

Production underwriters   Insurance company employees who work in the insurer's office in underwriting positions but who also travel to visit and maintain rapport with agents and sometimes clients.

Professional liability insurance   A type of insurance that protects physicians, accountants, architects, engineers, attorneys, insurance agents and brokers, and other professionals against liability arising out of their professional acts or omissions.

Property damage   Physical injury to, destruction of, or loss of use of tangible property.

Property insurance   Any type of insurance that indemnifies an insured who suffers a financial loss because property has been lost, stolen, damaged, or destroyed.

Property loss exposure   Any condition or situation that presents the possibility that a property loss will happen.

Proximate cause   The event that sets in motion an uninterrupted chain of events contributing to a loss.

Public adjuster   A person hired by an insured to represent the insured in handling a claim.

Punitive damages   Damages awarded by a court to punish wrongdoers who, through malicious or outrageous actions, cause injury or damage to others.

Rate   The price of insurance for each unit of exposure. The rate is multiplied by the number of exposure units to arrive at a premium.

Ratemaking   The process insurers use to calculate rates that determine the premium for insurance coverage.

Real property   Land, buildings, and other structures attached to the land or embedded in the land.

Rebating   Offering anything of value, other than the insurance itself, to an applicant as an inducement to buy or maintain insurance.

Reciprocal insurance exchange (interinsurance exchange)   An unincorporated association formed to provide insurance services to its members and managed by an attorney-in-fact.

Recreational vehicles   Vehicles (such as dune buggies and all-terrain vehicles) used for sports and recreational activities.

Reinsurance   A contractual relationship in which a reinsurer reimburses a primary insurer for some or all of the claim payments made by the primary insurer under policies written for its insureds.

Reinsurer   An insurer that insures a primary insurer.

Replacement cost The cost to repair or replace property using new materials of like kind and quality with no deduction for depreciation.

Reservation of rights letter A notice advising the insured that the insurer is investigating a claim. The reservation of rights letter is issued in order to inform the insured that a coverage problem might exist and to protect the insurer so it can deny coverage if necessary.

Residual market plan (shared market plan) A program that makes insurance available to those who cannot obtain coverage elsewhere because private insurers will not voluntarily provide such coverage for various reasons.

Retention A risk management technique that involves retaining all or part of a particular loss exposure.

Retroactive date In a claims-made policy, the date on or after which injury or damage must occur in order to be covered.

Risk management The process of making and implementing decisions to deal with loss exposures. It involves identifying loss exposures and then applying various techniques to eliminate, control, finance, or transfer those exposures.

Robbery The taking of property from a person by someone who has caused or threatened to cause the person harm.

Sales commission (commission) A percentage of the premium that the insurer pays to the agency or producer for new policies sold or existing policies renewed.

Salvage rights The rights of the insurer to recover and sell or otherwise dispose of insured property on which the insurer has paid a total loss.

Securities Written investment instruments representing either money or other property. Stocks and bonds are examples of securities.

Self-contained policy A single document that contains all the agreements between the insurer and the insured and that forms a complete policy by itself.

Self-insurance plan An arrangement in which an organization pays for some or all of its losses with its own resources rather than purchasing insurance.

Shared market plan. See **Residual market plan.**

Short rate refund A refund of premium that is less than the pro rata refund because of a penalty imposed upon the insured for canceling the policy mid-term.

Single limit The maximum amount an insurer will pay for the insured's liability for both bodily injury and property damage that arise from a single occurrence.

Sinkhole collapse   A cause of loss involving damage by the sudden sinking or collapse of land into underground empty spaces created by the action of water on limestone or dolomite.

Slander   An oral untrue statement that damages a person's reputation.

Social equity   A rating concept that considers rates to be unfairly discriminatory if they penalize an insured for characteristics (such as age or gender) that are beyond the insured's control.

Solvency   The ability of an insurance company to meet its financial obligations as they become due.

Solvency surveillance   The process, conducted by state insurance regulators, of verifying the solvency of insurance companies and determining whether the financial condition of the insurers enables them to remain in business in the long term.

Special damages   Compensatory damages allowed for specific, out-of-pocket expenses, such as doctor and hospital bills.

Special form coverage (open perils)   Provides coverage for "risk of direct loss" to property; coverage is provided for any direct loss to property unless the loss is caused by a peril specifically excluded by the policy.

Specific rates.   See **Individual rates**.

Specified causes of loss   A named perils coverage that covers loss to a covered vehicle caused by fire, lightning, theft, windstorm, hail, earthquake, flood, vandalism and other specifically listed perils.

Split limits   Separate limits that an insurer will pay for bodily injury and for property damage liability.

Sprinkler leakage   The accidental leakage or discharge of water or another substance from an automatic sprinkler system.

Staff claim representative   An insurance company employee who performs some or all of the insurer's claim handling activities.

Standard forms   Insurance forms that contain standardized policy wording. Insurance advisory organizations develop standard forms that many insurers use in their insurance policies. Some insurers develop their own standard forms that they use in policies for their insureds.

Standard market   Collectively, the insurers who voluntarily offer insurance coverages at rates designed for customers with average or better-than-average loss exposures.

State-mandated rates   State-specified rates that must be used by all insurers of a particular type of insurance in the state.

Statutory law   The formal laws (statutes) enacted by federal, state, or local legislative bodies.

Statutory liability   Legal liability imposed by a specific statute or law.

Stock insurance company   An insurer that is owned by its stockholders and formed as a corporation for the purpose of earning a profit for these stockholders.

Strict liability   A term sometimes used synonymously with **absolute liability**. Strict liability is also used to describe the liability imposed by certain statutes, such as workers compensation laws.

Subrogation   The insurer's right to recover payment for a loss it has paid to an insured from a negligent third party who caused the loss.

Subscribers   The members (policyholders) of a reciprocal insurance exchange who agree to insure each other.

Supplementary payments   Amounts covered in liability policies, in addition to the liability limits, for items such as premiums on bail bonds and appeal bonds, loss of the insured's earnings because of attendance at trials, and other reasonable expenses incurred by the insured at the insurer's request.

TPAs.   See **Third-party administrators.**

Term insurance   A type of life insurance that provides temporary protection (for a certain period) with no cash value.

Theft   Any act of stealing, including burglary and robbery.

Third-party administrators (TPAs)   Business firms that contract to provide administrative services, such as claim handling, to other businesses.

Time element loss (indirect loss)   The loss of income or the extra expenses resulting from direct loss to property. This type of loss takes place over a period of days, weeks, or even years following a direct loss.

Tort   A wrongful act, other than a crime or breach of contract, committed by one party against another.

Tort law   The branch of civil law that deals with civil wrongs other than breaches of contract.

Tortfeasor   A person, a business, or another party that has committed a tort.

Treaty reinsurance   An arrangement in which a reinsurer agrees to reinsure automatically a portion of all eligible insurance of the primary insurer.

Underwriter   An insurance company employee who evaluates applicants for insurance, selects those that are acceptable to the insurer, prices coverage, and determines policy terms and conditions.

Underwriting   The process of selecting insureds, pricing coverage, determining insurance policy terms and conditions, and then monitoring the underwriting decisions made.

Underwriting audit   A process in which members of an insurer's home office underwriting department examine files to see whether underwriters are following underwriting guidelines.

Underwriting authority   The limit on decisions that an underwriter can make without receiving approval from someone at a higher level.

Unearned premium   The portion of the written premium for a particular policy that applies to the part of the policy period that has not yet occurred.

Unearned premium reserve   The total of an insurer's unearned premiums on all policies at a particular time.

Unfair claim practices laws   State laws that specify claim practices that are illegal.

Unfair discrimination   Applying different standards or methods of treatment to insureds who have the same basic characteristics and loss potential.

Unfair trade practices laws   State laws that specify certain prohibited business practices.

Universal life insurance   A type of life insurance that combines protection with savings. A universal life insurance policy is a flexible-premium policy that separates the protection, savings, and expense components.

Unlicensed insurers.   See **Nonadmitted insurers**.

Use-and-file laws   State rating laws in which insurance rates must be filed with the state insurance department within a specified period after they are first used in the state.

Utmost good faith   An obligation to act in complete honesty.

Valued policy   A policy in which the insurer pays a stated amount in the event of a specified loss (usually a total loss), regardless of the actual value of the loss.

Vandalism   Willful and malicious damage to or destruction of property.

Vehicle damage   Damage done by a motor vehicle to some other kind of property.

Vicarious liability   Legal responsibility that occurs when one party is held liable for the actions of another party.

Volcanic action   A cause of loss by lava flow, ash, dust, particulate matter, airborne volcanic blast, or airborne shock waves resulting from a volcanic eruption.

Warranties   Promises, either written or implied, such as a promise by a seller to a buyer that a product is fit for a particular purpose.

Whole life insurance   A type of life insurance that provides lifetime protection (to age 100), has a level premium, and builds cash value.

Written premiums   Premiums on policies put into effect, or "written," during a given period.

Index

Page numbers in bold refer to definitions of Key Words and Phrases. Page numbers in italics refer to exhibits.

D

E

Standard forms, **5-11**, 7-18–7-20
Standard market, **2-22**
Standard & Poor's, 5-17
State government insurance programs, 1-11–1-12, 2-11–2-13
State-mandated rates, **2-19**
Statutory law, 9-5–9-6, **9-6**
Statutory liability, **9-13**, 9-13–9-14
Stock insurance companies, **2-4**, 2-4–2-5
Strict liability, **9-12**
Subrogation, **6-17**, 6-17–6-18, 7-27–7-28
Subscribers, **2-6**
Sudden and accidental water damage, 8-24
Supplementary payments, **9-26**, 9-26–9-27
Surplus
    policyholders', 3-12–3-13
Surplus lines insurance, 2-22–2-24, **2-23**
Surveys
    loss exposure, 10-7, *10-8*
Survivorship benefits, 2-10

T

TPAs (third-party administrators), **6-10**
Taxes, 3-9
    income, 3-10
Term insurance, **1-24**, 1-24–1-25
Theft, **8-25**
Third party, 6-4
Third-party administrators (TPAs), **6-10**
Tie-in sales, 4-22–4-23
Time element losses, **8-27**, 8-27–8-28
Tort law, **9-9**
Tortfeasors, **9-11**
Torts, **9-9**, 9-9–9-12
    intentional, 9-11–9-12
Trade associations
    producers', 4-18
Trailers, 8-7
Treaty reinsurance, **5-13**

U

Underwriters, **5-3**
    line, 5-14
    production, 4-19

Underwriting, **5-3**
    activities of, 5-4–5-12
    expenses of, 3-8–3-9
    guidelines for, 5-14–5-15
    history of, 5-3–5-4
    management of, 5-12–5-15
    process of, 5-15–5-22
    regulation of, 5-23–5-24
Underwriting audits, **5-15**
Underwriting authority, **5-14**
Unearned premium reserves, 3-12
Unearned premiums, **3-4**, 3-4–3-5
Unemployment insurance, 2-12
Unfair claim practices laws, 6-23–6-24, **6-24**
Unfair discrimination, 2-17–2-18, **2-18**
    underwriting and, 5-23–5-24
Unfair trade practices laws, **4-22**, 4-22–4-24
Uninsurable losses, 7-17
Universal life insurance, **1-25**
Unlicensed insurers, **2-24**
Use-and-file laws, **2-18**
Utmost good faith, **7-8**, 7-8–7-10

V

Valuation
    liability claim, 6-20–6-21
    property claim, 6-14–6-17
    provisions for, 8-32
Valued policies, **7-12**
Vandalism, **8-22**
Vehicles, 8-7
Vicarious liability, **9-11**
Void, 7-9
Volcanic action, **8-23**, 8-23–8-24

W

War, 8-25
Warranties, **9-13**
Water damage, 8-24
Wear and tear, 8-26
Weight of snow, ice, or sleet, 8-24
Whole life insurance, **1-24**
Windstorm, 8-19
Windstorm insurance pools, 2-13
Workers compensation insurance, 2-11–2-12
Written premiums, **3-4**